SOUL OF FIRE:
A BIOGRAPHY OF MARY MacSWINEY

D0897207

Soul of Fire

A Biography of Mary MacSwiney

CHARLOTTE H. FALLON

THE MERCIER PRESS
CORK AND DUBLIN

The Mercier Press Limited
4 Bridge Street, Cork
24 Lower Abbey Street, Dublin 1

© Charlotte H. Fallon, 1986

British Library Cataloguing in Publication Data
Fallon, Charlotte H.
    Soul of fire : a biography of Mary MacSwiney
    1. MacSwiney, Mary   2. Nationalists — Ireland — Biography
    3. Feminists — Ireland — Biography
    I. Title
    322.4'2'0924   DA965.M2/

ISBN 0-85342-797-6

To Benny and Elizabeth

Printed by Litho Press Co., Midleton, Co. Cork.

Contents

Introduction

*Nationalism is a theory of political legitimacy
which requires that ethnic boundaries should not
cut across political ones, and, in particular,
that ethnic boundaries within a given state. . .
should not separate the power holders from the rest.*[1]

THE HISTORY of Ireland in the twentieth century has revolved around
the struggle to establish an Irish national and cultural identity within an
independent country. Irish Nationalists waged an obstinate resistance
against the British and the experienced internecine conflict among
various Nationalist factions with differing concepts concerning the form
the Irish nation should take. Proposed variations were many: Arthur
Griffith gave early support to a dual monarchy for England and Ireland
using the Austro-Hungarian model; Patrick Pearse and the leaders of
the 1916 Uprising proclaimed an Irish Republic to encompass the entire
island; Eamon de Valera held several views, among them the concept
of an Irish dominion within the British Commonwealth; Michael Collins,
William Cosgrave, Richard Mulcahy and Kevin O'Higgins believed the
Treaty of 1921, creating the Free State for the twenty-six counties, was
the most viable plan for achieving an independent Ireland.

Mary MacSwiney became politically active in the early years of the
twentieth century, the time of the Irish cultural revival and renewal of
Nationalist aspirations. From among the choices proposed, she accepted
the declaration of the Republic in 1916. Her life became committed to
ensuring the implementation of Patrick Pearse's dream as she worked
energetically for Sinn Féin, Cumann na mBan, the Prisoners' Defence
League and the Second Dáil.

Though involved in the decision-making process of Republican politics for many years, particularly 1919 to 1932, Mary's important efforts
and contributions have gone largely unreported in the literature of the
period. Authors of three books encompassing Ireland's Civil War years,
George Dangerfield in *The Damnable Question*, Rex Taylor in *Michael
Collins* and Longford and O'Neill in *De Valera*, all refer to the 'redoubt-

able Mary MacSwiney' with no further explanation offered. Within the past few years, several authors have taken a more serious look at her political career. John Bowman in *De Valera and the Ulster Question*, refers to her as 'the guardian of Republicanism', while T. Ryle Dwyer in *De Valera's Darkest Hour* and Seán Cronin in *The McGarrity Papers* recognise both her prominence and her influence, particularly during the early years of the Free State.

Her life merits study for several reasons. First, she was one of the early suffragists in Ireland but cast this role aside in pursuit of nationalist ideals. From the early days of the women's emancipation movement, the cause of a free Ireland was perceived by most women as more important than the immediate extension of their own political rights.

Second, she was totally committed to the Republic as proclaimed in 1916 and remained so despite defection or rejection by some and dilution of commitment by others. Her intransigence provides a sharp contrast to the splinter groups that developed, to Mary's disdain and annoyance. Hers was not a blind following of a romantic leader; rather, her belief in the Republic had a firm ideological foundation that had developed over time through consultation with her brother Terence, examination of the writings of republican spokespersons and development of her own political philosophy.

Third, she came twice to the United States preaching the gospel of republicanism. These trips shed light on the complex relationship existing between the Irish and Irish-Americans the latter of whom were, and are continually, called upon to support the struggle in their ancestral homeland emotionally, politically and financially.

Fourth, the role of women in Irish society is illuminated. Public life in Ireland was dominated by men with the distinction in sex roles being legitimised by the state, the Roman Catholic Church and society generally. A few notable women emerge from this period, namely Maud Gonne, Countess Markievicz and Lady Gregory, all strong, influential women members of the ascendancy. In contrast, Mary MacSwiney was a Cork schoolteacher from a family of modest means. As one who chose not to be restricted by the dictates of her society, her life deals with feminism and its development, or lack thereof, in Ireland.

Fifth, the evolution of radical republican nationalism, the quality and virulence of which is still present, particularly in Northern Ireland, is illustrated. Is theirs a stubborn refusal to admit the ineffectiveness of political intransigence or is it an honourable adherence to principle – the breaking of which by other less committed participants has led to the continuing conflict in Ireland?

Sixth, a further look will be taken at the role of the Catholic Church vis-à-vis republicanism. Mary was a devout Catholic, a Third Order Benedictine, who aspired to lead a good and holy life in conformance with Catholic doctrine. The Irish hierarchy, however, were sharp and persistent in their condemnation of radical Republicanism. The resolution of the apparent paradox of being both a dedicated Catholic and a doctrinaire Republican follows Mary throughout her life.

Finally, Mary MacSwiney's interactions with the political players of this period should contribute to our understanding of twentieth-century Irish politics.

Acknowledgements

There are many people to whom I owe thanks for their help in preparing this manuscript. In Ireland, Dr Ronan Fanning who helped me continually with my MA thesis and offered constructive criticism about Mary MacSwiney; Mr and Mrs Ruarí Brugha, both of whom shared their insights and observations about the subject and welcomed me so graciously into their home; Mr and Mrs Cathal Brugha, who were so generous with their time and allowed me to examine private documents of Mary MacSwiney; Dr and Mrs Bernard Stuart without whom Sundays would have seemed endless.

In the United States: many thanks to Professor Jeffrey Cox without whose editing and suggestions I would still be labouring away; also Professor Lawrence Gelfand, a most kind and knowledgeable critic; Professors Linda Kerber, William Murray and the late Lawrence LaFore.

I most sincerely thank Elizabeth Nolan whose constant encouragement was invaluable as was that of my parents Gustava and Allan McCreary.

Lastly, and most importantly, I thank Benny and Elizabeth Fallon, who sacrificed much in order that I could pursue my goal. Without their love, encouragement and belief in me I would not have completed this manuscript.

1. From Suffragist to Nationalist

John MacSwiney, a native of Cork city, emigrated to England in the 1860s in search of employment. His was a situation often repeated as the Irish sought to break their shackles of poverty. Shortly after his arrival in London, MacSwiney obtained a teaching position and earned a small income, this modest success resulting despite the Fenian raids occurring in Ireland which only increased English suspicions about the unreliability of the Irish immigrant poor. John soon met, and later married, Mary Wilkinson, also a teacher, and a woman described as 'extremely English – Victorian.'[1] To them Mary Margarite MacSwiney was born in Surrey on 27 March 1872, the first of seven children.

Financial matters developed poorly for John MacSwiney. A low, sometimes unreliable, income made living difficult for the growing family which soon included Kit and Peter. In an effort to provide better for the family, the MacSwineys returned to Cork where John, with his brother's help, began a snuff and tobacco factory. For a man with a history of asthma, this was an unhealthy and unfortunate choice as well as a poor business decision. John, kind, gentle and generous, had little skill in financial or commercial matters. The business struggled as the young MacSwineys grew; the family soon included Terry, Margaret, Seán and Annie.

While the family atmosphere was one of austerity and modesty, the Irish national and political situation was in a state of excitement and flux. Though the MacSwineys were not politically active, young Mary, looking on through a window, felt excitement and exhilaration as she watched the frenzied activity caused by a Parnell procession through the streets of Cork. The waving banners and cheering crowds only accentuated the drawn, ascetic features of Charles Stewart Parnell, the man to whom the dreams of Irish freedom had been entrusted.

These public activities encouraged more overt displays of national pride within the MacSwiney home. John took particular enjoyment in listening to his eldest daughter recite 'The Death of Owen Roe'. The more energy Mary put into her delivery, the greater was her father's delight, cheering when Mary declared that 'God's wrath was brought upon the Saxon'.

Though the MacSwineys were encouraged to internalise Irish patriotism, externally their mother insisted upon traditional English manners, speech and deportment. Young Mary, in particular, had a marked British accent which brought jeers from her playmates.

As a child, Mary MacSwiney was considered serious, passing up dolls and tin soldiers in favour of playing school. As time progressed, she was a good student who enjoyed Latin and reading, particularly the works of Shakespeare. Because of problems of undetermined origin with her eyes at a young age, she was often found reading by the window where the light was best, a green eye shade in place.

Health problems would plague Mary through her life. At age seven she developed a seriously infected foot and fearing she would be kept home and miss her First Communion, this condition was hidden from her parents for a time. When treatment came it was ineffective. The result was a partial and then a complete amputation of the foot, after which Mary was fitted with a heavy, rather awkward surgical boot. The chronic pain had been relieved but she would go through life with a severe limp, a situation she accepted as she did all physical ailments, stoically and without complaint. Many who knew her well throughout her life, never knew the cause of her handicap.

As the 1880s progressed, the family's financial situation declined. After John's business failed completely, he emigrated to Australia in 1887 where he hoped to start a more financially successful life, at which time his family would join him. In his absence, Mrs MacSwiney opened a corner shop and sustained the family economically and emotionally.

Mary was educated at the Ursuline school in Cork. At the age of twenty, in 1892, having done extremely well academically, she obtained a teaching post in England at a small private school. While there, she learned of her father's death in Australia, after which she shared financial responsibility for the family. She soon took a teaching position in France but stayed only a short while as she felt cast in the role of a governess rather than a teacher.

Mary loved teaching and believed the road to her personal advancement lay with further education in this area. With a loan from the Students Aid Society in Ireland, she set off for Cambridge University to seek a teaching diploma. While there, she was one of two Irish Catholic women in the teaching programme that accepted one hundred, predominantly men.

As would be the case throughout her life, Mary spent little time pondering this pioneering role. She had seen her own mother take control of the family with little fuss and much competence. This positive role model, combined with her own values and ambition, imbued her with a belief in self-reliance and self-sufficiency. The fact of being a woman in a man's world seemed to faze her not at all. Her work was done thoroughly and conscientiously and she expected to be accepted by her colleagues on these merits. She had few, if any, thoughts about trail-blazing for future generations of women and was not inclined to break down barriers into male bastions. Rather, she had the straight-forward idea that each person should perform to his or her potential, gender not withstanding. Mary had traditional values about the role of women within the home, found no difficulty in accepting 'women's work', and sought a career in one of the few professional fields open to unmarried women.

While at Cambridge, Mary came to the defence of Ireland when called on to do so but was by no means a Victorian version of a student activist. The principal of her teacher-training described her as 'bright, energetic and enthusiastic'; one who would 'exercise an excellent influence over her pupils' and who had 'been on excellent terms both with the staff and with her fellow students'.[2]

With regard to Ireland, Mary considered the 1890s as 'the weary years of disappointment'.[3] Parnell had fallen, the Home Rule Party was divided by squabbling and unsure loyalties, and the British parliament adopted the 'win the Irish with compromise and concessions' attitude and philosophy, Prime Minister Balfour intending to 'kill Home Rule with kindness'.[4]

Having received her teaching diploma from Cambridge, Mary accepted a position at Hillside Convent in Farnboro, England, a boarding school directed by nuns of the Order of St Benedict. Here, she became familiar with their spiritual rule which included contemplative prayer, manual work, education and study. The Order had always maintained a belief in mysticism as well. This did not include any 'suggestion of those bodily phenomena of rapture and trance' but rather depended on 'the doctrine of the soul's possible union (i.e. in this life) with absolute reality, that is, with God'.[5] To better understand these concepts Mary read and studied the written works of the great Catholic mystics, St Teresa, St John of the Cross and Thomas à Kempis.

During these days she considered seriously entering the religious life. Though not tortured by the decision-making process, long hours were spent in consultation with her spiritual advisor, discussing her suitability for such a choice. As a means of preparation, a one year novitiate period was begun for the Oblates of St Benedict. At the end of this time, having decided her vocation was not the religious life, Mary became a member of a lay organisation, the Third Order of St Benedict. A solemn public promise was made at an investiture ceremony to dedicate herself to a life of greater Christian perfection, including 'detachment in the use of material things, generosity to the poor, chastity according to (one's) state in life and regular spiritual reading and study of sacred scripture'. Although this did not have the binding force of a solemn vow, Mary felt committed to her promises for the remainder of her life.[6]

Mary loved her time in Farnboro, as it combined teaching with study and prayer, all of which brought her to a full intellectual and philosophical acceptance of Christian doctrine. It was a time she nostalgically recalled for the rest of her life. After her mother died, in 1904, she returned to Cork and dutifully assumed a matriarchal role over the MacSwiney family.*

The Ireland of the early 1900s was one of renewed national awareness. The Gaelic movement had resurfaced following the tradition of the Young Irelanders of the 1840s and the Fenians of the 1860s. This time, however, with the cultural revival had come a broader base and subsequently greater support. The Gaelic Athletic Association had begun in 1882 and many local clubs and associations were promoting the native sports of hurling, camogie and football. The Gaelic League was similarly supporting things Irish, and Lady Gregory and W. B. Yeats had opened the Abbey Theatre in Dublin to much praise and support. Arthur Griffith had established Sinn Féin, (Ourselves), declaring that Ireland's independence had to be won in Ireland and suggesting a 'withdrawal of Irish representatives from Westminster'.[7]

The Gaelic revival was particularly successful in the cities, which would provide most of the leadership for the Republican and revolutionary movement. In the countryside, the traditional home of insurrection in Ireland, various Land Acts had given ownership of the land to the peasant proprietors. As the English leaders had hoped, this quieted the farmers considerably, gave impetus to farm improvements and left little time for political involvement.[8]

In Cork city, from 1904 to 1908, Mary was directing the MacSwiney

* Note for all of preceding, where not otherwise identified, sources include: Interviews with Mrs Máire Brugha and Mrs Maura Tyrell; Moirin Chavasse, *Terence MacSwiney*, Dublin, 1961; University College, Dublin Archives P48a/462, Mary MacSwiney's uncompleted memoirs.

family and pursuing her teaching career at St Angela's, an Ursuline Convent school. At this stage in her life, she was a low profile patriot, but her interest in Ireland was being awakened and revitalised by her brother Terence, an idealist, a poet and a dreamer. He studied the history of Ireland and became enchanted by Caitlín Ní Houlihan, transmitting enthusiasm throughout his family, but to Mary in particular.[9]

Mary's first political association was with the Irish suffrage movement. The suffrage movement in most western countries was conducted largely by the middle classes. In Ireland, the middle class was very small in a country that had been late to industrialise, remained largely rural, and thus provided a small pool from which to draw suffrage supporters. Ardent British feminist leaders such as Millicent Fawcett, Emmeline Pethick-Lawrence and Harriet Mill saw woman suffrage as a means of female escape from the bonds of domesticity, believing the vote would give women power in the political arena, to be followed by reforms in other areas such as property rights, divorce, education and employment. Unlike these women, Mary MacSwiney was in many ways a traditionalist. She had no intention of undermining the male role as head of the family and chief provider when possible and had little quarrel with many aspects of 'women's work' such as house-keeping, cooking and child care. She did believe, however, that women were the intellectual equals of men, capable of understanding the political process, and, as she herself had exemplified, capable of pursuing an independent career. At this time, she viewed suffrage as an end in itself, failing to consider the more long range goals of the women's movement.

The vote for women was a matter of justice to Mary. As contributing members of society, women should have the full rights of citizenship. To her, it was only logical that in a free society, women should share in the choice of governmental representatives. She rejected as illogical, and contrary to her own experience, the arguments of anti-suffragists that women were mentally inferior to men, that women's constitutions were too weak to withstand the rigours of politics, that God had put men at the top of the natural order, or that women were too emotional to be charged with choosing elected officials. She particularly resented the fact that denial of the vote placed all women on the 'level of imbeciles and lunatics'.[10] Her association with the suffrage movement, through membership in the Munster Women's Franchise League, was the first gate through which Mary passed on her way to involvement in Irish politics. She did not go forward reluctantly as much as unsuspectingly.

In 1910, the role of women in Ireland was particularly circumscribed.

With regard to women entering the professions, Francis Sheehy-Skeffington, an Irish feminist-activist, wrote that Ireland was one of 'the most backward countries'.[11] Three-quarters of female university graduates became teachers 'frequently at less than £100 per year',[12] while among urban working class women, pay was abysmally low, opportunity scarce and choices negligible. In a Dublin factory employing women in linen manufacturing, the average pay was 4/- per week. A typist might expect 12/6. The supplements to these meagre wages were closed windows, swirling lint, dirty lavatories and the 'brutal language' of foremen and shop overseers.[13]

The *Irish Citizen* reported a ludicrous situation in Dublin that exemplified prevalent attitudes. The paper stated that there was not a single public lavatory for women in Dublin while there were many for men. Any time such a structure for women was suggested it was met with 'strenuous opposition' by neighbourhood shopkeepers who feared that such a facility 'would lower the tone of the whole street and would materially injure their business'. It was stated at Dublin corporation meetings that respectable Dublin women would be too modest to use the lavatory, that the women 'of strong nerves' who would be altogether devoid of virtue would be attracted to the area and that 'ladies' had no need of public lavatories, as there were ladies' cloakrooms in every tea-shop.[14] This overlooked women coming and going from factory or office work, as well as the street vendors, flower sellers and the homeless poor.

Despite gross inequities perpetrated against women, members of the hierarchy scolded those activist women who sought redress. Bishop Kelly of Ross chided women who sought 'to escape from dependence on man, aping his dress, copying his social habits and displacing him in most callings'. He concluded: 'Many women, bitten by the higher education craze, openly and aggressively assert their own superiority and, revising God's order, attempt to exercise dominion over men.'[15] It was this type of rhetoric that led the editor of the *Irish Citizen* to ask, 'Is the Church woman's best friend? Do not all the facts point to the exact opposite?'[16]

Thus the two strongest social institutions in Ireland, the government, both national (through its refusal to grant women the vote among other things) and local, and the Catholic Church, had pronounced on what should be the place of women. This, coupled with a small middle class, the backbone of most feminist movements, resulted in the Irish suffrage movement having a small, albeit vocal, membership. By 1913, two years after its foundation, the Irish Women's Franchise League registered 828 names (668 women and 160 men), an increase of only 133 from the previous year.[17] The majority of Irish women, poor agriculturalists, found little in the suffrage movement which they believed to be relevant to their lives. There was little concern among them for obtaining the vote when the majority of their days were spent trying to provide the necessary food and shelter for their families through the meagre output of their land.

The years 1912-14 were particularly vital ones for both the Irish Home Rulers and the suffrage movement. Following the second election of 1910, the Irish Nationalists controlled 84 seats in parliament, with Liberals having 272, Conservatives 272, and Labour 42. Because the Nationalists held the balance, it was a propitious time to seek action on Ireland. The Liberals, under Asquith's leadership, promised Home Rule if the Irish would support the government on other issues, one being the denial of the franchise to women. Although many of the Irish Nationalists supported the idea of female enfranchisement, they fell in line behind their leader, John Redmond, rejecting the extension of the franchise on the promise of Home Rule which had been presented as an 'either-or' proposition. Many Irish parliamentarians echoed Mary MacSwiney's idea that 'if Ireland were free, women would get the vote'. This was a rather utopian belief, with little basis in reality, when the strong influence of the Church in Irish life is considered along with the poor support for the women's movement. Nonetheless it is illustrative of the rhetoric used in promotion of a free Ireland.[18]

This compromise brought dissension to the Irish suffrage movement. The purist suffragists, under the leadership of Francis and Hannah Sheehy-Skeffington, rejected the Redmondites for their refusal to support the suffrage issue. In so doing, the Sheehy-Skeffingtons were following the precedent of the Pankhursts in England who refused to support any elected party that did not actively support female suffrage. The Irish suffragists were committed to 'opposing every body of responsible politicians which is hostile to women's citizenship', contending that theirs was the only perspective 'consistent with self-respect'.[19]

It was at this juncture that Mary MacSwiney chose the path that would dominate the rest of her life. While realising the justice and relevance of woman suffrage, she believed that the cause of a free Ireland was more urgent. Mary did not consider herself a follower of John Redmond, but in 1914 she did consider that 'self-government for Ireland (was) the most important question in this country at present and must be paramount until Home Rule is attained'. She agreed with the editor of the *Irish Citizen* that there could be 'no free nation without free women' but continued that 'the world, women included, has taken some thousands of years to realise that fact. Three years more, in our very exceptional circumstances will not hurt us.'[20]

Mary objected to the adoption of militant suffrage tactics as being 'unsuitable to Ireland'. At a Cork suffrage meeting a sharp exchange ensued regarding this when one supporter of the Pankhurst policy, irritated with Mary's lack of enthusiasm, said, 'Oh Miss MacSwiney, Ireland's the centre of the universe to you.' Mary replied cryptically, 'Of course it is. Is it not so for you? I thought you claimed to be Irish.'[21]

The policy debate heated up between the two branches of the suffrage movement. The militants cited Mary and other supporters of the Irish Volunteers as having a 'slavish attitude' because they had agreed 'not to take any forward action themselves, but to help the men of the Irish Volunteers to raise money for their equipment, and in general to toady to them'. They said that 'women. . . who display this crawling servility to the men of their party, deserve nothing but contempt and will assuredly earn it – not only from the free-minded members of their own sex but also from the very men to whom they do homage.' The suffrage leaders were sensing that many supporters were drifting to the Nationalist camp and hoped to brow-beat them back to the place the suffragists considered all women belonged.[22]

These unkind references drew an immediate response from Mary who began a lively exchange of letters with the editor of the *Irish Citizen*. Her first letter began calmly enough and warned that if this name-calling persisted the militants would alienate 'Nationalist opinion from the suffrage cause'.[23] Up until this point, Mary and others believed that woman suffrage and Home Rule for Ireland were compatible goals. As both causes advanced and their strategies conflicted, choices had to be made.

The editor of the *Irish Citizen*, Francis Sheehy-Skeffington, would brook no diversity, however. His answer read:

Miss MacSwiney, though a suffragist, puts party first. Of course, she does not call it 'Party'; she attempts, as party camp followers always do, to persuade herself that she is upholding some great principle that is above party. For her it is 'Nationalism' that ties her to the chariot wheels of Mr Redmond.[24]

Despite these pugilistic rejoinders, Mary's reply was a calm one entitled 'A Plea for Common Sense', in which her belief that the suffrage issues in England and Ireland were very different was explained. In England, suffrage was the 'dominant need' which made opposition to the government in power a tenable position. Ireland, on the other hand 'was struggling to settle not a party question but a national one, and opposition to the government in the present crisis means opposition to Home Rule'. The suffrage issue had forced her and other Irish women into difficult decisions. By the end of her letter she slipped ever so slightly into the rhetoric that would typify her future as she could not resist accusing English women of using their Irish sisters for political gain. 'The suggestion made lately that Irish suffragists should help to drum Asquith out of Fife, shows so little grasp of the situation in Ireland that one almost asks if we are supposed to be content to be cats paws for English suffragists,' she wrote. As the letter went on, her Nationalist bias became increasingly apparent:

Englishwomen want to vote for themselves first and foremost. That is natural and we applaud and sympathise with their efforts. But in order to hasten their political enfranchisement – even by a year – they would not hesitate to wreck the cause of suffrage in Ireland for a generation or more. The sooner Irish women open their eyes to that fact, the sooner they will get back to sane methods. What is good for England is not good for Ireland in suffrage tactics, anymore than in other matters; and as Irishwomen we are concerned with our own country first.[25]

Mary MacSwiney's move away from the suffragists and towards Nationalism had been happening gradually and for some time, coinciding with her brother Terence's increasing involvement in Irish issues. Although not an early follower of Arthur Griffith, he had friends and associates in Sinn Féin. Often Terry and his friends would gather in the MacSwiney parlour to discuss literature but the conversation inevitably turned into heated debates over Ireland's future. Mary, as hostess, came in for criticism from the Sinn Féin contingent among the guests who labelled her suffragist friends a 'lot of Unionists'[26] and questioned her allegiance to them. Defensively, she responded that by her membership she 'did not accept king, lord, and commons, rather it was a protest against a manifest injustice which had nothing to do with Irish Nationality.'[27]

As the days and weeks passed, Mary became more and more imbued with Nationalist sentiment. At suffrage meetings she found herself giving the 'Irish point of view' on political matters in an effort to overcome the 'colossal ignorance' of those who always insisted, to Mary's dismay and fury, that they were Irish.[28]

Terence MacSwiney's activities, as one of the early leaders of the Cork Brigade of the newly formed Irish Volunteers, had a profound impact on Mary. Though older than Terry by seven years, she was in awe of her brother, doted on him as a loving mother, respected his intellect and was inspired by his politics. Following the formation of the Volunteers, some Irish women looked for a way to help in the fight for Irish freedom. This was realised in 1914 with the establishment of Cumann na mBan (Organisation of Women) which was to be the help-mate to the male organisation. Wife-like, it was to be watchful, supportive, faithful but not overtly active, particularly not in the military sense. To these women fell the task of taking care of the details of house-keeping such as running messages, sewing uniforms and wrapping bandages so that the men could be about the greater business of fomenting an Irish nation.

The militant suffragists, represented by the Sheehy-Skeffingtons, objected to this type of 'camp-following'. Mary viewed it in no such terms, however, objecting not at all to this 'help-mate' role. This was evidently an attitude shared by many other active Irish women as membership in Cumann na mBan quickly eclipsed that of the suffrage association which never exceeded 900. By October, this new women's organisation, begun just six months previously, had 63 branches 'some having as many as 100 members'.[29]

As the summer of 1914 approached, the Irish situation became more and more unsettled. There was disappointment in some cases, outrage in others, over the continual delays of Home Rule. The possibility of war in Europe was increasing daily. The Irish Volunteers strengthened greatly and tried to match the Ulster Defence Force, Unionist and predominantly Protestant, in men and weaponry. In Cork, the Volunteers were under the leadership of Tomás MacCurtain, a friend to all the MacSwineys, and Terence was soon his second in command thus increasing Mary's exposure to Nationalist sentiments and activities.

Her response to the situation in Ireland was not atypical. Many, including Eamon de Valera, Michael Collins and others who would become Irish heroes in the ensuing years, had not been raised in particularly Nationalistic homes. Most underwent a gradual transformation from being involved in the day to day struggle for home and family to believing that this same home and family should develop in a free Ireland. This belief was a reaction to various factors: the Gaelic revival, the continual delays of Home Rule, growing Irish perceptions of British deception and intransigence, the growth of avowedly Nationalist organisations, all of which were overlaid with the history of Irish Nationalist aspirations re-juvenated since 1798.

Cumann na mBan, established in Dublin in April 1914, sought to expand by establishing branches around the country, once firm in its foundations. By May of 1914, the same time as Mary's exchange of letters with the *Irish Citizen*, she was ready to begin a Cork branch for which the support of Tomás MacCurtain was immediately gained. He wrote: 'It is the desire of the members of the executive (of the Cork Volunteers) to give every possible assistance to Cumann na MBan.'[30]

The inaugural meeting of the Cork branch was held in the MacSwiney parlour, a room that was being made privy to more and more Nationalist plans and secrets. Ten women, including Mary's sister Annie, came together that May evening and discussed the various activities which the parent organisation suggested, such as first-aid, drill, organising boy scouts, home nursing, rifle practice, collecting money as well as canvassing for new members.[31] None of the women present expressed any indignation over the fact that they were being ascribed 'women's work'. Mary herself would have scoffed at any such quibbling, believing the important issue was that their work, whatever its nature, was being done for Ireland.

In June, Mary organised a mass meeting at Cork City Hall sponsored by Cumann na mBan 'in support of the Irish national Volunteers'. Those assembled heard Father Russell solicit funds and J. J. Walsh give a patriotic exhortation. Mrs O'Farrell, of the Dublin Cumann, told the audience not to be too dependent on MPs in England following which Bulmer Hobson suggested the feasibility of a Dublin parliament. The final speech of the evening, delivered by J. J. Horgan, was perhaps the most pragmatic when, in ringing tones, he called for 'defence not defiance', adding that the Irish 'must be armed to the belt'. The appeal to taking up the gun was being made and received with enthusiasm.[32]

Once the summer had arrived and classes had been dismissed at St Angela's, Mary had more time to devote to her cause. She spent her time increasingly on Nationalist issues, speaking at meetings, canvassing new members and generally espousing the need of a free Ireland. She was totally committed to upholding the manifesto of Cumann na mBan which read:

We are the women's section of the Irish Volunteers and have been working side by side with them from the beginning. We are the only women's organisation belonging to the Irish Volunteers and our activities and aims are solely national.[33]

Mary, as reflective of most of membership, was undisturbed by the rather contradictory assertion that the women were to work 'side by side with' but also 'belong to' the Volunteers. Again the similarity of the wife role surfaced.

The following months were a frenzy of partisan activity. Guns and ammunition were being 'run' and closeted by Ulster Unionists and Irish Volunteers. The MacSwiney family was drawn closer to partisan activities through the involvement of Terry in the Volunteers and Mary in Cumann na mBan, both of whom had completely internalised the Nationalist ideology.

With the outbreak of the First World War, many Irishmen and women were forced into an examination of conscience regarding their political alliance. The number of Irish men who joined the British forces was indicative of the commitment and attachment many Irish continued to feel toward Britain as large numbers of Irish left from Dun Laoghaire pier to fight with His Majesty's forces in France.[34]

Mary MacSwiney was appalled by the idea that young Irish lives were being sacrificed to ensure the stability of Ireland's oppressor. The war in Europe aggravated the tension among women in Sinn Féin and Cumann na mBan who were also active in the suffrage movement, their chant being, 'Give us an Irish parliament first and then we shall ask our own men to emancipate us.'[35]

The tension between suffragists and Nationalists grew when the former became involved in the war effort, a situation Mary MacSwiney could not abide quietly. In November 1914, she formally resigned from the Munster Women's Franchise League 'owing to the fact that they (were) devoting their money and energy to war propaganda, other than the purpose for which the society was founded'.[36]

Mary could not refrain from shrouding the suffragists in a Unionist cloak, to her mind the worst possible wardrobe. She wrote:

The conclusion has been forced upon me – very much against my will – that the majority of the members of the committee at any rate, are Britons first, suffragists second, and Irishwomen perhaps a bad third. As the reversal of that order is, to my mind, the only right one, our co-operation is no longer possible.[37]

One final rejoinder was added: 'May I recall that I stated my conviction that if trouble arose between England and Germany, English suffragists would sink their claims before the national need and that Christabel Pankhurst herself would be the first to do so. Let Irishwomen learn the particular lesson and put Ireland first and Ireland only; till Ireland is free.'[38] With these words Mary disassociated herself from suffrage activities and devoted her time exclusively to Nationalist issues.

She was encouraged in her position against the war by the proclamation of the Irish Volunteers in September 1914. At that time they repudiated 'the claim of any man to offer up the blood and lives of the sons of Irish men and Irish women to the services of the British Empire while no national government which could speak and act for the people of Ireland is allowed to exist.'[39]

In later years, when reflecting on this time, Mary wrote that her 'time in suffrage was interesting but more important issues were demanding attention.'[40]

With the coming of the war it is not too surprising that the suffrage movement should suffer vis-a-vis Nationalism. As David Fitzpatrick described in *Politics and Irish Life*, the network of Nationalist supporters was well developed throughout the country with shopkeepers, publicans and local newspaper editors being the main purveyors of information combined with a Nationalist ideological history of several centuries. In County Clare alone there were 150 Nationalist organisations between 1913 and 1916.[41] The movement was well entrenched and 'Nationalist demonstrations of all sorts offered forums, not only for speech-making, but also marching, holding flaming tar barrels aloft, waving flags and banging drums'. Fitzpatrick concluded that 'sometimes politics was an alternative to pub-drinking, sometimes the occasion for it. In either case, politics was an integral part of social life.'[42] It is little wonder that suffragists could not prevail against such an overwhelming competitor when the two groups were vying for support. Not surprisingly then, in Ireland, the cause with the most longevity and perceived relevance and importance was the one accepted as being the most meaningful and worthy of support.

The following year, 1915, was a time for politicising the Irish. The British had not brought the 'boys home for Christmas' as promised when the first soldiers set sail across the channel to engage the German enemy. The British now had their hands full dealing with the huge losses at the Dardanelles as well as German attacks on British coastal areas with the increasing threat of German submarines. The Irish Volunteers, for their part, sought to undermine British enlistment efforts in Ireland at every turn and engaged in active recruiting on their own behalf. Dorothy Macardle wrote that 'the Irish Volunteers were collecting arms; that was known at Dublin Castle but no legislation could be enforced against them which would not also affect Redmond's Volunteers and Redmond and his party must be conciliated because the last hope of securing recruits in Ireland depended on their goodwill.'[43] (John Redmond, in another unpopular move, had organised a contingent of Irish Volunteers to aid the British effort.) She continued with the most salient factor to the Nationalists: 'Every overt action taken against the separatists was an argument, in the minds of the Irish people, in favour of the separatist cause.'[44]

At the funeral of Fenian O'Donovan Rossa, Patrick Pearse, poet and inspirational Nationalist leader, pointed out to the British that they were providing the Nationalists with the most effective ammunition and propaganda. He declared openly '(The British) think they have foreseen everything, think that they have provided against everything; but the fools, the fools, the fools! They have left us our Fenian dead and while Ireland holds these graves, Ireland unfree shall never be at peace.'[45]

Mary MacSwiney had adopted the spirit of these words, becoming clearer in her own conception of where the future of Ireland lay. Unable to support the Arthur Griffith model of a dual-monarchy system in which Ireland would become a separate, independent country sharing its king with Britain, she had accepted the Redmondite version of Home Rule. This latter compromise meant that Ireland would have its own parliament within a federalist arrangement with Britain, terms which Mary agreed to reluctantly while cautioning that 'Mr Redmound does not loom so large on the horizon of the New Ireland',[46] and concluding that 'Mr Redmond is offering the Irish people very poor mouse after such years of labour'.[47] Despite these criticisms, Mary MacSwiney, as many other Irish patriot activists, had not yet delineated for herself the type of government structure that should exist within a free Ireland, a situation that would change with the Easter proclamation of 1916. Mary's own final convictions concerning the governmental form that the Irish state should assume were an amalgamation of her own evolving beliefs and principles, the influence of her brother Terry, and the views of Patrick Pearse, all of which were held together and encouraged by the continuing round of coercive British activities in Ireland.

While wrestling with her ideological position, Mary was faced with the daily realities of running a home and fulfilling her teaching obligations at St Angela's. Because she was devoted to teaching and strongly felt her obligations to her students, she never side-stepped her responsibilities to them to allow more time for her outside activities. She taught Latin with vigour and enthusiasm, prepared the senior girls for examinations, and helped to organise the annual social programme. In her history classes she strove to teach her students the full story of Ireland's past, glorifying in Ireland's ancient civilisation and culture and railing against foreign invaders who had sought to subjugate the Irish when unable to destroy them.[48]

Cumann na mBan activities filled the remainder of Mary's day. An organised, armed insurrection had not yet been planned in 1915, but there were vague stirrings and a continuing build-up among the Volunteers which made an uprising seem inevitable. In the likelihood of such an event, Mary organised Red Cross training for her branch members and by July, twelve women had 'qualified in proficiency in hygiene and emergency nursing'. The women's sphere was clearly delineated: when the shooting started the women were to remain away from the cross fire but be prepared to care for fallen warriors.

Despite this role behind the lines, Cumann na mBan was in no way shrinking from the use of physical force. Their insignia showed the words Cumann na mBan, inscribed in Celtic script, entwined around a rifle, demonstrating rather graphically the women's commitment to the Nationalist movement, their support for taking up the gun as well as with their acceptance of the necessity of violence if Ireland were to be free. It demonstrated a link with Ireland's violent past and a continuation of the fight begun by secret Irish societies in the eighteenth century.

In Cork, there was reputed to be a strong Unionist element within the community whose sentiments were not confined to the Protestant ascendants but were present among some prosperous Catholic families as well.[49] The Murphy family, wealthy Cork brewers from whom came the wife of Terence MacSwiney, were always staunch Unionists. When Mary, in later years, looked back on her associations with the Munster Franchise League, she concluded that many were Unionists at heart.[50]

The Nationalists and the Unionists represented the extremes within Irish society. Although the Volunteers, Cumann na mBan and the Irish Citizen Army were becoming increasingly more visible, the majority remained uninvolved. With unemployment and poverty rampant in Dublin and the housing situation abysmal, the business of daily living could be all consuming. Farm families lived on small, barely profitable holdings, although the coming of the war brought some degree of prosperity to farmers with their produce in high demand.

When considering the extent of expression of militant Nationalism or lack thereof, a review of the Irish contribution to the British war effort is useful. Certainly the Unionist members of the Ulster Volunteers enlisted in the British forces at a great rate. The numbers of recruits fell, however, when one left the Unionist strongholds of the northern counties. W. Allison Phillips in *The Revolution in Ireland, 1906-1923*, gives several reasons for the relatively poor success of the recruiting campaign including 'the recruiting advertisements, devised by publicity agents in London who had no knowledge of what appeals to Irishmen', which proved to be 'amazingly ineffective' and occasionally 'blatantly vulgar'.[51] There was also no 'honest effort made to conciliate the Irish Nationalist spirit' as shown by the British refusal to form the Irish Army Corps. When looking back over the previous century, particularly the famine years, this lack of British sensitivity was hardly new to the Irish but only another in a long series of insults. Phillips concluded that 'on the whole, the wonder is, not that Ireland did not provide more recruits, but that she provided so many'.[52]

David Fitzgerald reviewed the reaction to the war expressed in a provincial newspaper, *The Champion* of Clare and he concluded: '*The Champion's* waning enthusiasm for the war effort, to which the Irish Party leaders were irrevocably committed, accurately reflected the mood of the country.'[53] By 1915, this mood was beginning its swing toward Nationalism, but it would take several more years until the sentiment was overwhelming.

During 1915, Nationalist propaganda was disseminated through an astonishing mass of seditious literature including *Sinn Féin, Fianna Fáil, Ireland* and *Scissors and Paste*. The MacSwiney family not only read these sheets with enthusiasm and approval, they made frequent literary contributions. By this time Mary was dedicated to the goals of obtaining a free Ireland. If for any reason her zeal lagged, she was re-invigorated by her brother Terry although at this point, their relationship was symbiotic, each contributing to the other's Nationalist energy. While individually firm in their own commitment and beliefs, they continued to nurture one another in their pursuit of Irish statehood.

Mary had been deeply influenced by Terry's written words also. In *Principles of Freedom*, he called upon Irish women to join with Irish men, writing:

. . . the woman must stand in with (him) or help to pull him down. Let her understand this and her duty is present and urgent. The man so often wavers on the verge of the right path, the woman often decides him. If she is nobler than he, as is frequently the case, she can lift him to her level; if she is meaner, as she often is, she as surely drags him down. . . they are indispensable to each other; if they stand apart, neither can realise in its fullness the beauty and glory of life. . . If we are to put by national servitude, let us begin by driving out individual obsequiousness. Let the woman realise this, and at least as many women as men will prefer privation with self respect to comfort with contempt. Let us, then, in the name of our common nature, ask those who have her training in hand, to teach the woman to despise the man of menial soul and to loathe the luxury that is his price.[54]

One can speculate about the development of Terence MacSwiney's view of women. Certainly some of it sprang from his own deep rooted spirituality and commitment to justice and equality among all people. His family circumstances cannot be discounted. He had grown up in a home where his mother, though not dominant by force of personality, had shown herself to be a strong, competent woman, keeping the family together under stressful circumstances while encouraging each of her children to pursue fulfilment of their intellectual abilities. From his sister Mary, Terry had an extension of this model as she had overcome physical handicaps, enjoyed learning, pursued her own career and had proven a capable family manager when the need arose. Through the years, she had demonstrated strength and religiosity joined with pragmatism concerning daily events, a quality that Terence often lacked.

In all likelihood the brother and sister contributed to the development of one another. To what extent one gave or received more, it is impossible to delineate. Certainly, Terence verbalised his commitment to Nationalist issues earlier but Mary's feelings in this matter were an ember ready to ignite. Conversely perhaps, Mary, through example and encouragement, had allowed Terry's motivation to evolve.

By the end of 1915, the MacSwiney family was in the forefront of the growing Nationalist element in Ireland. Mary had gone from support of Home Rule to questioning its viability and credibility as she leaned towards greater separation from England. Firmly committed to Nationalist issues rather than purely feminist ones, she illustrated through her words and actions the role of Irish women and the social constraints upon them. Her lack of resistance to this situation demonstrated her own willingness to work within the established social system, a willingness that was accepted by many other Irish women. While staying within these constraints, she was straining more and more at the political restrictions placed on the Irish by England.

2. Martyrdoms, 1916-1920

The year 1916, the year of Patrick Pearse, James Connolly, James Plunkett and the other Easter martyrs, was a turning point for modern Ireland with increasing militarisation in both Unionist and Nationalist areas of the country. David Fitzpatrick wrote that the status of the RIC, in rural areas particularly, was gradually becoming adversarial in relation to the local population, especially in areas where the Irish Volunteers were most active and successful in recruiting.[1] These hostile feelings were further augmented by the passage of the Conscription Law for Great Britain. Dorothy Macardle wrote that with this action 'the government's dilemma in Ireland was complete', continuing that 'to force men into active service with an army which they regarded as their hereditary enemy was at all times a course full of danger; it was doubly precarious when the men were trained, armed and resolute to resist. On the other hand, these men if permitted to remain in Ireland, would create trouble. They were openly preparing for an insurrection, of which only the date remained in doubt.'[2]

Macardle somewhat overstated the case as many southern Catholics were not irretrievably 'hostile to Britain', the concluding evidence being the proportionately small number that actually took part in the military events of Easter week. Besides the partisans of either side, one must not discount those who viewed events without comment from the sidelines. Although it is difficult to assess the state of mind of this group, one might say that their attention had been garnered. For most, their deepest sympathies lay vaguely with Ireland, particularly if one considers the events of the nineteenth century: the mobilisation of the peasantry by Daniel O'Connell, the effects of the famine years, the Land War and continuing agrarian outrages. Nonetheless, pre-Rising in 1916, this group had not been radicalised.

The British were inadvertently contributing to Irish radicalisation, however. Arrests, under the Defence of the State Act, were continuing with 'nearly 500 prosecutions. . . between November 1914 and April 1916'.[3] Newspapers were being continually raided and closed down. Irish

ACTION VIDEO

406 Main St.
Avon, NJ 07717
(201) 988-0038

MEMBERSHIP NO.

1024

Name _Reilly_ Date _3-31-87_

Address _____

_____

Telephone _____

Driver's Lic. No. _____

DESCRIPTION	AMOUNT
Sleeping Beauty (4022)	94
Room with a view (3005)	1.98
tax	
TOTAL	3.10

THE UNDERSIGNED IS TOTALLY RESPONSIBLE
FOR RETURN OF ALL RENTAL TAPES IN GOOD
CONDITION. $1.00 PER DAY LATE CHARGE ON
ALL RENTALS. $2.00 PER DAY LATE CHARGE
ON ALL NEW RELEASES. 50¢ CHARGE FOR ALL
UN-REWOUND TAPES.

**PLEASE REWIND
ALL TAPES**

Signature _M Reilly_

reaction followed quickly: Clan na Gael in the United States was in a state of harried activity to supply arms to the Irish Volunteers; James Connolly and his small band, the Citizen Army, were threatening their own uprising if united action was not forthcoming; and Roger Casement was busy making arrangements with the Germans for a huge gun-running attempt which would ultimately turn into a fiasco. Amidst the growing turbulence, there was a lack of communication between the secret association IRB (Irish Republican Brotherhood) and the Irish Volunteers that would culminate in the disorganised efforts of Easter week.

In Cork, events were no less tumultuous. When the Rising had been agreed upon by the leadership in Dublin, it was decided 'the Cork Brigade was to move into positions on the north and north-west of the county'.[4] The Volunteers in Cork knew that an insurrection was being planned in Dublin but to them the operation was all rather nebulous, a situation for which Terence MacSwiney and Tomás MacCurtain sought clarification.

This was a time of increasing activity at the MacSwiney house. Terry was often gone from the home for varying lengths of time as military plans, drilling and operations advanced, leaving Mary occupied with her own round of activities including management of the house, teaching and Cumann na mBan. Although well aware of the nature of Terry's activities, she asked him no questions, looked for no explanations, expected no details, and supported him completely.[5] Accepting that the military aspects of resistance were his and having no quarrel with this aspect of separate spheres, she stated plainly that 'the guerilla warfare in Ireland is no affair for a woman to take part in. . . There are many things for the women to do besides taking part in the fighting.'[6]

Her concern was not about whose work was more important, believing each person, male or female, should fulfil the obligations necessary to secure a free Ireland. Freedom was the goal to which her gaze was transfixed, caring little for petty squabbling about 'camp followers' and the like, while having a grander view of each doing his or her part. It is unlikely that Mary ever considered that she was setting an example of following rather than leading for future generations of Irish women.

This acquiescence in military matters was in keeping with her own feminist ideology. While wishing for political and social equality, she did not believe it necessary for women to have access to all areas of society to protect this equality – separate but equal being viewed as an acceptable, workable concept. While her background had taught her to be self-reliant, capable and aggressive when necessary, it had also stressed more traditional values such as job differentiation in some areas for men and women. As an example of this, Mary's brothers were never expected to engage in such household tasks as cooking or cleaning just as she did not feel it her role to bear arms. Hers was not a desire to stand Irish society completely on its head, she did want to raise its consciousness about some areas of feminism, however.

Holy Week was filled with confusion and activity. As leaders of the Cork Volunteers, Terence MacSwiney and Tomás MacCurtain looked to the Dublin leadership for instruction, regarding the uprising while Terence, in keeping with his personality, sought to bring unity and cohesion between the IRB and the Volunteers. To this end, he dispatched his sister, Annie, to Dublin on Wednesday of Holy Week to visit and perhaps enhance co-operation among Seán MacDiarmada, Tom Clarke and James Connolly of IRB and Volunteer leader Eoin MacNeill.[7]

Throughout the week military confusion was rampant in Dublin and multiplied in Cork through unclear, delayed or misleading communications. After a series of orders and counter orders to attack or delay, word of the assault on the GPO in Dublin reached Cork late on Easter Monday afternoon. Of this time Chavasse wrote that 'the majority of the citizens of Cork emphatically did not want to see any fighting' while 'hostile groups gathered outside the Volunteers' Hall, watching those who went in and out.'[8]

MacCurtain and MacSwiney, upon returning to Cork HQ, were greeted by a throng of impatient, questioning Volunteers. 'The impression left by the records of the time is that the Volunteer leaders were too dazed and shaken, too possessed by the terrible trap in which they found themselves, to be able to plan and think clearly and effectively.'[9]

While these events were occurring, Mary MacSwiney remained active. In her home, she was ready to take messages if necessary, to house straggling Volunteers and to 'make cakes'.[10] By her own reckoning, this latter activity was engaged in for therapeutic as well as practical reasons. As president of Cumann na mBan, she was also in a state of readiness to fulfil the function of the organisation. Terence had told her that with the coming of the Rising, Cumann na mBan would be responsible for the care and maintenance of dependants. During Easter week, Mary had also been charged with hiring a car to meet Ginger O'Connell when he arrived in Cork, after which she had taken a note to Seán O'Hegarty in Ballingeary, about forty miles from Cork.[11]

The activities allotted to women, and to Mary in particular, were neither insignificant nor unimportant. They were integral for the co-ordination of Volunteer activity and at no time were they belittled or demeaned by the men. There was an overall feeling, though, that this arrangement of details fell within the scope of women's work. Neither in Cork nor in Dublin were women participants in or consulted about military planning or decision-making. Nor is there evidence that they wished to be included. There seemed to be no resentment or jealousy between the sexes about their role assignments.

Mary carried out her actions despite the fact that she did not whole-heartedly support the Rising, believing that the forces were not suitably prepared for combat. Though this was her personal belief, when it came to the time for action, she succumbed to the military discipline of obedience to her superiors for it was not without purpose that Cumann na mBan had been organised along military lines. By supporting the insurrection, however reluctantly, she separated herself from the major-ity of her countrymen, most of whom preferred to consider events rather suspiciously from the background. Her stand would put her in the polit-ical vanguard when the radical position was widely accepted in the 1918 election. Her background in the suffrage movement had prepared her to extol unpopular ideas.

Perhaps the most important event, which would have the most pro-found effect on Mary's life was the Declaration of the Irish Republic by Patrick Pearse. From the steps of the GPO he read his prepared state-ment to the people of Ireland:

We declare the right of the people of Ireland to the ownership of Ireland and to the unfettered control of Irish destinies to be sovereign and indefeasible. . . Standing on that fundamental right and again asserting it in arms in the face of the world, we hereby proclaim the Irish Republic as a Sovereign Independent State and we pledge our lives and the lives of our comrades in arms to the cause of its freedom.[12]

When word of the Proclamation reached Cork, Mary was not immediately caught up in a Republican fervour, receiving the news with gladness coupled with foreboding. Experience told her that the British would not relinquish control over Ireland because of an ill-fated coup attempt in Dublin. Once the Republic had been proclaimed, however, Mary accepted it as a *fait accompli*, the Republic then existing for her in a very real sense and for the remainder of her life she would give herself over to the cause of making the Republic a functioning reality. The leaders of the Irish uprising had made manifest the unarticulated vision of the Irish men and women, so Mary believed; the vision for which she herself had been struggling was clarified. Henceforth, she must do her part to secure the future of the Republic of Ireland.

The reality of the situation did not long escape Mary – the British would hardly accede to the demand for a Republic without protest, the arrest and imprisonment of the Dublin leaders giving credence to her fears rather quickly. The British did not confine themselves to Dublin in their pursuit of conspirators, however, as Cork was quickly awash with British troops whose orders were to maintain public order and to detain known dissidents.

On the morning of 2 May, a tired Mary MacSwiney set out from her home for her teaching post at St Angela's, the events of the past weeks having drained her physically and emotionally. The term was drawing to an end, however, and she had students to prepare for examinations.

Classes began on time as usual. Mary was in the midst of a maths class when the door burst open, British soldiers stepped in and arrested her before her dismayed students. The girls looked on in disbelief, some cried openly, others stood by bewildered. Mary was most annoyed at the fright given to her students and upbraided the young British recruits for their discourteousness. After a few words to the students in an attempt to calm them, Mary left St Angela's under military escort for the Cork jail.[13]

Upon arrival at the jail, Mary found herself in the company of several of her Cumann na mBan colleagues, as a widespread round-up of leaders had been carried out. Despite the general knowledge that the women were involved with this organisation, charges against them were weak at best.

The women were frightened by their first imprisonment but determined to show no trace of this to their British captors. For her part, Mary demanded that she be allowed to send a note to her sister, Annie, explaining her absence lest it cause worry. At first, Mary's demands were refused, but after her continued blustering the officer in charge agreed. Her note read: 'Here I am landed most unexpectedly.' Then, in order that Annie not be too distressed, Mary asked for school books, notes and paper, seeing this confinement as a good time to prepare examinations.[14]

This first imprisonment was to be of short duration. On learning of the plight of the women, Bishop Cohalan interceded on their behalf. It is not known whether the women were released because of lack of evidence or because the British did not wish to offend the hierarchy which was often the ally of the British government in attempts to maintain public order. Nonetheless, late that evening the women were released, much to their joy and relief. The damage had been done, however, as this arrest by the British hardened Mary's resolve to see to the removal of these invaders from England.

A further look at the actions of the Bishop is helpful in understanding the situation in Cork. Bishop Cohalan had been acting as a liaison between the British and the Volunteers to secure a release of arms by the latter. The original agreement had been to give arms to a third party, the Lord Mayor, the date for the transfer being 30 April. Because the Volunteer leaders were spread about and communications were difficult, the date was missed and reset by the Volunteers, but not the British, for 1 May. When the original time limit expired, the British considered all deals off, particularly the stipulation that there would be no arrests. When 2 May came, British officials decided on a show of strength, a quick lesson on who was in charge, by arresting Cumann na mBan and Volunteer leaders though all were released later that same day. Perhaps the intention was to show the Bishop that the British would not be beholden to the Catholic hierarchy while the quick releases were made in order that the churchmen not be hopelessly alienated. Chavasse suggests that once the roundup of insurrection leaders in Dublin was complete, there was less fear of rebellious acts in the other counties.[15]

As was the case with many other actions by the British during this time of trouble, the results were not as intended. The Irish activists were not impressed with this flexing of British muscle, as the brief interlude of imprisonment only served to harden the hearts of the Irish rebels against this foreign intruder. To Mary MacSwiney, one of those so moved, the Republic as declared by Patrick Pearse was the one, viable solution to Ireland's British problem.

Mary's arrest caused a crisis for her at St Angela's. Earlier that year, at the end of March, she had received notice from Sister Elizabeth, Superior of St Angela's, that she could not promise to retain Mary at the school for the scholastic year 1916-17 by citing 'changes that (were to) take place in the community.'[16] These changes included the imminent arrival of a new superior.

Mary had been a concern to the nuns for some time because of her radical politics. At one meeting with the Reverend Mother to discuss this situation, Mary had promised that she would not talk politics in the classroom and later stated: 'I had loyally kept my promise.'[17] Sister Elizabeth had two main concerns, however. The first was her desire not to alienate the parents of the pupils, many of whom retained British sympathies such as Cork Inspector Walsh who had his daughter enrolled at the school. The superior's second concern was to avoid handing on to her successor 'all that trouble about politics'.[18] With these reasons foremost, Mary received a letter in early April stating that her 'services would not be required after the holidays.'[19] The fact that her teaching performance was not in question was revealed in the final line of the note in which Sister Ursula, head mistress of St Angela's wrote: 'We shall be happy to send you any testimonial you may require.'[20]

Mary, determined to be heard, confronted the Mother Superior accusing her of attempting to assuage some parents by 'kow-towing only to the British element and ignoring the Irish element'. Sister Elizabeth replied: 'That's what we should call the rowdy element.'[21] Mary knew her case was lost against a 'West Briton' mentality such as that displayed by the Mother Superior.[22]

Upon learning of the arrest on 2 May, Sister Elizabeth foreshortened Mary's employment, informing her that 'not on any account' was she to enter the school again.[23] She was given £18 as her full salary up to 30 June.

The third of May was to prove even more calamitous to Mary. In the morning she was dismissed abruptly from her teaching post; by late afternoon, word reached her that her brother Terry had been arrested. His detention was no mere gesture on the part of the British and was a serious matter of grave concern to the MacSwiney family.

Shortly after his arrest, Terry, accompanied by a large group of Irish prisoners, was sent to a prison in Frongach, North Wales. Mary's first worry was for her brother's well-being. Release for these anxieties was found in her own activity as systematised efforts for prisoner relief were begun in Cork. Under Mary's direction, groups were organised to collect food, clothing, and personal items such as soap and razors for those imprisoned, while arrangements were made for priests to visit, say mass, hear confessions and, when possible, to convey messages.

In mid-June, Mary herself travelled to North Wales. She was most persistent in her demands and after various letters and meetings with camp officials was finally permitted to visit her brother and Tomás MacCurtain finding them well and in good spirits, to her immense relief. In the MacSwiney tradition, Terry had organised the prisoners for Irish classes and religious discussions. Mary was refused a second visit, even after an appeal to the Home Secretary through her Cork MP.[24]

Despite this final rejection, she was able to aid the prisoners in tangible ways. A £5 subscription for a harmonium was generated as well as foot-balls and a portable altar from a Manchester group.

During June, Mary had to deal with the prospects for her future teaching career. Despite promises of recommendations, new schools would be reluctant to employ a known political radical. She also had developed her own standards for educational material which included a strong Nationalist emphasis, and thus concluded that the most effective way to secure employment and assure the quality of education she wished was to open her own school. Thus, while journeying back and forth to Wales, spare moments were filled planning her school. At times the financial burden and the myriad of small details seemed overwhelming but the idea of a truly Irish school, under her own direction, sustained her.

As the summer progressed, plans for the new school solidified. Mary had arranged a loan of £250 from a friend in Drumcondra and approached Mrs Pearse about buying the furniture from St Enda's School though Patrick's mother was unsure about future plans.[25] The MacSwineys moved to 4 Belgrave Place, a large house that would serve the dual purpose of school and home.

The Bishop, Dr Cohalan, gave his blessing to the new venture and went so far as to suggest a prospective faculty member – a young woman with a BA and a teaching diploma. He reported that this candidate knew 'Irish, sings the traditional Irish and is keenly interested in Irish history'.[26] Even Dr Cohalan, a theological conservative, a dissenter against change and a person with whom Mary would conflict violently in the future, could have his Nationalist sentiments tapped by the idea of an Irish school in his diocese.

Mary contacted friends and acquaintances to disseminate information about the school. Advertisements were placed in the local press about the opening of St Ita's High School and Kindergarten for 'high class education on most modern lines . . . from a fully qualified staff'. The enrolment policy admitted girls up to the secondary grades and boys up to age ten.[27]

Meanwhile, the events of Easter had brought the Nationalist cause forward in Cork as well as around the country. Some middle class Cork families, though perhaps not overt in their Nationalism, believed in Ireland. From this segment, Mary probably drew her early students with the first years enrolment reaching thirty, in her mind a satisfactory number.

Easter Week and its aftermath further solidified Mary's belief that Ireland must become a Republic. Unlike most Irish citizens, she had been directly involved in the confrontation on two fronts: first, with the British authorities, who, recognising her potential for anti-government conspiracy, imprisoned her; second, she had lost her job because of her Nationalist zeal, subsequently meeting the challenge by opening her own school which reinforced her Nationalist beliefs. Her activities were becoming increasingly public, causing a spiral action as, in consequence of her public persona, she was compelled by herself and others to articulate Republican ideology more and more vigorously. From such a position, a proud woman would not retreat without bringing comparisons with Irish compromisers whom she so openly castigated.

St Ita's was a true reflection of Mary MacSwiney. Because it was her own, she could establish a philosophy of education in accordance with her beliefs, her aim for the school being 'to combine careful moral and religious training with a high standard of intellectual work'. She wished and felt confident that her students would 'always stand for what (was) best and noblest in the Irish race, worthy examples of Irish womanhood', and she hoped to graduate students 'of high character with a love of all that is beautiful in the spiritual and material world'.[28]

These were not just idle musings or optimistic dreams to Mary MacSwiney. Throughout her own school years she had exhibited a love of knowledge and enthusiasm for learning, convictions which were later transmitted to her own students, from whom were demanded truth and honesty in all things combined with respect for one another. Young children, preparing for their First Communion at the tender age of seven, were taught to distinguish between the sins of calumny and detraction, the latter being by far the worst in Mary's eyes. Calumny was a lie and the damage done could be rectified by confessing one's dishonesty. Detraction, however, was much harder to undo because it involved telling an unkind truth about another.

Mary treated her students with respect and disdained physical punishment, believing that children could be reasoned with and brought to see the error of their ways. She had a lively sense of humour which she shared with her students and was known to provide a comforting embrace when the need arose.[29]

Students at St Ita's were encouraged in independence of thought, not a common trait in Catholic education at the time. The classics were read and discussed at length. Often in the late afternoon the older pupils would gather in the parlour, oblivious of the disarray, to discuss philosophy and religion.

In the classroom, Mary and her sister Annie both taught with an emphasis on things Irish. Irish history was dealt with from ancient times, and not just as it related to England, while the Irish language was encouraged and taught to all age groups. Despite her own political convictions, however, Mary did not talk about contemporary political controversies. Certainly most, if not all, students were aware of her stance on Nationalist issues, but, perhaps drawing on her experience at St Angela's, such discussions were not to be taken up during class time. The issue came to a head during the first year of the school's operation. One student wore a British coloured rosette to the classroom, in memory of a relative just killed in the Great War. Another girl, in a fit of Republican zeal and possibly hoping to impress Miss MacSwiney, tore off the rosette and called the girl's loyalty to Ireland into question. Mary reacted quickly in dismissing the Irish sympathiser from the school for the insensitive treatment of her fellow student. Each was entitled to her own opinion and a debate was the proper forum for a display of differing views.[30]

To her students, Mary did not verbalise the need for women to achieve equality in the political arena. Her feminism took a more subtle approach, believing that each woman should fulfil her own potential, whatever that might be. Whether it did not occur to her or she did not believe that reaching this potential might be circumscribed by one's sex, is difficult to determine. One is inclined to believe that the question of sex differentiations was far from Mary's mind for she held no quarrel with women lawyers or politicians or homemakers. One did what one had to do. If obstacles were placed in one's path, a way was found either over or around them. No adjustments were made for those women who may be less determined, intelligent or aggressive than she.

The relationship between Mary's view of Irish womanhood and that held by her brother Terence was very close. Terence wrote in *Principles of Freedom*: 'The awakening consciousness of our womanhood is troubling itself rightly over the woman's place in the community. . . and is agitating for a more honourable and dignified place. We applaud the pioneers thus fighting for their honour and dignity.'[31] He went on to say that women 'must understand that greater than the need of the suffrage is the more urgent need of making her fellow woman spirited and self-reliant, ready rather to anticipate a danger than to evade it. When she is thus trained, not all the men of all the nations can deny her recognition and equality.'[32]

One cannot say definitively that this view was echoed exactly by Mary, but her unwritten attitudes were similar to those of her brother. Certainly, she had placed suffrage in a secondary position. The notable part of the passage is the prevalent attitude that before women could gain social equality they must prove their worth, while no such qualification of good and true behaviour was placed upon men. Also there is no reference to the justice argument as expounded by British women's rights crusaders John Stuart Mill and Millicent Fawcett whose argument stated that by nature the sexes were equal; it therefore followed that women should have equal rights with men in all phases of society.

Mary reflected the ideas of her brother in actions toward her students making a continuing effort to imbue the young women in her care with the type of virtues of which Terence would approve. There is the underlying strain, though it remains unspoken, that women must demonstrate their worth in their own social milieu and then, of course, for Ireland.

The events surrounding the Rising had been pivotal in Mary's life. She had her first official brush with the British authorities; she had been forced to leave her teaching post and start her own school; her brother's arrest and deportation to England resulted in her further entanglement in the cause of Ireland; the Republic had been proclaimed; and the British post-Rising activities had appalled her as well as many others. The cumulative result on Mary MacSwiney was the intensification of the belief that Ireland must be free and that she would play an active role in achieving this goal.

Through the autumn of 1916 and into 1917, Mary's involvement in Irish activities broadened, spurred in part by concern for Terence who was being pursued by the British authorities and imprisoned for varying periods of time. Mary remained active in the Prisoner's Relief Organisation and combined this with her Cumann na mBan role.

The women of Cumann na mBan were quickly learning the lessons of politics. In November, 1916, Mary received a letter from the Limerick Cumann urging a general policy of agitation for prisoner releases. The writer indicated that this would be a 'form of propaganda, it would influence American opinion and bring the women together'. [33] Mary heartily endorsed this policy, realising that it touched on the major needs of the movement: an issue, unity and money. It is notable that the Limerick Cumann first approached Mary MacSwiney with their request, a tribute to her work on behalf of prisoners as well as an acknowledgement of her leadership role within the Nationalist movement.

Though deeply involved with prisoner's issues, Mary was also determined that her school would be successful and students' abilities enhanced. While collecting socks and soap for Irish detainees in English prison camps, she was also organising the Christmas programme of St

Ita's. As Cork city was swarming with British soldiers, the junior children enacted an Irish fairy play, *The Shamrock Bell*, and the girls performed the trial scene from *The Merchant of Venice*. [Was Mary fancying herself a wry, Irish Shylock demanding a pound of flesh from the insolent British?] A semblance of balance was kept in her hectic life when for a few minutes she could set aside her National concerns and enjoy and take pride in the antics and achievements of her students.[34]

The new year, 1917, brought increasing organisational activity. In April, a Mansion House conference in Dublin brought together a wide variety of Irish leaders from Sinn Féin, the clergy, trade and labour which Mary attended as a representative of Cork Cumann na mBan. Just as the delegation was disparate in nature so too was the discussion of issues which included taxation, food, tillage and conscription. Although no definite conclusions were reached, the examination of these subjects served as a preparation for the 1918 election campaign, at which time candidates would have to be conversant in these areas and not be content to reiterate 'Brits Out' jingoism.[35]

As a follow-up to this, Mary was approached by Count Plunkett to join the newly formed Liberty League. The written aims required that members 'pledge to repudiate the English parliament, to deny its authority and to use evey available means to attain the complete independence of Ireland.'[36] Mary joined with enthusiasm, as she was only formalising those aims to which she had already pledged herself. Because the organisational headquarters were in Dublin, she felt she could offer only moral encouragement rather than substantive help but again her name was linked with the leadership of radical Republicanism.

In Cork, Cumann na mBan organised concerts, picnics and dances as fund-raisers for prisoners and their dependants. Mary took to the stump saying that 'these men fought for an ideal and it was the duty of the Irish nation to support their wives and children'.[37]

In June, Mary and Annie travelled to England to be present at Terry's wedding. Although a small affair and somewhat hastily prepared, as the groom was still a prisoner, it provided a brief respite from the tenseness and turmoil of 1917.

That year saw the rise of Sinn Féin accompanied by its recognition as the prime mover for Irish freedom. What Arthur Griffith had begun as a peaceful, national movement had now become radical and militarised with a close association with the IRB and the Volunteers. This union was due in part to by-election victories by four Sinn Féin candidates: Count Plunkett in Roscomon, Joseph McGuinness in South Longford,

Eamon de Valera in Clare and William Cosgrave in Kilkenny city, all of whom had committed their efforts on behalf of an Irish Republic. Arthur Griffith's original concepts for Sinn Féin had been changed dramatically; his belief in a dual monarchy had been jettisoned to be replaced by the idea that an Irish Republic, divested of all traces of British authority, was the only suitable solution for a peaceful, united Ireland. The election victories heightened British paranoia, the government responding with increased coercion and a new round of Public Safety Acts. Irish protestors were arrested for flying the tri-colour, holding marches or making inflammatory speeches. This was not an unusual response by the British considering the Great War in Europe was losing popularity on the home front, resulting in their need to demonstrate control and superiority over the nuisance Irish in an effort to shore up public confidence in England.

David Lloyd George, having taken over the government, was trying to maintain discipline and an unruly Ireland would only aggravate an already tumultuous British predicament. To maintain a semblance of stability within Ireland, Lloyd George continued his precarious balancing act between increasingly estranged Unionist and Nationalist populations. In the north, he wrapped his speeches in the Union Jack, reassuring Carson and his cohorts that Ulster would never be severed from the mother country. In the south he at least alluded to the tri-colour in an unsuccessful attempt to make conscription sound more palatable.

Unfortunately for the Prime Minister, the Irish were no longer convinced by British promises. Concurrently, the power of John Redmond was waning quickly with the rise of the Sinn Féin star. Lloyd George's added attempt at Irish appeasement was to call a Convention of Irishmen 'whose duty could be to submit to the cabinet proposals for the future government of Ireland within the empire'.[38] This was now viewed by many as but another in a long history of palliative measure, 'a bone thrown to a snarling dog'.[39] Irish Nationalists, under the suspicious eyes of Arthur Griffith, accused Lloyd George of changing sides once too often. Griffith suggested that when the convention could not reach consensus because of Unionist and Nationalist differences, the wily Welshman would proclaim to the world that 'England left the Irish to settle the question of government for themselves and they could not agree'.[40] Sinn Féin chose to ignore the convention giving credence among their members to the growing belief that violence was the only answer to rid Ireland of British domination, compromise and discussion having proven continually unsuccessful and disappointing.

Mary MacSwiney became a prominent voice in Cork espousing the Sinn Féin philosophy, once the principle of an Irish Republic had been officially adopted by the organisation. With radical Republican men becoming increasingly involved in military preparations, the door was open for women to assume political roles. Though most chose not to do so, in conformity with the values of the church and society, Mary did not hesitate to step forward, believing as she did in the cause. Unlike most Irish women, she had been given an opportunity for education which she seized upon and which in turn had helped in her definition of political justice. Positions of authority were not new to her as she had assumed them both in her home and school; she had gained public exposure, recognition and confidence through her work for women's suffrage, while her actions and beliefs were continually reinforced and encouraged by family members for whom she had great respect. Finally, she was an intelligent woman with a well developed social conscience arrived at through both her religious and secular education and background.

Through her efforts and those of her colleagues, Sinn Féin clubs soon numbered over 1,000. Membership increases were due not only to Republican organisation but were spurred by such events as the death in a Dublin prison of Republican hunger-striker Thomas Ashe and President Wilson's requests to the British government that more sincere efforts at a solution to the Irish problem be made. The Sinn Féin Ard-Fheis of 1917 brought together Republicans and Nationalists who proclaimed their rejection of subsequent co-operation with the British as a tack that had been tried repeatedly but had never succeeded in moving the Irish boat from the British harbour.

In Cork, under Mary MacSwiney's direction, Cumann na mBan became active in the anti-conscription campaign and in April, 1918, an anti-conscription demonstration was organised. She focused on the role of women in thwarting conscription efforts and 'proposed a resolution against the threatened industrial conscription of women'.[41] Cumann members were located at church doors at all masses, arranged at tables and chairs, disseminating information and encouraging all women to sign a pledge which directed that 'no woman would undertake a man's work, who was deprived of employment through refusing enforced military service'.[42] There is no evidence to suggest that Mary believed the women incapable of performing these jobs. Rather, this was a Nationalist issue with that which was best for Ireland as the primary concern. The question can be asked, however, if the unintended long term result of this policy was to keep women out of the male dominated work place and to re-emphasise the concept of separate spheres with deference to men in regard to jobs.

The post-war election brought concentrated activity as Sinn Féin, in a test of its political strength, put forward a full slate of candidates seeking election to the British House of Parliament. Cumann na mBan had the added incentive for being wholeheartedly committed to the election effort as women over thirty had been granted the vote and would participate for the first time as electors. In Cork, as president, Mary co-ordinated activity where the women seemed to be doing what Terence MacSwiney had recommended, proving that they deserved enfranchisement rather than accepting it as justice. Perhaps feeling the continual challenge to prove their worth and buoyed by the proscription of Cumann na mBan as 'a dangerous organisation', women canvassed, made speeches and distributed election material. In Dublin, Countess Markievicz won an election victory attributed largely to the work and persistence of women members of Sinn Féin and other women's organisations.[43]

Mary was particularly involved with the election in Cork because of the candidacy of her again imprisoned brother Terence. His wife was not given to public-speaking and in addition she was now the mother of a child, Máire, born in June. Mary, therefore, took to the campaign trail on her brother's behalf despite the fact that he was running unopposed. He was elected as a MP from Mid-Cork, one of 36 jailed candidates elected, a further illustration that the British were inflaming the Irish by continued military and police coercion.

The overwhelming electoral victory brought Anglo-Irish relations to a different plane as over 70% of the Irish electorate voted for Sinn Féin, thus repudiating British policy while delivering a stunning blow to the British as well as the Irish parliamentary party. Refusing to enter the British parliament, Sinn Féin established their own parliament, Dáil Éireann and immediately set about developing a governmental infrastructure, paralleling the British system by establishing an intricate court system and an extensive network of governmental departments. With Eamon de Valera as president, this new Irish government shadowed that established by the British, causing relations between the two to become even more chaotic. The British increased their military presence, the Irish countering with increased recruitment of Volunteers and more open military displays. The not too surprising outcome was the Anglo-Irish war.

In Cork, as throughout the country, there was a heightened sense of antagonism fuelled by the British troops and the Irish Volunteers. The British were being warned about the devilish Irish before they had even arrived in Ireland. A training manual for officers said that 'every soldier in Ireland must realise that the most harmless civilian may be armed and hostile' and that 'no inhabitant or civilian employee is really to be trusted.'[44] This latter notion was reinforced by the ever present Irish informer. Obviously, a people who would spy on one another lacked honour and trustworthiness. Because the British soldiers lived in a state of suspicion and fear, their own behaviour was adjusted. Innocent pedestrians were stopped on town streets and subjected to verbal harassment and rough searches. Drunken soldiers roamed Cork streets in the evening firing their revolvers at random,[45] activities in part a response to an increasing Volunteer presence. In this situation action and reaction became cyclical so that after a short while it was no longer relevant who had been the provocateur. To assuage their own discomfort in this foreign land, British soldiers acted in brutal ways that strengthened the resolve of convinced Irish Nationalists and converted the uncertain to a hatred of the British. The citizens of Cork had not been committed to revolution in 1916. By 1921, Cork was a Republican stronghold.

British actions continued to antagonise Mary MacSwiney directly: on at least three occasions her house had been searched by the British; she had seen her adored brother, his colleagues, and scores of young men carted off to British prisons where families had to beg and plead for information or visiting rights; as a teacher she was rebuffed in her efforts to present a curriculum directed towards Irish history, literature and culture; when her efforts to change this offended some in her school she had lost her teaching position; she had been jailed without charge; and all around her she saw families in financial distress and material deprivation because a family member had chosen to fight for Irish freedom.

Mary became a functionary in the Sinn Féin government in Cork, further augmenting her increasingly public presence to both the Irish and the British. On 1 February, 1919, under a Cumann na mBan committee, School Meals Flag Day was held. There was a two fold purpose for the collection: first, to encompass children outside the school meals' programme enacted by the British government (In Ireland, those excluded were often the poorest of the poor who attended Christian Brothers' schools, not qualified under the act); second, to supplement the national schools many of which were not sufficiently funded.

The British again showed a lack of sensitivity and abysmally poor judgment when they took names and levied fines because the collection had been held without a permit. As one whose name was taken, Mary was livid at this display of callousness by the British directed at Irish children. She wrote to the Dublin organising committee protesting vehemently 'against any of the money so collected being paid as fines to the English government'. She went on to admonish them against paying at all and if the committee insisted on doing so that 'the committee should (bear) the loss of the money themselves and not use that of the poor children'.[46]

Mary's outrage was increased because Cork had been placed under military rule since the killings of two members of the RIC at Soloheadbeg in January, a situation that added another oppressive dimension to daily life. Citizens were required to obey the curfew laws and dare not transgress by remaining out past eight or nine o'clock in the evening on pain of detention. The continuing display of military equipment and the unending round of searches and detainments were augmenting the work of Sinn Féin, the Volunteers and Cumann na mBan.

Sinn Féin had begun to edge its way into the consciousness of the local citizenry as reported in a study from the English Society of Friends which stated that by 1920, 80% of Ireland rendered allegiance to the Irish Republic. This optimistic figure, which may have been derived from a less than scientific investigation, contained an important qualifier. The report stated that while 'extreme Sinn Féiners were apparently irreconcilable and would be content only by the formation of an Irish Republic, there was still 'a large mass of moderate opinion which would accept a well conceived, liberal measure of self government'.[47] Mary MacSwiney, as an extreme Republican, was on the radical fringe of the Nationalist movement.

Meanwhile, Sinn Féin courts were in full operation and were reported by the Society of Friends as 'efficient and impartial' in dealing with 'criminal offences, questions of rent, ownership and occupation of land'. In rural areas, land questions were still the most hotly contested, due, in part, to land hunger from post-famine displacement. Even in the north-east, where 'Unionists abounded', many from the 'anti-Nationalist party, in their capacity as merchants, found it expedient to use the Dáil courts rather than British courts for the settlement of their bills'.[48]

Sinn Féin gained support among the predominately rural population by helping to establish co-operative creameries, teaching modern agricultural methods, and settling disputes among labourers and farmers. The frequency of the occurrences of the latter demonstrated that the political issues of Home Rule, Republicanism and 'Brits Out' were not the only concerns in much of the countryside. To make sure that the gospel according to Sinn Féin was spread, those in charge made appeals to disputing parties to set aside these internecine squabbles and unite against their common enemy and the cause of their problem, the British and their unwanted representatives in Ireland.[49]

Reflecting on the situation, Mary saw it in clear, precise terms: 'Once 1916 was fought and once the Republican government was established constitutionally, there could be no acceptance of English Home Rule.'[50] Although the Society of Friends had observed that these sentiments were not universal in Ireland, they observed that under the prevailing conditions 'tempers were hardening, the door of opportunity (was) closing'.[51]

Normal conditions were in a state of decline as evidenced during 12 March, when a group of British soldiers looted and destroyed a row of shops on Patrick Street in Cork city, perhaps in fearful reaction to the knowledge that the Cork Volunteers numbered 8,000. On the night of 19 March, Tomás MacCurtain, Lord Mayor of Cork and long time friend and associate of the MacSwiney's, was murdered by the RIC who had burst into his bedroom and shot the Volunteer leader before the eyes of his wife, in an ill-conceived attempt to counter Irish terror, intimidate the population and display British authority.

The MacSwineys, as many of the citizens of Cork, mourned the death through public processions and private promises of revenge. Mary's initial grief was increased when she considered that Terence was second-in-command of the Cork Brigade. One side of her wanted to remove her brother to safety, an unrealistic thought she knew because he would never allow it, while her more stoic side saw MacCurtain's death in an acceptable light if it could help Ireland be free. Her conflict intensified when her brother was appointed Lord Mayor on 20 March, 1920.[52]

Mary listened with mixed feelings to her brother's speech after his investiture with the chain of office. He spoke of the murder of his predecessor and the British attempts to terrorise and added: 'Our first duty is to answer that threat in the only fitting manner, by showing ourselves unterrified, cool and inflexible for the fulfilment of our chief purpose, the establishment of the independence and integrity of the country, the peace and happiness of the Irish Republic.'[53]

Mary's fears for her brother's safety were increased on 11 August,

1920, when he was arrested at Cork City Hall and taken into custody. Although upset by the news, it was incumbent that she remain calm, as the family relied upon her good judgment, common sense and reliability. Having tried to reassure Annie, who paced the house railing against the British and swearing vengeance upon their blackened souls, Mary went the next day to Terry's wife, Muriel, and daughter, Máire Óg, who were on holidays by the sea.[54] Her sister-in-law was told of the arrest and given the court-martial date of 16 August. Muriel then went to Cork city, while Mary stayed with her godchild, then two years old.

Quite as expected, Terence MacSwiney was convicted on various charges including possession of an RIC numerical cypher and 'being in possession of (documents the publication of which would be) likely to cause disaffection to his majesty'.[55] What was unexpected was that Terence MacSwiney had begun fasting from the time of his arrest to protest the illegality of these British actions on Irish soil. He was sentenced to two years' imprisonment and during the pre-dawn hours of the following morning he was transported by boat to South Wales and then taken by train to London. He was driven to Brixton Prison, the gates of which he would not again pass through alive. This was the fifth day of his hunger-strike.[56]

The prisoner's health deteriorated rapidly, probably due to the exhausting schedule he had been maintaining, the emotional trauma surrounding his arrest and trial, and the physical trauma of undergoing these intense stresses while fasting. When the family received word of Terry's condition, wife Muriel, sisters Annie and Mary, and brother Seán left imediately for London. They would all stay throughout the ordeal that was to come.

Mary organised a rotating schedule for the family so that someone could be with Terence through the day. Deference was given to Muriel, who chose to be at her husband's bedside during the evening hours while Mary and Annie were usually at the prison in the afternoon. Mary read to her brother often from Thomas à Kempis' *Imitation of Christ*, a book of which they never tired. They were intrigued by the mystical qualities of the author and discussed him in relation to Teresa of Avila and John Divine.[57]

While not at her brother's bedside, Mary debated with herself concerning the best course of action to pursue and was immediately in touch with Art O'Brien, the representative of the Irish Republic in London. Together, they understood that they must put aside their own pain and try to make as much political capital from the situation as possible.

In consequence of this decision, Mary met almost daily with the press, providing them with details of her brother's deteriorating condition. As the days of the hunger-strike wore on, the coverage in the British press became more and more extensive though rarely sympathetic. Gradually, the foreign press also adopted the story as it was a most intriguing, easily romanticised tale: the young, beautiful, and frail Muriel going each day to be at the bedside of her starving husband who himself was a modern day martyr giving away his life, an inch at a time, that Ireland might be free; at home in Cork, an innocent two-year-old awaited the return of her father who had gone away so abruptly.

Reporters began to converge on London from thoughout the western world. The European press asked why, considering the promises made after the Great War to free the small nations of the world, Ireland was still manacled to Britain. American reporters, particularly from cities with high Irish-American populations, wired graphic reports to their home offices. Australia and Canada, from within the empire, asked why this man could not be released.

As the story spread, it had the effect for which Mary had hoped. Letters and telegrams of support for the prisoner flooded the mail room at Brixton prison while David Lloyd George was deluged with requests, some threatening in nature, to free the prisoner in the name of all that was right and just. Máire Óg received dolls from around the world as tokens of consolation from people who could do little to secure her father's release but felt the need to give expression of their support for his fight.

During these days Mary gathered her strength for two purposes: to sustain her brother's morale and to do good for Ireland. To see her brother wrung her heart as she loved him dearly. His suffering moved her to tears of pain and anxiety but only when she was alone, her public persona remaining stern and inflexible.

Mary hoped to gain support from organised labour in order to bring further pressure to bear on the politicians to release Terence. On 9 September, she travelled to Portsmouth to meet with the Trades Union Congress, a group that had been supportive of Irish labour in the past, particularly in 1913. Earlier in the week, the Congress had asked the Prime Minister, through a telegraph, to release Terence MacSwiney. Mary hoped to convince the Congress to take a giant step in their support of the Lord Mayor by calling a general strike. She was refused permission to address the Congress, however, the president of the body giving her a verbal pat on the head as he rejected her requests. Referring to her desire to speak, Mr Thomas, the president, said patronisingly: 'If any of you think for a moment of the torture that this woman has been through for the past three weeks, you ought to know quite well that it would be madness to allow anything of the kind. . . The torture she is going through naturally imposes a strain that becomes difficult to bear.' He suggested that in lieu of an address by Mary MacSwiney, another telegram of protest be sent to Lloyd George despite the fact that the first one had brought no response, the Prime Minister saying generally that the entire issue belonged before a parliamentary committee. Mr Thomas turned aside a request from the floor suggesting that the parliamentary committee be asked to interview the Prime Minister.[58]

Mary was enraged by the condescending attitude of the Congress President, not considering his motivations, only his lack of a favourable response. Mr Thomas may have been reacting to both Mary's sex and her nationality. Although Marxist Socialism called for the barrier of Nationalism to be cast aside, that which existed between the British and the Irish was very high and very resistant. The British had come to scorn the poor Irish who had flooded English cities and displaced British workers by under-cutting their wages. Mr Thomas and his organisation were willing to give lip-service and token support to the Lord Mayor who lay dying slowly in Brixton Prison but were not willing to go any further with their protest than the issuing of a telegram. They would save their strike threats and industrial actions for causes that were more immediate to themselves.

Mary was disappointed with, but not immobilised by, this negative response. She herself wrote a letter to David Lloyd George chastising him for his inactivity and insensitivity to the Irish cause adding that he need not make emotional appeals to women about the losses that they could suffer: 'Ireland's women stand side by side with Ireland's men in the demand for absolute independence.'[59] Never one to grovel before the British Prime Minister, she demanded justice, couching her remarks with barely veiled threats of the woe that would betide him and his country if they did not accede to the wishes of the Irish.

The British government initially was caught unaware by the hunger-strike, expecting that Terence MacSwiney would agree to take food once his health became seriously impaired. As the days went on and the letter campaign grew, their rather cavalier demeanour became one of concern. The government had no wish to be depicted around the world as an uncaring oaf who turned a blind eye while an upstanding young man, albeit an Irishman, starved himself to death. Conversely, they felt obliged and pressured by the Irish Unionists, led by Edward Carson, to remain firm in the face of Irish Nationalist threats. To maintain credibility under such circumstances, Lloyd George was again called upon to display his dazzling political foot work.

Mary had long since ceased to be beguiled by the conciliatory words of David Lloyd George and, as her brother lay dying, she saw excessively cynical motivation behind the Prime Minister's intransigence. She believed that the Prime Minister hoped the Lord Mayor's death would cause such fierce outbreaks in Ireland that the British would be forced to invoke coercionist measures just as they had done in 1798.[60]

Mary became increasingly irritable when a British priest, Father Bernard Vaughan, questioned the rectitude of providing the sacraments to a person who was in effect committing suicide, a mortal sin in the eyes of the Church. A public response was made, indicating that, in fact, her brother was sacrificing his life for his fellow countrymen. Because, 'greater love than this hath no man, to give his life for a friend' her brother's actions were 'heroic in the highest degree'. Her strength and patience wearing thin, Mary was in no mood for subtlety. She addressed the priest tersely: 'How then, can one be so stupid or malicious as to suggest that the Lord Mayor of Cork, or any other man in a similar state for the sake of a great principle, is guilty of self-murder.' In what was becoming more and more her aggressive style, with overtones of moral superiority, she again went on the offensive, concluding that 'Father Vaughan, as an Englishman, must share the guilt of his government's crime. Let him then preserve a shamed silence while a hero dies.'[61]

As international coverage of the hunger-strike increased, Mary looked to the United States for official support. Unofficial support was mounting as demonstrated by the refusal of New York longshoremen to unload British ships. A letter, drafted to the two presidential candidates, Senator Harding and Governor Cox, illustrated Mary's emerging political style, righteous and aggressive, believing that God and justice were on her side. She would never assume the role of a humble supplicant while fighting for Ireland. Her style was combative, challenging others to do what she perceived as right. In this spirit she wrote to the candidates:

There is a country, which though small, has helped more than any other to build up the greatness of your country and which materially supported your country's fight for freedom. That country, Ireland, is the victim of the same tyrannous oppression which your country had to combat. Ireland is the victim of England's unbridled tyranny and terrorism today and 25 million Irish, throughout the world, would like to hear from him, who may be America's president, what he is prepared to do against the foreign forces of brutality and inhumanity in Ireland. . . Give now, through your press, some message of hope to the Irish population of the world, that the inhumanity practised by England on Irish prisoners and on Ireland, cannot continue with the tacit consent of the free nations of the world.[62]

In her life until this point, Mary had deferred to men in some political areas as demonstrated by the role of Cumann na mBan. She quite readily assumed the place of assistant or perhaps co-operative associate, in doing what was required. In the public arena now, she would again do what was required – be seen as a forceful presence, one with whom to be reckoned, all Victorian notions or deceptions about delicacy or a woman's place being dismissed. Because Mary emerged so readily into the national limelight during her brother's hunger-strike, it can be believed that she harboured no thought about the innate subservience of women. Again, no time was wasted quibbling about divisions of labour as she forged ahead with the task at hand. She remembered Terence's words concerning the qualities distinctive to women: 'gentleness, sensibility, sympathy and tenderness and when we have these qualities intensified in any woman and with them combined the endurance, courage and daring that are taken as the manly virtues, we have a woman of the heroic type.'[63]

As the hunger-strike progressed and was prolonged, Mary felt the responsibility to exhibit all of these qualities. The family members looked to her for strength and leadership just as they had after the death of their mother. Art O'Brien could serve as a guide through the political maze of prison officials and public servants, but Mary herself would represent the MacSwineys.

Because of her public posture, Mary was thought by many to be rigid and unfeeling, a stereo-typical spinster schoolteacher of the early twentieth century. During and after the hunger-strike, there were those, including the Bishop of Cork, who held Mary responsible for her brother's death. These accusers pictured her with shoulders set, speaking through pinched lips, prodding Terence to do his duty, maintain his fast and be a hero for Ireland. If it had not been for her stern admonishments, some believed, Terence would have forsaken his fast.[64]

This picture does little justice to either Terence or Mary. Was Terence so cowed by his older sister, now the family matriarch, that he conceded his life so as not to disobey and hence receive her wrath? This was hardly the case. The two loved each other deeply but their love was rooted in mutual respect. As independence of thought was a valued characteristic within their family, neither would force their opinions on the other although without doubt they were mutually influential. The hunger-strike, however, belonged to Terence alone. When he began, he believed that it would be short-lived, release would be secured, and it would be a victory for Ireland. When this planned scenario was thwarted by the British authorities, his resolve to maintain the hunger-strike remained. He was committed to it as a matter of principle, a principle that was inextricably woven with the fate of Ireland.[65]

Mary understood the rationale behind her brother's action, an understanding that became clearer as they read together the words of Thomas à Kempis, from whom Terence had developed the philosophy that 'it was not he that could inflict the most but the one that could endure the most that would prevail'. This expression brought determination to Terence and understanding to Mary as with her family and Muriel, she watched daily her brother's body shrink but his spirit grow. Mary would not tamper with the ideals that her brother saw so clearly. When she refused to have him force fed, some believed her heartless and callous whereas, in reality, she would have loved to end her brother's suffering as she had always sought to mitigate any of his pain as they were growing up. She had too much respect for his commitment to do so, however. Her brother's wishes would not be countermanded because as long as he was conscious and in control of his faculties, no amount of pressure would change his mind.

On 20 September, Mary had written to the Home Office to clarify the position of her brother. She wished it understood that he was not seeking political prisoner status, rather, his was a protest 'against the act of imprisoning him' at all.[66] Because Dáil Éireann was the duly elected government of Ireland, the British had no authority, either moral or legal, to make the arrest. It was important to the MacSwineys that the larger issue be made clear to both the government and the public.

As the hunger-strike continued into October, far surpassing the length any one thought possible, the British sought explanations. Not surprisingly, they accused the family, friends, and spiritual advisor Father Dominic, of surreptitiously bringing food to the prisoner. Mary, outraged at such assaults on her honour, continually denied these allegations in the press, attributing them to the British, who being without conscience or honour themselves, could not understand these virtues in others.[67]

The most dramatic confrontation came late in October, as Terence was drifting in and out of consciousness. Citing his deteriorating health and the subsequent need for more intensive medical attention, family visiting privileges were being shortened. On 20 October, Edward Short, Secretary for Home Affairs, speaking before the House of Commons, said that Terence MacSwiney, though unconscious, had voluntarily swallowed the food administered to him. He added that although the prison doctors did not feed him until he became unconscious, he (Minister Short) could not answer for what Terence's friends were doing.

Mary, enraged by these remarks, again vented her emotions and hostility in a letter to the secretary with copies to the press in which she called Mr Short's innuendoes 'as despicable as the rest of (his) government's campaign of lies by implication against (the MacSwineys)'. She added tersely: 'We have ceased to hope for any sign of honour or fair play from any member of the English government, but you will not succeed in discrediting us or the cause for which we stand – Ireland's independence among the civilised nations of the world.'[68]

The seventy-third day of Terence's hunger-strike was one of confrontation and frustration for Mary, her family and friends. As the prisoner was on the verge of death, Mary and Annie were refused entrance to their brother's cell while Seán and Muriel were allowed in for short periods. Mary verbally assaulted the prison doctor, the warden and any prison official with whom she came in contact. Finally, because of their disruptive behaviour, Annie and Mary were not allowed past the prison gates. In a display of anger, sorrow and frustration, they spent the day at the prison gates, alternating prayers with press interviews.

The following day, Terence's ordeal ended. He died on the seventy-fourth day of his prolonged, well publicised, hunger-strike. Mary was relieved that his suffering was over and determined that his death would not be in vain.

Art O'Brien had received permission from Bishop Amigo for the body to be taken to lie in state in Southwark Cathedral, the one condition set by the bishop being that the proceeding should be apolitical. After the body was taken to the church, several of Terry's Volunteer comrades slipped in and dressed their dead colleague in his uniform. Mary was hardly naive about the need to exploit her brother's death for Nationalist gain but was upset over the uniform incident, making her displeasure known to Art O'Brien. As a family, they had given their word of honour to the Bishop to abide by his conditions and the uniform was a violation of that agreement.[69]

Mary accompanied the coffin containing her brother's body on its procession through the streets of London, on the boat across the Irish Sea to Dublin and finally by train back to the family home in Cork. Everywhere the outpouring of emotion was overwhelming, more than the Nationalist leaders could have hoped for. Through it all Mary wore black and the traditional veil of mourning. From that time on she would rarely wear any colour other than black.

To say that this hunger-strike had a part in shaping Mary's future would be an understatement as the effects on her were many. Personally, she would mourn the loss of her brother until her own death as an emptiness had been left that could never be filled. She was also given new personal responsibilities. As her brother lay dying, he had given Mary joint custody of his daughter Máire Óg perhaps realising that Muriel's mental health was too fragile to cope with all that had happened and raise the child as well. Mary felt very deeply the responsibility toward her niece, Terry's living legacy.

Mary had become more aware of political realities, realising that Ireland needed additional leverage, both financial and political, in dealing with Britain. She looked to America for this assistance, her thoughts guided in that direction by Eamon de Valera who had been in America for over a year.

Her belief that the press was a powerful medium for circulating information had been reaffirmed and in the future she would use this channel often. Experience had been gained in the public forum as reporters and other questioners had been faced daily. Although they were generally supportive, some had been hostile interrogators, particularly those representatives from the British press.

While drafting letters and giving interviews, Mary had been compelled to crystallise her own ideas about the Irish crisis and set an agenda for the future. Since the Easter Proclamation of Patrick Pearse, she too had proclaimed the Republic. Her hatred of the British intrusion had been galvanised. What had previously been a grand dream, an independent Irish nation, was now an ideal just waiting to be grasped and made a reality.

After the death of Terence, Mary believed that she was the custodian of his dream. Not to continue to demonstrate service and dedication in the cause of Irish freedom would be to somehow discredit his name and dishonour his memory. The family torch had been passed to her now and she must hold it high and go forward. His heroic death had served to further sanctify Terence in Mary's eyes, adding further pressure on her to seek to fulfil his dream for Ireland. Not to do so would be a desecration of his memory and would make a mockery of his death.

Mary took time to re-read her dead brother's essays. By reading them carefully and combining them with her own beliefs, she was able to set her work for the Republic on a firm ideological foundation. Terence had written that 'the end of Freedom is to realise the salvation and happiness of all peoples'. Mary believed that this must be the goal of the Irish separatists. It was necessary that Republicans show that their policy would 'harmonise, unify and develop national life' as well as restore the Irish race to 'its place among the nations, enabling them to fulfil a national destiny'. Mary concluded that in a 'free state each citizen is in the natural environment for full self development. In an enslaved state it is the reverse.'

Terence had not withdrawn in fear or indignation from the thought of war, writing that 'war must be faced and blood shed not gleefully but as a terrible necessity because there were moral horrors worse than any physical horror'. Freedom was necessary to develop the soul and 'the soul is greater than the body'. This latter belief had been part of Mary's life for many years. She had struggled to reach a satisfactory compromise with the Catholic teaching that one must endure unhappiness in this life to be happy in the next. Finally, she had set it aside as too simplistic, too passive, adopting instead a philosophy of improvement through action, action that would sometimes, regrettably, have to go beyond self-actualisation into the public arena ending in armed conflict. Mary concluded that 'moral force does not exclude physical force, it but inspires and ennobles it', believing unequivocally that the fight for Irish separation was a 'just war'.[70]

Mary went forward from her brother's death armed with the under-standing of her own beliefs and a need to go on in the struggle to secure a free Ireland. Her vision of what the future should be was clear and cloudless, an Irish Republic, the government of which was Dáil Éireann. This was the only satisfactory answer; anything less than that may be easier but it would represent a compromise of principle, of what was right, just and honourable. Mary would be forced to reject any such compromise, believing one could not bargain away one's soul.

As the hunger-strike ended, a new phase of Mary's life began. She emerged from the seventy-four days with her Republicanism resolute, her political acumen increased and matured and her name known throughout Ireland, as well as in Irish circles in Britain and the United States. No longer would she be seen as an extension of her brother in Republican matters, the role typically ascribed to most Irish women.

Though still beholden to Terence for name recognition, she was developing a political career independent of him.

The MacSwineys were not given long to mourn their loss privately after their return to Cork. While Muriel was reunited with her daughter, Annie and Mary had to tend to their school which the other teachers had conducted in their absence. Meanwhile, outside their doors, military rule was still the order of the day, with troops patrolling the streets while Volunteers continued their hit and run attacks from back alleys. Daily life went on against a backdrop of escalating fear, distrust and violence.

3. The First American Tour, 1920-1921

During November, the MacSwiney family was approached by a representative of an American group, organised to establish a commission to examine conditions in Ireland, under the sponsorship of the New York based, Irish-American newspaper, *The Nation*. Although the organisers sought to present a front of objectivity, the proposed commission's nature and origins were Irish and Nationalist. It was believed that Muriel MacSwiney, the bereaved young widow, could be a star witness with Mary also invited as a witness but more particularly as a companion to her sister-in-law. The MacSwineys saw this mission as their duty to Ireland and agreed to participate.

On 26 November, 1920, Muriel and Mary MacSwiney boarded *The Celtic* at Queenstown (Cobh) and set sail for America. Both women, wrapped in their black coats and hats against the late autumn wind, waved solemnly to their friends and family who had come to see them off. Neither of the women knew what to expect from this trip to America, a journey so many of their countrymen had been forced, through economic hardship, to make before them. The voyage was a quiet time for the two women, a time of reflection on what had passed and what was to come.[1]

The solitude of the journey was broken abruptly when the ship sailed into New York harbour on 5 December as crowds had been amassing since early in the day to greet the widow and sister of Ireland's latest hero. Bands struck up Irish tunes while a confused police guard sought to sort out conflicting information about the pier at which the ship would dock. Streamers were tossed in the air and banners were held high to identify various Irish-American organisations as the two women emerged to this crowd of boisterous enthusiasts. Their welcoming party was sufficiently large to block the exit of financier J. P. Morgan, who had been travelling aboard the same ship.

When the official party had been gathered together, they formed a motorcade procession to the St Regis Hotel, led by 'three automobiles bearing wounded soldiers'. The initial group was followed by 70 more cars, each adorned with the 'stars and stripes and the orange, green, and white, of the Irish Republic'. This was but the beginning. 'In the procession were more than 5,000 marchers from the various Irish societies and children from the Carmelite school in costumes.' The marchers were preceded by 'the band of the 69th Regiment which played the Sinn Féin Soldiers Song and other airs.'[2]

Mary appeared both bewildered and bemused as the parade continued up Fifth Avenue towards the hotel. She may well have pondered the sentiments of her associate from the Irish Women's Suffrage League, Hannah Sheehy-Skeffington, who, after her own trip to America, had written:

The Americans are incurably sentimental, they like rather blatant appeals to the emotions and are very eager for thrills. The human interest, as they call it, particularly appeals to them and usually, as everywhere in America, a woman has a good show and is more sure of sympathy and kindliness in the States than usually would be the case in another country.[3]

Once the cars reached the hotel, the two women, though physically tired and emotionally drained, were taken into a hall for another official reception. When asked her impression of New York, Mary, too weary for subtlety, exhibited the candour for which she was known, replying bluntly: 'I think it's very wonderful. I think the tall buildings are very remarkable, but very ugly from an artistic point of view.'[4]

The following morning, planned activities began in earnest with morning mass at St Patrick's followed by a meeting with Archbishop Hayes. The Irish situation was discussed briefly, with Mary encouraging the Archbishop to lend moral and verbal support to the cause of an Irish Republic.

Then it was on to a reception hosted by Mrs Henry Villard, whose husband was editor of *The Nation*, the sponsor of the trip. Local Irish-American leaders were anxious to meet the wife and sister of the Irish hero about whom they had read so much and supported so earnestly.

This was followed by a brief meeting with Eamon de Valera who had himself been on an extended tour in the United States. He gave his sympathies over the recent bereavement but discussed little of substance, being somewhat wary of women and, as yet, not taking too seriously Mary's political abilities.[5]

The two women arrived in Washington, DC late that evening probably anxious only for some solitude and rest after their tiring schedule. At this stop they were greeted by 5,000 supporters who remained silent as a mark of respect for the Lord Mayor and his family. The two were then taken from the station by motorcade along Pennsylvania Avenue, past the White House, and on to their hotel via Rhode Island Avenue.[6]

It was an irony, not lost on Mary, that the procession was led by 200 veterans of the First World War, a war scorned and belittled by Irish Republicans. This was lost on many of the Irish-Americans who had an emotional attachment to the land of their forefathers rather than an intellectual understanding of the political situation. The response to the arrival of the MacSwineys illustrated the continuing readiness by Irish-Americans to exhibit sentimentality over their homeland by becoming caught up in the spirit of such moments. Perhaps these supporters were acting from latent guilt about leaving their homeland in its time of crisis, resulting in their extreme reactions to and emphasis on the sacrifices of those who remained behind to continue Ireland's fight. Certainly, Irish-Americans had felt helpless during the hunger-strike of Terence MacSwiney, so by honouring his wife and sister, they could at last feel that they were overtly expressing their appreciation and support while acknowledging his martyrdom. While salving the Irish-American conscience, this outpouring of sentiment added to the bond being established between them and radical Republicans, begun by the Easter martyrs of 1916, encouraged by the tour of Eamon de Valera, and strengthened by the arrival, reception and rhetoric of the MacSwineys.

The following day, Muriel and Mary went before the Committee on Conditions in Ireland. The membership of the committee consisted of one hundred and fifty persons of varied backgrounds including eight American senators, varied congressmen, governors of five states, mayors, representatives of the Catholic and Protestant clergy, teachers, trade unionists, writers and merchants. Among the panel were Jane Addams, feminist leader and social activist, and Rose Schneiderman of the Women's Trade Union League, the organisers intending that the body be 'representative of all shades of American opinion'. The list of witnesses indicated that the same cross section of opinion was not so sought after among those testifying. Among the witnesses were the MacSwineys, relatives of Tomás MacCurtain, the current mayor of Cork, various town councillors and five former members of the RIC. The American witnesses were primarily reporters who had investigated the Irish situation and filed reports sympathetic to the Irish Nationalists. From England, the Committee sought to secure witnesses from the British Labour Party, the British Society of Friends, and the Women's International League, each of whom had previously undertaken examination of the

Irish situation and been dismayed by British policy and continuing atrocities perpetrated against the Irish. The Committee spokesperson stated that attempts to call pro-British witnesses had been thwarted by the British government which would not co-operate, believing the groups' findings were pre-determined.

Muriel, the first of the MacSwineys called to testify, recounted the details of her husband's arrest, detention and death. An emotional climax was reached when she told, in a quiet voice, of their two year old's last visit with her father as he lay dying, too weak to take his child in his arms. Although her time on the stand was brief, the tragic figure, cloaked in mourning, her face a picture of sorrow, her voice continually on the edge of a tearful breakdown, was all the Committee had hoped for.

Mary was called as the following witness, her demeanour a contrast to that of her sister-in-law. *The New York Evening Post* described her as 'an Irish schoolteacher, clear of complexion, radiating enthusiasm, perfectly composed', who went on for two hours giving a 'word-picture-lecture of Ireland's fight against a government her Irish people have never accepted'.[7] She discussed the situation since Easter week, describing the Sinn Féin government, Dáil Éireann, and the positive response to it among the Irish people and the continuing breakdown of British civil authority coupled with their coercive efforts to maintain some semblance of authority. British court authorities were described as sitting 'behind barbed wire barricades and sandbags, surrounded by a regiment of soldiers waiting for cases which never came'.[8] The outrages of the British forces in Ireland were detailed, coupled with descriptions of governmental insensitivity exemplified particularly during the final days of her brother's life. Mary commended the Irish Republican leaders for their upright character and well defined moral sense, a sharp contrast, indeed, to their British counterparts. She concluded, her voice having not wavered throughout her oration, by stating emphatically: 'We are not rebels and it is not rebellion but insurrection that disturbs Ireland. A rebellion is an uprising against a lawful government.'[9] This recitation had not been in the least objective nor had the witness any intention of making it so. She had no personal interest in British explanations of their presence in Ireland or their reasons for continuing military actions. Her mind was set on bringing about their removal from her homeland and it was the necessity for this action she wished to convey, in no uncertain terms, to her American audiences.

The following day, Mary was back in the witness chair. This time her words came less in the narrative style of her previous account, being more directed towards ways to change the situation in Ireland. To the panel before her she said clearly and with conviction that the 'United States had not lived up to its ideal of making the world safe for democracy'. Spurning the notion that the Irish conflict had its roots in religious intolerance, she said that the British government was 'deliberately firing religious hatreds' adding that there would be no religious differences 'if Protestants and Catholics were left without outside interference'.[10]

Mary's abilities as a speaker did not go unnoticed outside the committee room for, following her testimony, she was asked to make a public address at Central High School in Washington, an invitation accepted without hesitation. Mary spent this occasion clarifying what she perceived to be America's role in the Irish situation, admitting realistically: 'Ireland does not expect America to go to war on her account.' However, America could help in the most obvious manner: 'Ireland does ask aid from the richest country in the world.' She stopped short of implying that money collected would be used for guns, ammunition and other military supplies. Rather, the request was put on a more humanitarian plane as she told how the British destruction of crops and food supplies would bring starvation during the coming winter unless aid was forthcoming. To leave no heart-string unplucked, she declared in a sermonistic style: 'The men can get on; the women can stand the suffering. But it is for the children I plead.' To complete the allusion to Britain as their common enemy, the upcoming winter was referred to as 'Ireland's Valley Forge'.[11]

Although, in retrospect, these speeches may seem orchestrated, carefully charted and planned, this was hardly the case. Sometimes a few notes were jotted on a piece of paper about points she wished not to overlook but this was the extent of formal preparation. Mary always knew she would speak about the tyranny of the British and the need of an Irish Republic but aside from these basics, speeches were extemporaneous, often increasing in fervour as her audience reacted. She had clarified her stand completely in her own mind, and was convinced of the truth and justice of her argument and most important, perhaps, its rightness. Mary always spoke with an air of righteousness which cast any would-be detractors in the role of morally defective opponents of good.

Within the next days she was asked again to speak to a group of Irish sympathisers at Gonzaga Hall in Washington. Immediately before coming forward to the podium, Mary was handed a dispatch that told of the burning of Cork city. It had been a horrible, destructive blaze set by the British troops that did over $30,000,000 damage to the city centre. Mary was overcome! Her first worry was about her sister Annie, but she trusted that their home was far enough removed to keep her safe. The thought of the Cork she loved lying now in cinders brought feelings of desolation and isolation. Looking up from the paper that bore the dreadful news she said: 'It is unspeakably horrible. Those devils. How I wish I could get at them.'[12] As it turned out, Mary spent the remainder of her life attempting to 'get at them'. But that evening in December, her mind in turmoil, she went before the audience, spoke for but a few minutes and, for perhaps the only time in her life, stepped down, at a loss for words, with tears in her eyes.

From Washington, Mary was called back to New York to meet with Eamon de Valera, the President of the Irish Republic, who had been on a long tour of the United States lasting over one and a half years. During his stay he had had serious conflicts with the leaders of Clann na Gael, Judge Cohalan and John Devoy, over who would be responsible for policy-making for Ireland. The two Americans believed that, as the main providers of funds, they should also be the decision-makers. De Valera believed the Americans should provide money because they were in a position to do so, but that they should then have the good sense to stand aside and let the leadership in Ireland take over, as they were on the front lines, often having to react quickly to a fluctuating political and military environment. When a compromise solution could not be reached with the American leadership, De Valera founded his own organisation in November 1920, appropriately called The American Association for the Recognition of an Irish Republic.[13]

In mid-December, after his long absence and the war in Ireland escalating, De Valera felt compelled to return home. He spoke to Mary briefly, explaining his own situation and asking her to stay on in America, continuing the task he had begun. As might be expected, he put the request in terms of Mary's duty to the Republic and her martyred brother, an offer Mary could not in conscience refuse, though she would have preferred to return home.[14]

When De Valera issued this request, he knew the importance of American support, both political and financial. Therefore, the position with which he was entrusting Mary MacSwiney was an important one, one crucial to Irish efforts in the United States. Certainly Mary would not be the sole representative, but would be venturing into many areas new to the Irish cause.

De Valera, as reported by his biographers Longford and O'Neill, had an ambivalent attitude toward women in public life. He was a traditional Pauline in his view and interpretation of the family, believing women should be subject to their husbands, bear children, maintain the home and support their husband's endeavours. De Valera had seen the effect that Mary had achieved after her short stay in Washington. She was shrewd, articulate and unintimidated by group or media attention. More than this, she was the sister of a bona fide Irish martyr. For De Valera, these positive attributes outweighed the fact that she was female and hence, by his interpretation, not well acquainted with the wily world of politics. De Valera also had few other alternatives at hand. His close male colleagues were needed in Ireland for the final push against the British while Mary was present, primed and ready. All factors considered, she was the best possible candidate available.

Mary wasted no time in beginning her new duties. After the meeting with De Valera, she proceeded to Boston, where she was received by a crowd estimated at between 8,000 and 10,000.[15] With her Washington experience as a guide, she stepped to the podium with enthusiasm and authority, making a speech *The Boston Globe* reported as one 'which those in the hall will long remember because of the impressive manner in which it was delivered and the unusual character of the address itself.' The story went on to comment on Mary's 'great power as a speaker, her remarkable diction and (her) comprehensive knowledge of every phase of American history in its relation to Ireland.' The element of surprise for the audience was compounded because 'there were few in that vast audience who... knew anything of this remarkable woman'.[16]

Mary chose this opportunity to go on the attack, telling her American supporters that if they had stayed with the ideals for which the United States had entered the First World War, Ireland would be free. Not content to leave the subject with that brief accusation, she increased her volume and added:

You sheathed the sword and you left Ireland a slave. You fought for freedom for small nations and left the biggest of the small nations, the oldest of the small nations and the most important of the small nations to Christianity and civilisation; she is the only one you left enslaved.[17]

Mary stepped down from the speakers' platform amid thunderous applause and cheers for herself and for Ireland.

During the days preceding Christmas, meetings continued with leaders of the Irish-American constituency. She was eager to press the cause of the Irish Republic which, in the future, would be referred to simply as 'recognition'.

As the new year began, Muriel MacSwiney decided to return to Ireland. Her mental health had always been fragile, punctuated with periods of acute depression. The events surrounding her husband's death and the subsequent trip to America, where she was continually asked to recall the events of the hunger-strike, proved a strain on her physical well-being and she returned home in a state of complete exhaustion.

Mary's personal worries were not inconsequential. She was joint guardian to the young Máire Óg; she had long been the source of strength and dependability to her more highly-strung sister Annie; her brother Seán, who fought a continual battle with alcoholism, looked to Mary for both guidance and shelter at various times; and her school was progressing but was not yet financially solvent. Mary kept her own counsel concerning these matters. Because she had always been the one to whom others turned, she herself turned to no one, only praying often and devoutly for strength and finding release and relief in her religious convictions.

One disconcerting note had arrived from home during December. The Bishop of Cork, Dr Cohalan, had issued an edict of excommunication against those who belonged to the IRA, an action taken up by other bishops around the country.[18] The hierarchy had never supported radical politics but had come to realise that Home Rule could serve the Church's interests as it would mean a Catholic government, one from which the Church could expect co-operation and even compliance, particularly in regard to moral matters such as divorce as well as education. Churchmen were worried that Sinn Féin, with its radical leadership, might limit the role of the Church by being less conforming with regard to Church directives and perhaps limiting Church control of education, a power it guarded most jealously.

Mary was incensed by this clerical interference. She took her religion very seriously and never quarrelled with the hierarchy over matters of faith but believed that when the clergy, and particularly the hierarchy, preached against Republicanism, they were well out of the bounds of Church authority. Mary was quite blunt in her statements, writing: 'Our people are not in a mood to stand injustice under the guise of religious direction.' No time was wasted in sending off a snappy letter to Cardinal Logue in which she respectfully but firmly asked him to stop interfering.[19]

Mary would not let the matter stop with this letter and some private outrage. Having stored it in her memory, she found an occasion to bring it forward in February of 1921. While talking with Archbishop

Mundelein of New Orleans, who was en route to Rome, she broached the subject of the IRA. Having explained the legitimacy and relevance of this organisation within the Irish Republican government, she asked the Archbishop to intervene with the Pope not to condemn them or their cause.[20]

This disagreement with the Irish bishops was another issue that Mary would have to set aside, at least temporarily, realising the inherent difficulties in trans-Atlantic arguing. In January, 1921, her speaking tour of the United States began, during which time Mary travelled by train in the company of Catherine Flanagan, her appointed companion and secretary. The reasons given to Mary for the tour were two-fold: to argue the cause of 'recognition', hence enlisting membership in the AARIR; and to solicit funds to aid in the support of the Irish Republican Government.

The latter purpose never sat comfortably with Mary. To De Valera she explained her discomfort in asking for money, writing: 'I am not much good as a beggar but I can always talk for recognition and let them infer the necessity for supplying the sinews of war.'[21] Nonetheless, she did participate in the bond-drive begun by De Valera to pay for the loan he had floated. These were $10 bonds that might be 'reclaimed one month after the international recognition of the Republic of Ireland – at 5% interest per annum from the first day of the 7th month after the freeing of the Republic of Ireland from British military control and said Bond to be redeemable at par within one year thereafter'.[22]

The first stop of Mary's tour was Buffalo, NY, where she spoke to an overflow crowd of about 1,800 gathered in a parish hall. A procession of forty priests led Mary into the hall, along with a band and a boy's choir. She shook hands, posed for pictures, gave autographs, reminisced about her brother but mainly argued for American involvement in the Irish cause. Having spoken, she met with local leaders and members of the press. The AARIR was new to Buffalo and after Mary's speech some members were taken with the promise of a door to door canvass to obtain more.[23]

From Buffalo, it was on to Pittsburgh. Here, the organisation and support were stronger and a rousing address was delivered to 18,000. Despite the larger numbers, Mary's agenda changed little, as the subject matter of her public speeches and private conversations was constant.[24]

The attendance at these first two stops illustrated the ready interest Irish-Americans had in supporting visitors with news from their homeland. It gave them an opportunity to join their voices in protest against the British, always the villain in the piece, and the focus of Irish hatred for centuries, as the cause of their poverty, subservient status in their own land, and hence, their emigration. These gatherings served to reinforce these perceptions, while the subsequent sharing of ideas for success against the dastardly British created an atmosphere ready to accept increased Irish militarism. Whereas one or two people seemed insignificant and ineffectual, large groups portended activism and power.

After these two stops, Mary understood her role more clearly and became more comfortable with it. Certainly, she knew the necessity of obtaining money to facilitate both military and humanitarian efforts in Ireland as the war against the British escalated. It was hoped that by encouraging 'recognition' of the Irish Republic by the United States, in some official capacity, pressure could be brought to bear against the British to do likewise. The Irish leadership believed that American pressure plus the doctrine and philosophy of the League of Nations could prevail against the previous British intransigence over the Irish question. The United States government could be convinced of the viability of 'recognition' only if the electorate demanded it. It was toward the voters then that Mary turned her attention, attempting to convince them that an Irish Republic was mandatory and had in fact been mandated by the citizens of Ireland in the election of 1918.

With these concepts clear to herself, Mary went to Cleveland where another huge rally, accompanied by a full page of coverage in *Cleveland Plain Dealer*, awaited her. Catherine Flanagan described the publicity they gathered as 'the best ever', having 'three full days of front pages'.[25]

With success came publicity ideas and a new promotional tool was added to the campaign. The AARIR had cards printed with a picture of Terence MacSwiney on one side and his sister Mary on the other, the end of the card was perforated so it could be torn off and then used as a membership card. Ms Flanagan described this effort as 'very effective'.[26]

In Columbus, to her delighted surprise, Mary was given the opportunity to address the state legislature. If she failed to convince her audience that aid for Ireland was tantamount, she did succeed in making them aware of a situation about which many had little knowledge.

After Cincinnati, Springfield was the last Ohio stop before moving to Lexington, Kentucky. Support here was strong and despite the AARIR being only two weeks old, it already had 300 members. Both the local newspapers had given editorial support to the cause and greeted Mary warmly. One well-meaning editor called on Mary at her hotel, offering his own solution to the Irish question, the United States should buy

Ireland. Mary corrected his mis-interpretation of the desires of the Irish people in no uncertain terms, while inwardly amused by his American chauvinism.[27]

In Tennessee, visits were made to Knoxville, Nashville and Memphis, where a total of more than 10,000 people were addressed following which Mary left for St Louis.

The pace of the tour was demanding and arduous with the continuous public pressure giving Mary little free time for reading or reflection. Often her leg ached after long hours spent in receiving lines, her throat hurt, her voice rasped and the desire for sleep was overwhelming. Despite this, she was energised by the level of enthusiasm of her audiences as the two seemed to have a symbiotic relationship, each gaining strength from the other. Though not allowed the luxury of rest, her public demeanour was ever hopeful and energetic.

Mary's speeches changed little although on various occasions she chose to emphasise one particular aspect of the Irish situation. She always repudiated the statement that the Irish were rebels. Indeed, to Mary, the British were the invaders and since their coming they had perpetrated untold violence and brutality upon the Irish as well as denying political, religious and educational freedom. These dastardly British were now using money borrowed from the United States for propaganda against Ireland. Amongst the lies they promulgated was the untruth that the trouble in Ireland was a religious struggle. Mary assured each audience that if the Irish were left to manage their own affairs, freed from British instigation of religious strife, there would be no problems between Catholics and Protestants. In her concluding condemnation of the British, Mary recited, in a calm, reasoned voice, the atrocities of the Black and Tans and the questionable convictions of Irish lads by British officials. When speaking of Edward Carson, she could not withold her venom and her voice rose in anger at the mention of his name. Upon this champion of Unionism and Protestant rights the most derogatory epithet in her vocabulary was bestowed; Carson was the anti-Christ.

Listeners were reminded that the true, elected government of the Republic of Ireland had been established in 1919 with the First Dáil Éireann. It was to this body that the Irish people overwhelmingly gave their support as their representatives. It was as spokesperson for this group that Mary was in America seeking recognition for the young Republic. She went on to say that the Irish sought recognition by the United States because of the latter's position as a world power, reminding those present of the influence of Irish-Americans including their considerable voting power. In an overstatement, the belief was voiced that the United States could set Ireland free without firing a shot, if it would bring pressure to bear upon England and provide financial support to the new government of Ireland.[28]

In an effort to make her speeches more meaningful, Mary made many analogies to the United States struggle for freedom and independence, quoting freely from a small handbook written by John X. Regan in 1919 entitled *Ireland and Presidents of the United States.* She was particularly fond of the quotations from Washington and Jefferson that championed the Irish cause: the former stating, 'Patriots of Ireland!. . . Be strong in hope! Your cause is identical with mine'; the latter writing, 'Ireland – may she soon burst her fetters and take her rank among the free Republics of the earth.' Her final appeal was that Ireland too wanted to be a Republican democracy.[29]

Invariably, the audience responded positively to Mary's oratory though perhaps it was a case of preaching to the converted. This aside, however, perhaps they could sense that this was not some paid politico who had rehearsed her delivery and struggled for words that would provide the highest emotional impact. Mary did indeed stray into hyperbolic phrases particularly when condemning the British. These flourishes aside, she spoke with honesty, sincerity and a depth of emotion that conveyed her overwhelming belief in the cause for which she fought. The lingering sorrow from her brother's death still lay close to the surface, bringing empathy for the middle-aged woman dressed in black. But it was her sorrow for the present state of Ireland that evoked the positive response from those who listened and heard. She was neither brash nor bold, speaking from her heart but her head was in control.

After this first successful run through the eastern states, Mary's itinerary sped up even more reaching a fever pitch as she zig-zagged back and forth across the country in a reckless geographic pattern. She travelled like a whirlwind in the south and west visiting Lincoln, Los Angeles, Spokane, Tulsa, Fort Worth, Dallas, Houston, Anaconda, San Francisco, Portland, Butte, Des Moines, Sioux City and Oklahoma City; while receptions gained in size and enthusiasm as her growing reputation preceded her. Further illustrating her increasing popularity, newspapers greeted her arrival with headlines and accolades. *The Anaconda Standard* reported: 'Miss MacSwiney is not an unworthy successor of Grattan, Burke and O'Connell.'[30] *The New Orleans Item* enthusiastically described her as the 'vividly alive sister of the martyred Irish mayor (who) shows thrilling zeal and ability to command and inspire. . . eager as a school girl'.[31] *The American Industrial Liberator* summed up Mary's southern swing in one inch headlines that read 'Southern States Give Remarkable Welcome to Miss MacSwiney.'[32] *The San Francisco Examiner* reported that at 'an immense meeting. . . San Francisco paid tribute to Mary MacSwiney'.[33] An Irish leader on the west coast cabled a colleague that 'Miss MacSwiney has swept LA as no other visitor from the east or from Ireland has ever done. Her argument is the most intellectual, convincing and persuasive we have ever heard down here.'[34] In Galveston, Mary MacSwiney's visit and cause were reported on the front page, the first time ever for the Irish situation.[35]

Mary took no personal responsibility for her overwhelming success, attributing the turnouts to the fame achieved by her brother Terence and believing she was but riding his coat-tails. In a letter home to a friend she wrote: 'That I reached them was mainly due to Terry's death and the interest it excited.'[36] This humility may be admirable but somewhat misplaced. Though this may have been the truth when she entered America, since then her own energy, oratory and indefatigability had created its own momentum. She was no longer a replacement for the dead Lord Mayor, having emerged as a recognisable personality in her own right with an identity separated from that of her brother. Whatever the causation for the crowds, it held little interest to Mary. She was delighted with the turnouts and even more impressed by the blossoming membership in the AARIR and the money flowing into Republican coffers.

Despite the growing number of superlatives written about her, Mary's head remained unturned. She joked about her secretary, writing that 'Catherine is delighted at the publicity everywhere. She has reached a point now that she feels like calling out the editor if we do not get the front page. The "Joan of Arc" and "Idol of the Irish people" stunt nearly did for me, but thank God for the sense of humour and proportion anyhow which He has given me.'[37]

During her tour, Mary's awareness of the role of women was sharpened. The Dublin Cumann H.Q. sent a letter reminding her to 'assure the American nation that the women of Ireland are standing with the soldiers and that "no surrender" is the watchword'. The organisation did not want women represented as a pacifist group urging the men to lay down their arms. Mary needed no reminder of this and her audience were never given even a hint of this image. She had no philosophical disagreement about taking up the gun and conveyed this clearly to her listeners.

In the same letter from Cumann headquarters, the first writer added rather wistfully that 'perhaps for the first time since its inception Cumann na mBan is getting a chance to do the work for which it was started – taking its place beside the IRA'.[38] Mary herself had never had difficulty accepting the role of Cumann na mBan, rejecting the 'camp-follower' image as inappropriate and untrue but believing in the synthesis of IRA and Cumann na mBan activity for the sake of Ireland. As the letter indicates, there were a few, or at least one, within the Cumann, who choked under the bridle of male leadership and wished for equality. In keeping with the tradition defined by Irish society and the Catholic Curch, however, the majority of women deferred to the male organisation.

Mary further illustrated her lack of appreciation for or understanding of this one Cumann member's concerns in an interview with a *Washington Times* reporter, stating:

(A feminist movement) is not necessary in our country. The women of Ireland are on full equality with the men and are comrades in everything. Even in ancient times women in Ireland had the right to their own property. We move along with men. When our Republic was formed, women were given equal rights in all things. The men are not disturbed when women are given high offices. We are the only country in the world with a woman in the cabinet of the government. Some day, no doubt, a woman will be president of our Republic.[39]

It is difficult to understand Mary's statements about equality when only a few short years before, she had been a vigorous spokeswoman for woman suffrage. Did she really believe that the declaration of the Republic had swept away all injustices against women or was she merely trying to illustrate the utopian nature of a free Ireland? Although Mary was never consumed with the notion of female inequities, the latter suggestion seems more viable.

Mary was not reluctant to tap the female resources in the United States. While in Washington, DC, she received letters of introduction to the heads of all the suffrage clubs, to the business and professional women's clubs and to the women lawyers.[40] At home, Mary had seen the accomplishments of Irish women in taking care of organisational details while the men engaged in war. She knew that maintaining lists, typing letters and door to door canvassing were essential to the success of the movement in America. She had noted in a letter to Máirín Nic Danbiac that 'in every town I continue to get a large audience of non-Irish, non-Catholic women', observing further, after three months of effort, that 'the women are better than the men' as they came forward more readily to join the AARIR and were indefatigable in their effort for Ireland.[41]

Perhaps the women received extra inspiration from the Irish school teacher, most plain in appearance, who, aside from the Irish accent, could have been one of them. Perhaps, too, despite Mary's enormous public and personal popularity, men were reluctant to give their unreserved support to a woman. After all, this was 1921, just a short time after the enfranchisement of women in both Ireland and America, at which time all the arguments about the inferiority of women, or at least their separate sphere, had been rehashed.

While in America, Mary was also able to smooth some of the feathers that had been ruffled by Eamon de Valera. In New York, visiting the humble hotel room home of the ageing John Devoy, Mary saw an old and lonely man and immediately felt sorry for him despite the 'venom' he wrote in some of his reports.[42] The time-worn Fenian responded well to Mary personally. Although he often disagreed with her approach, he listened to her statements and never spoke ill of her as he had done so many times of De Valera.

Mary's meeting with Judge Cohalan yielded similar results. In San Francisco, she tried to entice him to give his whole hearted support to President De Valera but was rejected firmly. Regretting that her efforts had failed, she wrote to De Valera that 'Cohalan could have been useful if he did not want to be Emperor of the Irish Republic'.[43]

Mary made other efforts to assuage these two American leaders and while not deferring to them, remained non-combative. On occasion, to accommodate their sensibilities, she would send drafts of her speeches or statements to them for their perusal. This uncharacteristic cultivation of American leaders would serve her well in the future and at the time it aided in the unity of Irish-American effort, tenuous though it may be. Mary's conciliatory actions also came from her firm belief that all of the Irish must present a united front if they were to be successful in their political campaign against the British. Her actions which had called for no compromise in principle on her part, were believed to be the best for Ireland, and thus were personally acceptable to her.

It was during this foray into America that Mary MacSwiney and Eamon de Valera first came into conflict. Because of the response received around the country, Mary was convinced that America was ripe for the picking and no effort, either personal or financial, should be spared. She believed that Ireland could gain almost unlimited financial support if the field were saturated with Irish workers, preaching the word and passing the hat. Such efforts would also make new converts to the cause of recognition who would, in turn, bring pressure to bear upon their representatives in Congress. Mary suggested more Irish lobbyists should be in place in Washington while the grass roots movement was forming in the countryside. She wrote to James O'Mara on a note of urgency: 'I do not advocate a continuously lavish expenditure but suggest spending generously, lavishly if you like, for two months. . . Take advantage, at once, of all the enthusiasm which our visits are arousing.' She encouraged a flood of literature including copies of her speeches which were in demand as well as reprints of the testimony given in Washington the previous December. By way of convincing her reader, she added: 'Harding said here, when asked his attitude on the Irish recognition, that he would do what the majority of the people wanted.' Was not this reason enough to increase speakers and lobbying efforts in the capital? She pleaded with O'Mara to 'get An Dáil's consent for the necessary expenditure inmediately' as all allotments had to be made through him. Once more her plea was reiterated: 'It is a real crime not to crystalise all this sentiment while we have the chance.'[44]

Mary sent the same plea, less formally presented, to her old friend Harry Boland. Having stated her case, she added: 'Write to me like a good boy and tell me you will be a brick and shell out generously.'[45]

Despite what Mary believed to be the convincing nature of her case, her wishes did not prevail. The pronouncement from Dublin and De Valera, to her great chagrin, was a refusal to commit any more money, from a rapidly depleting treasury, to champion the cause in America. Mary was bewildered and duly annoyed by what she perceived as De Valera's political short-sightedness. Perhaps part of his motivation lay with the difficulties he had undergone in America, no longer wishing to waste money on what he saw as an intransigent American leadership. He had also made his best political effort to win party approval from both Democrats and Republicans during his American tour, and had failed in both camps, gaining sympathy but no firm commitment for recognition. Mary saw this denial of funds as a loss of a great ally for Ireland. Though she tried to be submissive to Republican authority, she burned over De Valera's decision, firmly believing that she knew better. Again, it was her conviction that the Irish must appear unified and not as a group riddled with conflict, that helped her to maintain public silence over this issue.

Mary continued her tour of the United States until August, 1921. She criss-crossed the country with occasional stops in Washington, DC where she called upon congressional representatives and senators, ever hopeful of gaining their support for recognition. She visited them believing that no country in Europe was in a position to give Ireland recognition unless the United States led the way.[46]

When the summer months arrived, Mary's pace did not falter though she was much bothered by the warm temperatures. The gruelling schedule of three to four speeches a day was kept up but by day's end she wished to 'go into cold storage'.[47] Conscientious not to offend her American audiences even though their questions were often tedious, she explained to a friend that 'they really did not mean to be offensive. On the whole I was "nice" and "good" and patient to a degree'.[48]

She missed her sister Annie and would have preferred to be in her school but mused rather pragmatically that 'if I did go back I should probably be locked up. There's no doubt that they are feeling the effect of my campaign here – the enemy I mean. I have reached many people who have never before heard a word.'[49]

Indeed, the 'enemy' was aware of Mary MacSwiney. At one point during her tour the British Ambassador was following in her wake, trying to dispel the impression of the British that Mary was creating.[50]

As the tour came to an end, Mary, counting the days until she would set sail for home, reflected on her experience. She regretted that she had not seen more tourist attractions but said simply and precisely: 'It has been wonderful – this first big tour of mine.'[51]

The results of her tour were broad in scope: the money collected would help the Sinn Féin shadow government supply food, clothing and shelter for those in need and provide more guns and ammunition for the Nationalists; with the great number of new members in the AARIR, more pressure to help solve the Irish question could be brought to bear on the United States Congress.

For Mary herself, it provided her with name recognition in many areas throughout the United States and to many her name became inextricably linked with the fight for Irish freedom. She became personally acquainted with most of the leaders of the Irish movement in America and got on well with most, if not all, of them, who found her a dedicated and devoted spokesperson whose sincerity was unquestionable. Mary was now in personal touch with the large and influential American organisation, many of whose members were devoted to her. These things taken together, would be to her advantage in the future.

Mary was also the one Irish person who had not shied from the issue of the Republic as had De Valera. Her position was clear and unequivocal and known to all with whom she came in contact. De Valera, on the other hand, had left himself manoeuvring room, while claiming the right to choose the type of government for Ireland rather than specifically advocating a Republic, politically and diplomatically the sensible approach. In contrast, Mary MacSwiney was irrevocably committed to a Republic and hers was the last impression left with Americans.

With the American tours of Eamon de Valera and Mary MacSwiney, the precedent had been established that Americans would give money without being in total command of the facts. Certainly, many Irish-Americans were clear in their desire for a free Ireland, but now Mary MacSwiney had come and told them that the only way Ireland could be free would be to have a Republic just as the United States had. America contributed generously, asked few questions and trusted that those responsible would use the funds to obtain a suitable solution to Ireland's problems. This flow of American money to Irish Republicans continues under the same terms up to the present.

The Americans had been acquainted almost solely with radical Irish politics and politicians. In 1921, Mary MacSwiney spoke for the majority of the Irish in desiring freedom as they had shown in the Sinn Féin election of 1919. As time passed, however, Irish opinion moderated in its demands for a Republic but this change was not conveyed convincingly to Irish-Americans. They had been transfixed by the MacSwiney view of a Republic and it would seem somehow disloyal to accept less.

Despite her many accomplishments in the United States which included substantial financial contributions, enlarged membership in the AARIR and a semblance of Irish-American unity, Mary did not view her tour as an overwhelming success. Personal aggrandisement meant little to her and though her ego had been flattered continually by her new American friends, she considered only the benefits that Ireland could derive from the tour. She retained the belief that these benefits had been diminished through De Valera's lack of financial commitment to the American effort. The much sought after 'recognition' had not come to fruition, with little likelihood that this dream would be realised in the near future. Mary continually regretted that the opportunity afforded them had not been 'taken at the tide', leaving Sinn Féin with many supporters in the USA but an under-staffed organisational headquarters resulting in disorganisation in the field. In Mary's mind, Ireland's most influential ally had not been adequately tapped.

Despite her regrets, on the eve of the Civil War, the last words heard in America were those of a radical Republican. The large audiences of Mary MacSwiney would remember her words, her philosophy, her view of Ireland and her rejection of all things British. Amongst her last public statements in the United States, Mary said: 'If Ireland does not win recognition as a Republic at the conference table she will on the battlefield.'[52]

4. The Civil War Years

The months of June and July, 1921, had been a time of frequent, often urgent political exchanges between England and Ireland. On 22 June, the Parliament of Northen Ireland was officially opened by the King in Belfast, a bitter moment for Irish Nationalists and a triumph for northern Unionists. The King, having agreed to this new source of contention, sought to mitigate the sting to the south by adopting a conciliatory, almost plaintive tone in his formal address. Having established the new parliament, a monument to factionalism, he enjoined 'all Irishmen to pause, to stretch out the hand to forebearance and conciliation, to forgive and forget.'[1]

David Lloyd George followed up on this appeal of the King. The designer of this new parliament that legitimised the split between north and south, Lloyd George called up Eamon de Valera to join Unionist leader James Craig in London for a conference with the Prime Minister. Considering Lloyd George's role in supporting the Unionist parliament, his letter to De Valera is ironic indeed, as he wrote with an air of innocence: 'We make this invitation with a fervent desire to end the ruinous conflict which has for centuries divided Ireland.'[2] After a meeting between Lloyd George and De Valera was arranged and as a gesture of goodwill, a truce was called in Ireland on 11 July, the eve of Orangemen's Day.

In Ireland the news of the truce was greeted with joy and relief. Macardle wrote: 'It felt like victory – the removal of curfew, freedom to walk at night in the streets, to light bonfires, fly the Tri-colour, shout "Up the Republic" and sing "The Soldiers' Song."'[3] Among the civilian population there was the belief that victory had been achieved. The political and military leaders were less convinced, ever mindful of the divisive nature of the northern parliament and the tenuousness of the upcoming discussion. De Valera and his colleagues made detailed arrangements to maintain vigilance and preparedness until the negotiations with the British became a reality.[4]

It was into this scene that Mary MacSwiney returned from America.

Remaining unconvinced about the sincerity of the British, she considered it a 'deadly blunder' that her people 'had permitted the opening of the Belfast parliament so quietly,' believing that it gave the King a platform from which to address the world at a time, she believed, when world opinion had become 'too much' for the British. To her increasingly suspicious mind, the English had 'suggested a cessation of hostilities, making the speech of King George V at Belfast a pretext to save their faces in the hopes of extricating themselves from a difficult situation.'[5]

Mary had returned to Ireland with increased importance in Nationalist circles. First, she had distinguished herself in 1916 as one who had undergone hardship willingly by supporting the concept of an independent Ireland before this had mass appeal. Being thus in the vanguard, she was associated with the early leaders of the Republican movement, not one who climbed aboard the train once it gained momentum. She was one of the relatively few who had suffered personally during the Easter Rising as she had lost her job and her freedom, albeit the latter for only a short period. Second, during her brother's hunger-strike and death, she had been interviewed and written about continually, at which times she repeatedly explained the Irish situation and pressed for independence, deflecting any personal attention to the cause of freedom for Ireland. Third, her triumphs in America had been duly noted, particularly by Sinn Féin officers, well aware of the financial benefits she had wrought. Her prominence was recognised in the parliamentary election, held during her absence in America, at which time Mary was put forward as the candidate for Cork city, the area previously represented by Terence. Mary easily won victory, becoming a representative to the British Parliament. This body was boycotted by all the Sinn Féin members elected who preferred to meet as Dáil Éireann, the legislative body established by Republicans elected in 1918. Mary and her recently elected colleagues, called TD's (Teachta Dála – deputies) now constituted the Second Dáil, a body to which all constitutionally elected Irish representatives were invited, but was in turn boycotted by Unionists.

Upon arriving back in Ireland, Mary went to Dublin for a meeting of the Second Dáil, where the deputies listened to De Valera and discussed at length Home Rule proposals. She chatted and exchanged information about her American tour with her colleagues, many of whom were growing increasingly optimistic about the British proposals. Mary remained sceptical, however, feeling less than exuberant about the truce and not happy 'about the vagueness surrounding the procedure.'[6]

Despite her increasing prominence, Mary was quickly brought face to face with her role as a woman in a predominantly male organisation when she returned home to Cork. On 8 August 1921, a note was sent to the MacSwineys from Richard Mulcahy, Volunteer officer and friend, explaining that De Valera would be spending one or two days travelling incognito around Cork. Mulcahy wrote: 'We want to involve you in the matter of itinerary to the following extent,' explaining that four men would 'descend' at about 12:30 'looking for a bit of dinner.' They would return at about 7 pm for tea after which the president 'may wish to have some interviews or some general chat.' The final request was 'he and I will take a bed from you for the night.'[7] It was an honour to entertain the President of the Republic and perhaps some Nationalist strategy was plotted during or after the meals, with Mary present. On this occasion, though, Mary MacSwiney was assigned 'women's work' rather than that of a Dáil deputy. Though a male deputy may also have been excluded from secret military matters, it is doubtful he would have been asked to prepare tea. Perhaps too, De Valera was recognising Mary's growing prominence and was unconsciously providing a lesson on who was in control. Mary herself was unconcerned, her confidence was not jarred as she felt no personal ambition, only ambition for Ireland.

As the summer progressed and autumn arrived, official cables and letters continued to pass between Ireland and England concerning the establishment of treaty negotiations. As the time for the beginning of the formal talks drew closer, Mary could not rid herself of the suspicions she harboured toward the British. Perhaps as a way of venting her feelings in some concrete manner she resigned her membership in the Catholic Women's Suffrage Society, an organisation based in England, giving as her reason the general untoward actions of the British government in its dealings with Ireland.[8]

While in Dublin, Mary had met with De Valera at the Mansion House and once again quizzed him about his theory of external association which he had been touting as an acceptable solution to Anglo-Irish separation. In keeping with his training as a mathematician, De Valera explained it graphically on paper. While a sceptical Mary MacSwiney looked on, he drew two circles side by side, one representing England, the other Ireland, encasing both in one large circle. De Valera believed that if this relationship was adopted he would feel content 'that the sovereignty and integrity of the nation would be safeguarded.'[9]

Mary MacSwiney could not be convinced. She wanted a Republic clear and unequivocal, believing the concept of 'external association' to be 'insidious and dangerous' while it limited 'Ireland's freedoms' and most important it was 'inconsistent with the Republican position.' She was torn about what to do. While the negotiations were beginning, it was important that the Irish present a united front and not one riddled with factionalism. Finally, lest intransigence over the Republic further delay the formation of an Irish negotiating team, she put aside further criticism of De Valera's concept so as 'to avoid a desperate situation.'[10]

After a considerable amount of discussion and argument, the Irish delegates to the London meeting were selected. In a letter to Joseph McGarrity in Philadelphia, Eamon de Valera revealed that he would have liked to see Mary MacSwiney 'facing Lloyd George across the table. . . not merely because of her own personality and political ability but because Lloyd George could not fail to see beside her the spirit of her dead brother.' Despite treating her as a bed and breakfast lady while in Cork, he was not immune to her political or oratorical talents. He concluded with another telling remark: 'She was also ruled out by Arthur Griffith and Michael Collins' attitude towards her – women in general I suppose.'[11]

The president may have based Mary's exclusion on sexism alone, but this would seem to be only part of the explanation. Griffith had long been dealing with the British and Michael Collins was noted for his pragmatism. Both men must have realised that Mary MacSwiney would not negotiate as she was a total intransigent, firm about the Irish Republic, whose presence at the London talks would have stalled progress from the opening day. Surely Eamon de Valera, after his valiant, though fruitless, efforts to convince Mary of the viability of external association, was well appraised of her intractability.

Excluded from the main action of the talks, Mary looked on in worry from the periphery. One hopeful thought for her was that the negotiations had 'regularised' the position of the Irish. She believed that 'England, having once made a truce with (the) army and entered a conference with (the Irish) government' could never again refer to them as 'a murder gang.'[12]

Despite this glimmer of hope, Mary wished to make sure the delegates were certain of their commission. She wrote to Arthur Griffith in late October wishing him well, while reminding him of his heavy responsibility, and, as a none too subtle hint, enclosed mortuary cards of Terry, one for each of the delegates.[13] She was not about to let them forget that her brother had died for a Republic. Griffith replied with thanks, confirming that the outlook 'was not very bright.'[14]

On 9 November, as news from the London discussion was filtering back to Ireland, Mary was becoming increasingly alarmed. The talk of oaths to the King and dominion status for Ireland were completely outside the range of what was acceptable to her. She wrote again to Arthur Griffith, realising he was head of the delegation but also suspicious because he was the one with whom Lloyd George seemed most comfortable. Not wanting the English to feel that a lack of response from the Irish at home meant that Lloyd George's proposals were acceptable, Mary concluded with long distance advice: 'Our silence is only a proof of our confidence in our delegates but may deceive people in England and elsewhere if no protest is made now.'[15]

Despite these letter warnings and her own uneasiness, Mary believed that there was not in Ireland a man better able to cope with the wily Lloyd George than Arthur Griffith. [16]

Arthur Griffith responded quickly to Mary's second letter. Perhaps he recognised her growing influence at home or he may have felt a genuine concern for her misgivings. For whatever reason, he told her not to be 'influenced by press reports,' going on in a reassuring tone that they would bring nothing home 'that we believe the Irish people cannot accept. Possibly we shall bring home nothing at all.'[17] Arthur Griffith may also have been remembering how only one year before he had stood at the grave of Terence MacSwiney and declared that 'the last man in Ireland would die before the Republic which he and his comrades died for should be abandoned.[18]

Despite the admonitions and warnings of Mary MacSwiney and other resolute Republicans, the Treaty was signed by the plenipotentiaries on 6 December, 1921. While the delegates were relieved that the long process was over, they were not so naive as to believe that the Treaty would be universally well received in Ireland, particularly as it contained the necessity of an oath of allegiance to the King by Irish parliamentarians, provisions for the division of Ireland into north and south with the south having far less than independent status and the need for the south to pay annuities to Britain.

Mary MacSwiney, as might have been predicted, was incredulous over the signing. She wasted no time in sending a letter to each of the delegates, reminding them, as a school teacher might, that they had made a mistake. She went on: 'But you will, I hope, tell us also that you realise that you are bound to submit to An Dáil and that you will cheerfully and gladly accept the rejection of this mistaken Treaty.' The letter, up until this point, had a rather optimistic tone. Certainly, Mary believed, the wrong could be righted, because of her own bitterness however, she could hardly keep from slipping into some harsh rhetoric, continuing: 'The English atmosphere must be indeed poisonous if its venom has infected you.' She concluded with a patriotic appeal: 'Your oath to the Republic is a prior claim and more binding that any word given to the enemies of your country.'[19] A final addendum was added to the letter, in which, in an effort to establish her bona fides, she wrote uncharacteristically and almost defensively: 'I have earned my right to speak.' Perhaps she believed that this reminder would revitalise the memory of her dead brother and then play havoc with the consciences of the delegates.

Mary had by now made her own lasting judgments about Arthur Griffith and Michael Collins. She remembered how once Arthur Griffith had espoused a dual monarchy for England and Ireland, a concept she would 'not touch with a forty foot pole,' while recalling that, despite his words at Terry's funeral, he 'was never a convinced Republican.'[20] Initially, she had believed him to be most capable but, following the negotiations and his failure in her eyes, she mused that 'want of faith in your cause is a fatal barrier to success.'[21] Similarly, she wrote to a friend that Michael Collins 'never really believed in the reality of the Republican government of which he formed a part.' Even more disenchanting was her belief that Collins harboured rather base political motives as she concluded that there was 'a large share of personal ambition at the bottom of his conduct as well as want of faith and vision.'[22]

Mary was beginning to do to the Irish who disagreed with her what she had always done to the British – accuse them of being self-seeking, unreliable and untrustworthy. With her singularity of vision and faith, that she believed Collins lacked, her interpretation of what was best for Ireland was the only one that was right and defensible. Anyone who disagreed had a 'slave mind' somehow wrought by the British; hence her enemies, English and Irish, were now joined in some unholy alliance.

Mary was clear on where the negotiations had gone astray, concluding that 'the delegates' mistake was in attempting to give away essentials. Money they might give, special agreements with regard to defence or trade, but they should not have given away the vital principle of independence.'[23]

With the signing of the Treaty, battle had been joined between doctrinaire Republicans and those who believed, with Michael Collins, that the Treaty was the best available stepping stone to Irish freedom. The war of words was carried on within the Dáil chamber as members rose to proclaim their allegiance to one side or the other.

Mary MacSwiney took this opportunity to speak in the public arena against signing the Treaty. And speak she did. She is remembered for delivering the longest oration of the debate, going on for almost three hours as a TD in the Dáil chamber. Essentially, she reviewed the Republican position and exhorted her fellow TDs to stand firm in their rejection of the insulting Treaty that was being perpetrated upon them by the despicable British led by that 'unscrupulous trickster' David Lloyd George.[24]

Opinions on her oratory split along party lines. Those supporting the Treaty found her words strident and overbearing, the half-crazed meanderings of an hysterical woman. Arthur Griffith as one opposed, continually tried to interrupt and poked fun at the length of her address. Republicans were more charitable. J. J. O'Kelly was filled with praise, declaring, 'What a surpassing feat of eloquence and reasoning. . . everyone with a mind to appreciate the most brilliant address we had ever heard was spell-bound.'[25] Dorothy Macardle, strongly entrenched in the Republican camp, called the speech 'a masterpiece of logic and eloquence. . . uncompromising in tone.'[26]

Despite varying opinions as to the content, Mary MacSwiney's reputation as an orator was only enhanced by her performance before the Dáil. Because of the length of her discourse, members came and went, some being surprised, upon their return after a lengthy break, to find Mary still proceeding in top form. As the time passed, she warmed to the task physically as well as mentally and gradually shed various pieces of her apparel. Her hat was doffed, then her scarf-collar and then her jacket. Sceilig (J J O'Kelly) described her as ending up looking 'somewhat as on the mortuary cart.'[27]

Her message to An Dáil and to Ireland was loud and clear. Ireland had fought long and hard and now the only thing that would satisfy their Nationalist hunger was a Republic. She reminded all that 'On the 21st of January, 1919, this assembly, elected by the will of the sovereign people of Ireland, declared by the will of the people the Republican form of government as best for Ireland and cast off forever their allegiance to any foreigner.' She remained mindful of the oath of allegiance that had been sworn by members of both the First and Second Dáil, each deputy swearing to 'defend the Irish Republic and the government of the Republic of Ireland which is Dáil Éireann against all enemies foreign and domestic.'[28]

Despite the best efforts of Mary MacSwiney and her ideological colleagues, the Treaty was approved by the Dáil. Mary joined De Valera as they walked out of the Dáil chamber after their defeat.

The anti-Treatyites were not immobilised by their defeat, however. They quickly met in a separate session and evolved a strategy for the future. The first item on their agenda was to send representatives to America 'to place (the) present position before the people and secure their support.' After support was achieved it was essential to secure enough American funds 'to enable the Republic to meet essential expenses until general elections and in case of a defeat, to maintain the Republican Party.' Finally, all envoys were to avoid 'communication with (the) Free State, holding it an usurping government.'[29] There was also the upcoming election to be considered, which would in fact be a referendum on the Treaty, so Mary MacSwiney returned to Cork, to canvass and electioneer among her constituents.

To the people of Cork, she gave her view of some of the mistaken reasons of those who signed or supported the Treaty. First, she looked to some members of the IRA and their 'thoughtless enthusiasm,' saying some cared not at all for their oath of allegiance but were 'keen only on getting arms and equipment.' Her second group she labelled 'doubting Thomases.' These were the people 'so oppressed with England's power that they scarcely believe their own.' Third, she turned to those supporters of Michael Collins who called the Treaty a 'step towards the Republic,' not realising they were turning down the Republic already established. Fourth, she spoke of those whom she considered particularly lack-lustre, those uninvolved people 'who never lifted a finger to help their country through its time of suffering, but who (were) now loud in their clamours for peace and safety.'[30]

Beside the issue of the Republic, Mary was equally firm in rejecting partition, writing that partition was England's 'greatest crime in Ireland.' Reflecting on it in later years, she re-echoed her sentiments of the time saying that on the part of the British 'it was a dastardly trick deliberately planned not only to create a new pole from which she might launch a new attack on any freedom she might be forced to grant, but to continue and perpetuate the bigotry and bitterness which for generations she has fostered'.[31]

She continually railed against the terms of the Treaty, believing it to be a sign of surrender to the British and an unacceptable compromise, while saying that 'compromise has never succeeded in Ireland. Wherever it has been tried it has but dragged our cause down and the next generation had to begin all over again.'[32]

There was surely truth in Mary's words, as the history of Catholic emancipation in O'Connell's time and Home Rule in 1910-14 had shown. The difference in 1922 was that finally the Irish were left to deal with their internal problems alone; but again the compromises were great. Ireland would not be united and the Free State would remain under the British umbrella who would retain military installations. History has recorded that the partition compromise would fulfil Mary MacSwiney's prediction, and leave an unresolved problem for the future. She was correct in believing that a final solution should be reached at that time. Unhappily for Mary, the majority saw the Treaty as that solution.

In February, while both pro- and anti-Treaty supporters were trying to solidify their support around the country, prior to the election, Cumann na mBan held its annual convention in Dublin. As was the case throughout Ireland, opinions about the acceptability of the Treaty were polarised in this women's organisation. Mary MacSwiney declared before this meeting of her peers that 'women were the backbone of the nation'. After a long harangue against the British and those whom Mary considered their supporters in Ireland, she urged all members to reaffirm their allegiance to the Republic. Jenny Wyse-Power spoke in favour of the Treaty, adopting the Michael Collins position that 'it seemed easier to get the Republic from a government working in Ireland by Irishmen than from an Ireland under British rule.'[33] Unlike the situation in the Dáil, Cumann na mBan voted overwhelmingly to reject the Treaty, the final count being 419 to 63, after which the pro-Treaty members were asked to resign, leaving the organisation totally in control of the radical Republicans. Its non-compromising, non-tolerant attitude was re-affirmed.[34]

The outcome of the convention was not surprising as the leadership of Cumann na mBan was composed of doctrinaire Republicans, many of whom had lost family members or other loved ones in the fight for Irish freedom. Perhaps because these women were unable to bear arms themselves, they felt a stronger commitment to maintain the Republican ideal. It seemed to many that any compromise on their part would shame the heroic dead or somehow lessen their sacrifice. Ireland, indeed, is often ruled from the grave.

Mary MacSwiney gave voice to this sentiment when she was speaking with the Terence MacSwiney Memorial Committee, telling them firmly that 'the tragedies of Cork and Brixton gaols would never have been endured for Dominion Home Rule.' To emphasise her point, she declined to give her support to any type of monument to her brother saying, 'There will be no memorial to commemorate that sacrifice while

Irishmen give fidelity to an English king.'[35]

During March and April, Irish society become more factionalised. The army was in turmoil as the military leadership was divided over the Treaty with individual soldiers tending to follow their commander's lead. The army leaders opposed to the Treaty met in convention in late March, established their own executive, thus giving the anti-Treaty politicians firm military support. In April, the Four Courts were seized by this group, necessitating their removal by government troops. The Provisional Irish government was under continual pressure from the British to maintain law and order, only to see the situation around them deteriorating as the election rhetoric intensified and the call to arms was growing louder.

In an effort to defuse the situation, Michael Collins and Eamon de Valera agreed to the election pact by which Sinn Féin, to which they both still claimed allegiance, would put forth one panel of candidates. The number of pro- and anti-Treaty candidates permitted would be proportionate to the representation of each in the Dáil. However, on the eve of the election Michael Collins, in what appeared to many as a repudiation of the pact, told Irish men and women to vote according to their consciences and not feel bound to Sinn Féin. It was later argued that Collins' statement encouraged voters to turn away from Sinn Féin, in favour of Labour and Farmers party candidates.

Mary MacSwiney denounced Michael Collins for his policy reversal, believing that if the pact had been 'faithfully kept, it would have saved the country, defeated English machinations and strengthened a united Ireland.'[36] Mary's views of the power of the pact seem overly optimistic. In fact, word of Collins message did not reach most of the country until after the polls closed on election day. In looking for a scapegoat, Mary MacSwiney was engaging in post-election hyperbole.

She and the other women deputies in the Dáil (appropriately enough dubbed 'the black women' as they all wore mourning) were engaged in their own campaign exploits. The five (excluding Countess Markievicz) wrote an appeal in the Republican paper, *Poblacht na h-Éireann*, forecasting the dire consequences if the Treaty were upheld. They foreshadowed the future when they asked, 'Do you think the material benefits it brings are worth the risk of Civil War?' This was reminiscent of the threat that Lloyd George had held over the heads of the Treaty negotiators promising immediate war if the Treaty were rejected. Unfortunately, in this case it was not a bluff. The women went on to conclude: 'There can be no unity on the Treaty; why then force it. If we stand together the enemy will be powerless against us.'[37]

When the election results were in, the anti-Treatyites were despondent. The return showed: TCD (Trinity College, Dublin) members – four, Labour – seventeen, Farmers – seven, Independents – six, Sinn Féin Panel – ninety-four, including fifty-eight favouring the Treaty and thirty-six opposed. Although Mary MacSwiney was re-elected in Cork, the country was indicating a majority acceptance of the Treaty. Considering those who rejected the pact candidates altogether, many wished to establish peace and turn attention towards the economic and social needs of the country.

In Cork, Mary MacSwiney cast about looking for reasons other than the rejection of the pact, for the defeat. She challenged the honour of Michael Collins, rejecting him completely, asserting that he was doing England's bidding, adding, 'What service (he) rendered Ireland in earlier years was nullified by (his) later action.'[38] This total disregard for Collins was the beginning of a long pattern – for to maintain Mary's support, one had to share her vision of the Republic and entertain no alternatives or half measures. If one did stray from this narrow path, Mary lost all respect for him or her and would have no further personal contact. On the Republican principle she could tolerate no differences or even varying shades of opinion.

In the search for a scapegoat in the electoral defeat, Mary also blamed the Labour movement. The Labour leaders had called a one day strike on 24 April, somewhat ironically 'in the interests of Peace.' Mary felt this to be inadequate and declared that 'if Labour had definitely declared for unity of the National forces above all things, whatever happened to the Treaty, Labour could have brought about unity and would have laid the country under a deep debt of gratitude.' She then continued with what seems the real reason for her tirade, saying, 'By helping break the pact the Labour leaders helped the horrors that followed.'[39] Mary had wanted the Labour party to withdraw from the election altogether leaving the voters with a clear choice within Sinn Féin. To her mind, if the Labour party truly wanted peace for Ireland, that is what they would have done. Just as with Michael Collins' rejection of the pact, Mary was attributing more power to Labour than they possessed. They did elect seventeen deputies to the Dáil but overall that was a small representation as Ireland remained predominantly agricultural.

Mary had one other blame-worthy group, the signers of the Treaty and those that supported it in the Dáil. Forecasting the coming war again, she wrote to her former friend and colleague, Richard Mulcahy, that if blood were shed in a civil strife, 'then before God and our martyred dead, I hold Griffith and Collins primarily responsible and with them every one of you 'that is supporting the Treaty.'[40]

Finally, Mary turned to the electorate itself. She could not be convinced, however, that the election results were a true indication of the beliefs of most Irish citizens believing somehow they had been duped or misinformed. Others pointed out that the majority had spoken and if democratic processes were to be heeded, then the Treaty should stand. Mary was ready with an answer that she was called upon to give through the remainder of her life. She said:

The people of a nation may not voluntarily surrender their independence; they may not vote it away in the ballot box even under duress and if some, even a majority be found, who through force or cupidity, would vote for such a surrender, the vote is invalid legally and morally and a minority is justified in upholding the independence of their country.[41]

This political theory was certainly subject to criticism by many in Ireland. The independence, so proudly hailed by Mary, was the de jure independence proclaimed by a small group of radicals in 1916, then reiterated by the majority in the 1918 election but had never existed de facto. The election, however, could also be viewed as a frustrated rejection of British hesitancy and delay in granting some form of Home Rule, rather than as an acceptance of Republican ideology. In 1922, in voting in favour of the Treaty, the majority voted to give a degree of de facto independence to a part of Ireland, seeing this as an improvement, however small, over their total lack of independence previously. Thus, contrary to Mary's statement, now, in the view of the majority, independence was not being surrendered but rather seized upon, choosing de facto over de jure freedom. In clinging to the Republic, Mary and her ideological colleagues were insisting on a government form that had been instituted by a very small group of active Republicans numbering less than 1,000, which had become much more popular by 1922, but was still clearly of minority status.

After various false starts, the much dreaded but much expected Civil War began. Mary herself did not recoil from the war as some others did, believing it to be a just war and the only way left for achieving a Republic. Though not inclined to take up weapons herself, she did not consider this renewed violence as inherently evil, rather as necessary in preventing further evil.

As the war went on outside her house and rather frightening exchanges of bullets could be heard, Mary mulled over her own situation. She wrote in her diary: 'Many people are quite confident that I shall be one of the first shot "accidentally on purpose". I doubt it.' After further thought about her own safety she concluded, 'I should be surprised if they stooped so low as to shoot Terry's sister for no other reason than fidelity to him and his principles.'[42]

With this imaginary bullet-proof coat encasing her, Mary MacSwiney continued to tour Ireland, decrying the Treaty, the leaders of the Free State and the British government. Regarding the latter, she saw Bonar Law's succession of David Lloyd George as of little concern to Ireland. To a Sinn Féin club in London she said that whether the English government was Liberal or Conservative, Radical or Labour, mattered not at all to Ireland as they were 'tweedledum and tweedledee'.[43] In referring to the Free State government and its soldiers, she declared sharply that the English had 'returned to Ireland in a different uniform.'[44]

As the Civil War continued, the Republicans were faced with another enemy, the Church. In a sermon in Killarney, Father Fitzgerald summed up the Church's position in language all could understand: 'Some of the so-called IRA were men once, but despite the pleadings of the bishops of Ireland they have left their homes and have gone to the hills, to murder, plunder and rob. We don't want their Republic.'[45]

In a letter to the *Cork Examiner*, Mary MacSwiney cried foul over this interference. She asked if 'young men (were) to be driven from the Church because they (were) following their conscience?' concluding that 'in many churches – the pulpit is used as a political platform to denounce all who are faithful in deed and word to the Republic.'[46] Mary saw no conflict between one's desire to fight for an Irish Republic and to practice the Catholic religion in contrast to many of the clergy and virtually all of the hierarchy who did. The Republicans were a continuing threat to stability. The Free State government had indicated to the Church that they would not interfere with the moral teachings of the Church or with their grip on education which the Church sought to tighten, particularly now that the British had left. There also remained the lingering suspicion among the hierarachy that the Republicans were Socialists and would somehow seek to diminish the power of the Church in Ireland. If these things were not worrisome enough to the bishops, there remained the fear of the Republicans as an unknown quantity who might seek to impinge on Church authority in a multitude of ways not yet considered.

In August the violence escalated in Ireland. The army of the Provisional Free State government was pitted against the 'Irregulars' and forced to counteract the latter's guerrilla operations. August also brought the deaths of Arthur Griffith and Michael Collins, both of whom were mourned throughout the country although Michael Collins, young, aggressive and charismatic, was considered perhaps the more tragic loss of the two.

Mary MacSwiney had only harsh words for the dead Collins, believing he had betrayed the Republic at the Treaty negotiations thus making his name anathema. When asked about the death of Collins, she replied abruptly, 'Michael Collins was not murdered. He was killed in a fight – like many other men as good or better.' Not being content with this, she added that his death had resulted from a war for which 'he himself was mainly responsible.' As always she concluded by casting him in the role as a puppet of the British saying, 'He obeyed England's orders and took England's guns to fight his own countrymen.'[47] It was this type of rhetoric that led many to believe that Mary MacSwiney was cold, bitter and unfeeling. Those close to her believed just the opposite. It remains, however, that Mary was completely inflexible in her moral judgments of those who sought a   path divergent from her own by which to solve Ireland's problems.

During September and October of 1922, Mary delegated many of her teaching duties to others and again toured the country speaking on behalf of the Republicans. It was urgent that she and other women did this as most Republican men were engaged in military activities or were 'on the run'. A growing number were also being captured and imprisoned to begin their term, in author Frank O'Connor's phrase, as guests of the nation.

In October, the hierarchy made another serious attack on Republicanism when Cardinal Logue issued the now famous 'joint pastoral letter' in which Republicans who persisted in acting against the state were excommunicated. It condemned the Republican side as 'morally only a system of murder and assassination of the National forces.' Besides this condemnation, the letter contained directives important on a personal level, as it continued that 'all those who. . . participate in such crimes, are guilty of grievous sins and may not be absolved in confession, nor admitted to Holy Communion.' This message was read at all Sunday masses, thereby reaching the great majority of Free State residents.[48]

Mary MacSwiney took her usual stand against the Church interfering in secular matters, adding these sentiments to her speeches while warning her listeners not to be cowed by the clergy. These new statements joined her increasingly vituperative remarks about the government in which she referred to the pro-Treatyites as 'perjurers, job hunters and materialists,' while she and her Republican colleagues stood 'for truth, honour and the sanctity of oaths.'[49] The increasingly inflammatory nature of her speeches caused the *Morning Post* to refer to her as 'the world's champion, long distance, non-stop venom hurler, Miss Mary MacSwiney.'[50]

While opponents sought to rebut Mary's accusations and diminish her effectiveness, the president of the Republic, Eamon de Valera, took this time to reward her. She was nominated to the Republican Council of State, one of twelve persons charged with the responsibility of maintaining a functioning Republic during these troubled times.[51]

During the first days of November, Mary MacSwiney went to Dublin to consult with the Prisoners Defence Association, an organisation she had helped found during her brother's imprisonments. Here, in an effort to counter-attack the bishops, she called for the Republican cause and subsequent victory to be 'a holy one as well as a great one.'[52]

While in Dublin, Mary stayed at the Herbert Park home of Madame O'Rahilly, also a Republican activist who was suspected by Free State officials of harbouring fugitives. Late in the evening of 4 November, the house was raided by Free State soldiers, an action carried out simultaneously with a raid on the home of Mrs Humphries, where the long sought-after Ernie O'Malley was taken into custody. He was believed to have been hiding in one of the two homes. When he was not found at Madame O'Rahilly's, Mary MacSwiney, alone in the house, was taken in lieu of a larger Republican catch.[53] This is the most likely explanation of Mary's arrest at this particular time, as she had never sought to avoid arrest by either being elusive or leaving her whereabouts uncertain. She had been available for arrest at almost any time.

Taken into custody and driven to Mountjoy Jail, she was imprisoned without charge as was permissible under the Emergency Powers Act. Immediately, Mary declared that she was on a hunger-strike as a protest against the illegality of her imprisonment. Citing Terence MacSwiney's example, hers was a 'protest against any claim of a foreign king to authority in this country.'[54] This action was a result of a strategy that had already been developed as she had written earlier, 'If I am imprisoned I will go on hunger-strike.' Obviously influenced in this by her brother, she continued, 'Pray for me that I may be as brave as those who have gone before me.'[55]

Once word of Mary MacSwiney's hunger-strike was made known, Cumann na mBan understood that there was a need to mount a publicity campaign on behalf of their imprisoned sister. In Cork, they organised a march through the main streets led by a pipers' band, while women marchers with placards and banners urged the release of the hunger-striking Mary MacSwiney.[56] This was accompanied by a letter-writing campaign to the Cork and Dublin newspapers as well as to the Free State government.

It was in Dublin, the site of the prison, that the activities were most intense. Here Cumann na mBan, under the leadership of Maud Gonne MacBride and Mrs Despard, organised a monster rally. The demonstration began with a march past the government offices in Merrion Square and then to Sackville Street where speakers were arranged.[57] The women also gathered a deputation to seek an audience with Archbishop Byrne to urge his intercession on the prisoner's behalf.[58] They arranged nightly prayer vigils at the gates of the prison where the rosary was recited for religious purposes as well as to convince onlookers of their Catholicism in light of recent castigation of Republicans by the hierarchy.[59]

Free State soldiers obliged the women in their search for publicity. At various times the soldiers ran cars into groups of protestors, fired shots over their heads, turned water hoses on the women, and generally harassed them physically and verbally.[60]

The publicity gained began to reap benefits very quickly. From all around the country, cables from county and town councils, unions, civic organisations and private individuals were being sent to President Cosgrave and his Free State ministers. A typical one came from David Neenan of Cork, which read: 'In God's name and in the name of all Ireland's martyrs do not disgrace the Irish by permitting Mary MacSwiney to die of starvation.'[61] These cables were often accompanied by petitions signed by hundreds of citizens calling for Mary MacSwiney's release.[62]

The hunger-strike received international attention from Canada, Australia and particularly from the United States as the organisational work Mary MacSwiney had done in America was not forgotten. AARIR groups from Jamaica, Long Island to San Francisco, accusing the Free State government of all manner of atrocities, demanded the release of their friend. One of the cables read: 'We deplore and deprecate your inhuman and barbarous treatment of the sister of Terence MacSwiney and trust that a just Providence will mete out to both of you (Cosgrave and Mulcahy) proper retribution if she dies.'[63] This radicalism that Mary MacSwiney preached in the United States was bearing fruit on her behalf.

Despite these attempts to threaten the stability of the government and hence to coerce it, President Cosgrave remained firm in his decision not to release the prisoner unless she signed an undertaking swearing to abstain from future anti-government activity. The government believed that Mary MacSwiney was 'one of over 6,000 prisoners and if a concession were granted to her there was nothing to prevent other prisoners going on hunger-strike and making cases for release.'[64]

A new dimension was added to the case when Annie MacSwiney, having journeyed from Cork, sought to visit her fasting sister. In a display of particularly poor judgment, prison officials, acting on government instruction, refused to permit the visit. As expected, Annie MacSwiney was not amenable to the idea of returning quietly to Cork after her request was rejected. Instead, arriving with a deck chair and screen, she encamped herself at the gates of the prison and in what was fast becoming a family tradition, began a hunger-strike of her own.[65] She presented an intriguing picture as she sat in her chair, 'wearing a fur coat with a rug about her knees... supported by small relays of women friends.'[66] Now the Cosgrave government could be cast in the role of a bureaucratic monster, bent on obliterating the entire MacSwiney family.

From inside the prison, Mary MacSwiney sought to augment the publicity campaign raging around her by engaging in a letter-writing campaign of her own. In an attempt to shame her old friend Richard Mulcahy, now Defence Minister in the Free State government, into compliance by appealing to his emotions, patriotism and anti-British sentiments, she wrote, 'As Birkenhead said... why should they keep one hundred or one hundred and fifty thousand English soldiers here at enormous expense when that can get you and the rest of yours to do it for them... Shame on you, Dick.'[67] Letters were also sent to the *Irish Independent*, explaining her situation. Despite threats by the government to censor the paper more heavily in the future, the paper printed two of Mary's letters with the addendum, 'we are obliged to delete passages from the foregoing which we are not in a position to publish.'[68] The condensation notwithstanding, her message was not lost.

To the Archbishop of Dublin, Mary wrote a long scathing letter in which she explained the origins of her present protest and decried the injustice of the joint pastoral of October. She wrote, 'If our fight is wrong today then every fight ever carried on for freedom in Ireland was wrong.' She declared that the army of the Republic would be victorious in the end, proving to the hierarchy 'that God is not always on the side of the biggest battalions.'[69]

She also wrote an open letter to Free State soldiers who were once in the IRA. At this point, any attempt at publicity was abandoned as the letter read: 'Remember that every Irishman who supports King George's Irish government and continues to wear the uniform that Terence MacSwiney lies buried in, is having his share in my death.'[70]

As the days went on, the hierarchy joined the debate about Mary MacSwiney's future. Archbishop Byrne wrote in confidence to the president saying, 'Personally, I have little sympathy for this lady and politically none.' His own feelings aside, he continued that allowing her to die 'would be a thoroughly unwise policy,' as it would make a heroine of her.[71] In a similar vein, Cardinal Logue believed that Mary MacSwiney, along with other women prisoners, were 'doing more harm in prison than they could do outside.'[72] In response to the cardinal, President Cosgrave wrote that he could not permit 'the extension of any special consideration to a person like Mary MacSwiney who is so largely responsible for the prevailing anarchy and crime.'[73]

President Cosgrave and his Minister of Home Affairs, Kevin O'Higgins, rejected all clerical requests politely but firmly, insisting that the situation was 'too serious to permit leniency which would be interpreted alike by opponents and supporters as weakness.'[74]

The confrontation remained a stalemate until 24 November, the twentieth day of the hunger-strike. Up until that time, Mary MacSwiney had impressed her fellow prisoners with her vigour and stamina, remaining remarkably vital, reading, writing, conversing while 'her mind was alert, cheerful and at peace.'[75] On the twentieth day, however, her condition changed abruptly. Her pulse became weak and thready, her temperature sub-normal and her sleep restless and disturbed. At this time, a priest was summoned, and Extreme Unction was administered.[76]

The Free State government was faced with the dilemma of exhibiting weakness by allowing release or of creating a new Republican talisman, an Irish heroine, if Mary MacSwiney was allowed to die. The cabinet debate must have been intense, particularly between the authoritarian Kevin O'Higgins and the more conciliatory Richard Mulcahy who retained sympathy with many Republicans, his colleagues of a few short months before.

The debate was resolved abruptly and without explanation when, on 28 November, Mary MacSwiney was released. The government gave no reasons for its decision and the following day at his weekly press conference, Kevin O'Higgins would entertain no questions about the matter.[77]

It is likely that prior to release, Richard Mulcahy had argued that clemency in this case would reflect positively on the Free State government. The time for this was most auspicious, as just a few days earlier, on 17 November four young Republican soldiers had died before a Free State firing squad at Kilmainham prison,[78] the government intending these deaths to serve as a deterrent to recruits and potential recruits of the Republican forces. These deaths had been followed on 24 November by the execution of Erskine Childers. If Mary MacSwiney had also been allowed to die this might have proved too harsh an obstacle to overcome in maintaining governmental credibility. She was well known at home and abroad, the sister of a genuine Irish martyr and a woman involved in a man's war. Her death would have given the radical Nationalists another symbol, a model of courage and intransigence.

The Republican press identified the government's situation, though expressing it with suitable partisan rhetoric: '(Cosgrave's) action in murdering one sister would have undoubtedly led to the death of the other and even the blatant voices of the Free State champions could hardly drown the outcry that would follow these murders.'[79]

The risk proved too great for the Free State government as they did not want to antagonise public opinion further as many supporters of the government were now calling for Mary's release. It remained, also, that she was held without charge. To let one die under such circumstances would have been a tactical error and would have brought the government more harm than good.

Speaking the following spring, Kevin O'Higgins stated what may have in fact been the deciding factor in granting release. He said that 'Deputy MacSwiney was given back her life once. It might have been thought that that was due to her family, that a life was owing them.'[80]

When the release was issued, Mary MacSwiney was taken by a military ambulance to a private nursing home on Eccles Street.[81] Here she was nursed by two Republican nurse colleagues until her health was sufficiently restored to withstand the trip home to Cork where she would live to fight another day.

Mary MacSwiney felt victorious in this battle of wills, which indeed she had been. She believed, further, that the Free State could be coerced again in the future, with hunger-strikes a ready tool. Mary may have considered the political reasons for the government's decision as she was hardly naive in this area, in public, however, she claimed victory had been achieved because of the rightness of the Republican cause and the weakness of the Free State in the face of a greater moral presence.

The negative publicity over the hunger-strike, though minimal, did not cease with Mary's release from prison. Contrary to the supplications on her behalf by Archbishop Byrne and Cardinal Logue, there were clergymen who did not share this position. Mary's nemesis in Cork, Bishop Cohalan, who had participated in Terry's funeral rites, had said tersely that Mary was involved in an act of 'self-murder' and 'if she dies she has only herself to blame.'[82] With a similar view, the *Catholic Herald* editorialised that 'no humanitarian consideration should blind us to the immorality of the act itself.'[83] Mary's continuing controversy with the hierarchy had only been increased by her hunger-strike.

The hunger-strike provides information into the perceptions and place of Irish women in 1922. One letter to President Cosgrave from George Lyons stated that Mary MacSwiney was 'a woman – according to feminine psychology, being unfitted to inflict hurt upon a man, she inflicts hurt upon herself.'[84] A more telling letter came from Dr O'Connor, senior Medical Officer at Mountjoy, who wrote, 'This present additional strain of facing a long hunger-strike combined with her past experience in this same trouble and her present disturbed mental equilibriun from the climacteric, may conceivably culminate in unhinging her mind.'[85]

The hunger-strike occurred just four years after the enfranchisement of women. Throughout the period that women sought the vote, there were continuing references made to the inferiority or at least the 'separate sphere' of women. Considering this, as well as the Catholic Church's view of women, it is not surprising that the Free State government was somewhat perplexed or unsure as to how they should proceed with Mary MacSwiney. Cardinal Logue had identified this particular sensitivity toward women when he had written to Cosgrave that the imprisoned women, by virtue of their sex, gained public sympathy. Although it was never stated in government council, the woman issue, regardless of noted relatives, may well have been influential in obtaining release.

Meanwhile Mary MacSwiney, weak but victorious, returned to Cork where she regained her strength. To the Irish people, she had presented a picture of Republican will and commitment coupled with a determination not to compromise, making her name synonymous with the Republic. While Mary was recuperating, she was mourning the loss of her good friend, Erskine Childers, an Englishman who had vigorously adopted the Irish Republican cause, took part in the Treaty talks and had joined the doctrinaires in the battle against the Free State government. Having been being captured by government forces and charged with possession of a hand gun, he died before a government firing squad, during Mary's hunger-strike. She said of him that 'if ever a pure and gentle soul went straight to his Maker, he did.' Before and during the Civil War, he had stayed at St Ita's when in Cork during which times Mary 'learned to know him better and love him dearly,' as 'a whole-hearted convert,' totally dedicated to the Republic.[86] It was this latter commitment that made him accepted and respected by Mary MacSwiney as anything less brought only her unswerving enmity. After his death, Mary reserved one side of the fireplace mantle in her sitting room for Erskine Childers' memorabilia, the other side for remembrances of her brother Terence, these areas then appropriately dubbed shrines by onlookers. These were the only two men on whom Mary would lavish such devotion.[87]

The new year, 1923, brought with it more ill fortune for the Republican forces as they were outmanned and outarmed by the Free State soldiers. Realising this and with the hope of avoiding more bloodshed, Liam Deasy, Republican military leader, called for an arms' surrender.

Despite the inevitability of defeat, Mary MacSwiney maintained her fight. Once she was fully recovered, her speech-making and letter-writing were resumed in earnest. Amid mounting criticism and questioning about failure to accept the majority vote of the Irish people, Mary insisted that the majority were wrong in infringing on a fundamental right, continuing, 'There has always been in Ireland a loyal and fearless minority. . . (Hence) the cause of Ireland has never been lost.'[88]

Mary's activities brought her continued attention from the government. In an interview with the *Daily Mail*, President Cosgrave identified Eamon de Valera and Mary MacSwiney as two prime 'political malcontents,' adding derisively that 'the latter's ambition is. . . to be Queen of Ireland,'[89]

The new year also brought conflict between Mary MacSwiney and Eamon de Valera. De Valera, ever the pragmatist, could see the direction in which the country was moving and was thus considering his options, trying to decide which political course to pursue. His decision was to issue a 'personal public statement' in which he would reiterate the sovereign rights of Ireland as inalienable, calling for a plebiscite about the Treaty and renegotiations with England. To sidestep the tricky issue of the oath, he said that 'no one who accepts principles of order can be justly excluded by any political oath.' It was essentially an attempt at peace with honour illustrating De Valera's assumption that concessions on the part of Republicans were necessary.[90]

Mary MacSwiney was appalled at the content of the statement, which De Valera had sent to her as a courtesy before its publication. She wrote back hastily, encouraging him to rethink, urging him to speak only as 'the head of the nation – the Republic and as that only in conjunction with his ministers.' She understood that this proposed statement could only fragment the already dispirited Republicans and concluded that 'a personal statement (would) be a bigger blow than Liam Deasy's and do more harm.'[91]

De Valera believed that it was more important that he engage in political fence-mending with the mainstream of Irish opinion than with the dwindling ranks of the doctrinaire Republicans. He wrote to a friend explaining his differences with Mary MacSwiney, citing a 'genuine desire for peace everywhere,' adding: 'Miss MacSwiney would probably feel justified in taking the initiative in starting this war. I would not.' He believed that it was a war of defence, as 'force and unjustifiable methods' had been used against him and his colleagues. To Mary he wrote a snappy letter criticising her criticism of the oath he had proposed in lieu of the one negotiated in London, the letter assuming a patronising tone: 'It is clear. . . you didn't read it properly. A little knowledge is a dangerous thing. . . my oath could be framed in accordance with our own proposals.'[92]

What particularly annoyed De Valera was that Mary had allowed his letter to her to be seized during a raid on Sinn Féin headquarters in Suffolk Street. One of Mary's responses was also confiscated and reprinted in the *Freeman's Journal*.[93]

De Valera finally decided against the statement. Dwyer, in *De Valera's Darkest Hour*, attributes this to the 'hardline opposition he had received at the hands of Mary MacSwiney.'[94] It was this, combined with the knowledge that the Free State already had documents in their possession and might try to exploit the apparent dissension within the Republican camp, that persuaded him.

Mary MacSwiney was unconvinced now about De Valera's intentions. She had tried to remain loyal to him in order to maintain Republican unity. These statements of De Valera's were increasingly worrisome to her, however, as they hinted at some form of co-operation with the Free State and any type of oath of allegiance to Britain or the king, no matter how vague, was unacceptable. Mary believed herself duty-bound to support the president but before this she had two greater commitments, to herself and to the Republic.

These misgivings were set aside when, in early April, Mary MacSwiney once again found herself a guest of the state. She and her Dáil colleague, Catherine O'Callaghan, had been travelling by train to Tipperary to attend the funeral of the popular IRA leader Liam Lynch who had been killed in a shootout with Free State troops. Government leaders feared that the funeral would serve as a rallying point for the sagging Republican forces. The presence of Mary MacSwiney, who was bound to hurl more venom at the government, was therefore to be blocked. The two women, along with the ageing Count Plunkett, were arrested as they were leaving the train.[95]

The women were taken to Kilmainham Jail in Dublin where a hunger-strike had already been begun by three other Republican women prisoners. Probably no one was surprised when Mary MacSwiney immediately declared that she was once again on a hunger-strike.

Her colleagues in this action were Annie O'Neill, Kitty Costello, Nellie Ryan (sister-in-law to Richard Mulcahy), Catherine O'Callaghan TD and widow of the mayor of Limerick and Maud Gonne MacBride, an important figure in the national cultural revival, Caitlín Ní Houlihan herself. Considering the reputations and relatives of these women, the Cosgrave government was in a very precarious position.

One reminder in particular was difficult to avoid. Just a few short months before, all of those involved, government ministers and hunger-strikers, had been united in their fight against the British. Once again, Richard Mulcahy was torn by ties of blood and friendship. Father Costello, the brother of Kitty, reminded President Cosgrave of the days when he had hidden in the Costello home and borrowed his priest-friend's clothes as a disguise against the British.[96]

The first public response from the government reiterated their stand not to be coerced by hunger-strikers. But the women involved had not forgotten what Mary MacSwiney had done just five months earlier. President Cosgrave was accused of 'making war on women',[97] leaving the impression that war was the proper domain of men only. President Cosgrave replied that 'the mainstay of the trouble we have had was the activity of women'; recognising the important role that women played in carrying petrol, making bombs, distributing literature and hiding fugitives.[98]

The president added that it was not possible 'to consider these women as ordinary females.'[99] They were most assuredly female but they were not similar to the majority of Irish women. The hunger-strikers, including Mary MacSwiney, were middle-class, well-educated urbanites, deeply involved in and committed to Republicanism. Most Irish women were poor agricultural workers who, according to election results, believed with Michael Collins that the Treaty was the most viable route to Irish freedom.

As the hunger-strike continued, the members of Cumann na mBan once again sought to maximise publicity. To their chagrin, public opinion was now difficult to mobilise. The large groups who had gathered the previous autumn in support of Mary MacSwiney could not be roused again. Mrs Despard now kept a lone vigil at the gates of the prison, and even she became discouraged after a few lonely days and abandoned her watch.[100]

The newspapers gave the incident little notice. Among the few public reactions were motions passed by the Dublin and Cork corporations urging release of all the women. Republican fanaticism was waning and being replaced by a more conciliatory approach.

The hierarchy once again requested that President Cosgrave consider releasing the women. Archbishop Byrne, noting the government's 'view as to the machinations of women in the movement' still argued that 'their deaths would cause a wave of sympathy throughout the country.'[101] Despite this apparent, though privately expressed, concern for the hunger-strikers, the hierarchy continued its public barrage of words against Republicans. Cardinal Logue, in his lenten pastoral 'especially deplored that a number of women and girls have become involved in this wild orgy of violence.'[102] There was, to him, something particularly unseemly in female involvement.

The government remained unmoved, perhaps considering the lack of public outcry as indicating support for their position. This was combined with their election victory, the military defeat of Republicans and the general feeling throughout the country, as noted by De Valera, in favour of peace.

Inside the prison, things looked bleak. The women's conditions deteriorated rapidly, this time providing 'a regular gloom over the place.'[103] Mary MacSwiney was described by one of her prisoner-nurses as being 'the same grand spirit but ever so much weaker this time on her twelfth day than in Mountjoy.'[104] This general air of despair was a reflection of the intransigent governmental attitude and the lack of public support.

The government was able to conclude a more satisfactory end to these hunger-strikes than it had to the previous one of Mary MacSwiney when a legislative deal was struck between Kevin O'Higgins and Partick McCartan TD. The government agreed to release the women if Dr

McCartan would introduce a resolution stating that in the future, 'the fact of a prisoner being on hunger-strike should not affect the merits of the question of detention or release.'[105] The arrangement was made and the resolution to be proposed was formulated.

With this settled, four of the six women were released immediately, all except Catherine O'Callaghan and Mary MacSwiney. For some reason, unexplained, these two women were kept for extra days. Inside the prison, all the interned women grew increasingly bitter over the government's effort to flex its muscle while the health of the strikers deteriorated. One prisoner-attendant summed up the anger and frustration of her colleagues, writing to her mother, 'We are all amazed at their being detained, knowing that their release is intended and the cruelty of the delay is appalling to us.'[106] The Free State government was only solidifying Republican resistance through their actions, just as their British predecessors had done.

Finally, on 1 May, Mrs O'Callaghan was released but Mary MacSwiney remained. Mary's health was much more seriously affected during this fast than it had been the previous autumn. She was reported to have neuritis as well as having experienced several episodes of fainting.[107] Finally, at 6 pm on 2 May, Mary MacSwiney was released. When she was taken to Miss O'Donnell's private nursing home on Eccles Street she was 'almost unconscious'. Remaining stable during the evening and improved slightly during the night, making a gradual recovery after her nineteen-day fast.[108]

The Free State government may have released the women gradually to prevent the spectacle of six ambulances carrying wan, exhausted women through the streets of Dublin. The hunger-strike had no great popular appeal, however, leaving this rationale frail at best. Perhaps it was believed that despite the pending resolution, Mary MacSwiney had in fact won again, leaving the government with one last opportunity to exert their authority over her. Perhaps those making the decisions, Kevin O'Higgins in particular, wanted to be absolutely certain that the resolution would be placed before and passed by the Dáil prior to releasing the recalcitrant Mary MacSwiney. Most likely, it had been intended that she remain imprisoned until after the resolution had been enacted and only her rapidly deteriorating health caused her to be released beforehand. It would have reflected extremely poorly on the government if she had died when a settlement had been reached. The resolution was introduced into the Dáil on 3 May, and after some debate concerning the exact wording, was passed.

Mary MacSwiney once again considered herself the victor as the resolution of the hunger-strike called for no compromise on her part. What may have been most disturbing to her was the lack of public support for her cause. She and her colleagues were clearly out of step with the majority of Irish women, the population as a whole seeming tired. They wanted an end to the armed conflict in order that their lives could proceed in peace and resolve the pressing economic problems that plagued the country. Mary MacSwiney, as one might expect, did not accept this popular choice. She continued to see herself, and those of her philosophy, as the guardians of Ireland's honour and its commitment to Republicanism. Her resolve was not diminished in the least, despite her growing ideological isolation, her sense of responsibility may even have been strengthened by this realisation.

Her recovery was spurred by what was happening around the country, particularly the actions of Eamon de Valera. During the last days of April and early May, while the women fasted for Republican ideals, Eamon de Valera was approaching government members in an effort to bring the conflicting parties 'into the non-violent and democratic channels of parliamentary procedure, leaving the central problem to be settled eventually by the people's votes.'[109] He was suggesting that Republicans could operate generally under the Treaty if some adjustment could be made in the oath.[110]

Not surprisingly, Mary MacSwiney was left aghast by De Valera's proposals. This cosying up to the Free State government was intolerable to her and totally dishonest. Disregarding medical advice, she began letter-writing and speech-making again. She did not openly defy De Valera's approach, rather she preached loyalty to the Republic and its martyred dead.

De Valera did not want his plans tampered with through the untimely remarks of Mary MacSwiney. He rebuked her assumption of authority, writing, 'A definite decision has not been taken on the course which is to be followed if this offer is definitely turned down,' while reminding her that the final decision was up to a 'united cabinet and army council'. He then addressed her latest activities: 'A report has just come to me that you. . . are engaged in getting a number of our soldiers to pledge themselves to violate GHQ orders and to renew hostilities.' He went on to appeal to her loyalty: 'I cannot imagine that you who spoke to me on one occasion of discipline can be guilty of such an act.'[111]

Mary MacSwiney and Eamon de Valera were becoming increasingly disenchanted with each other. Prior to the latest hunger-strike, De

Valera had upbraided Mary for her continuing over-estimation of 'Republican strength and under-estimate of that of the Free State' while admitting that he tended to do the opposite. 'Of the two' he continued, 'I have no doubt than an omniscient being would rate my error but a small fraction of yours – vanity?'[112] His use of a question mark was the only subtlety in his remark.

For her part, Mary MacSwiney had her priorities ordered. She wanted to be loyal to De Valera as president of the Republic and had made concessions to this end particularly regarding his Document No. 2. Her first duty was to the Republic, however, which was greater than any individual. She had written to Richard Mulcahy, 'if De Valera were on your side we should still fight on. We do not stand for men but for principles.'[113]

Things were not going well for Mary MacSwiney and her cause. The military forces of the Free State had been triumphant in the field to such an extent that IRA leaders were calling for a cessation of fighting. The political forces of the Free State had legitimised their claim as the duly elected government of the people both by their 1922 election victory and the declining support for radicalism. Now, too, Eamon de Valera was making conciliatory overtures on behalf of Sinn Féin. Mary MacSwiney's response to these reverses was to work harder at spreading the Republican gospel, continuing to believe that if the public were presented with the facts as she saw them, they too would be convinced. She never lacked the faith, however contrary to reality, that she had once accused Michael Collins of lacking.

With the zeal of a young missionary, she revitalised her speaking tour, preparing for the election upcoming in August, continuing to find reasons for the failure of the Republic and never hesitating to lay blame. She pounded away at the notion that Michael Collins and Arthur Griffith had buckled to the wishes of Lloyd George under the threat of war, believing that the Irish should have recognised this as the blind threat it was. The English would not have started war anew. She described how Lord Birkenhead, speaking in Liverpool, 'stated that the war in Ireland could not be launched because it would cost 199,000 lives and 250 million pounds.'[114] She added that Lord Birkenhead and David Lloyd George 'were at that time preparing the English people to accept the fact that war could not be renewed against the Irish and that Ireland would have to be allowed to leave the British Empire.'[115] She concluded that those who signed the Treaty illustrated only great weakness particularly knowing 'as they did, that the Treaty would split the country from top to bottom.'[116]

This rather innovative interpretation of events by Mary MacSwiney was largely inaccurate and unfair to those who had negotiated for Ireland in good faith and had signed the Treaty reluctantly but with good intentions. First, at no time had the British indicated that anything more than dominion status would be given to Ireland. Second, those negotiating in London, particularly Michael Collins who had a ready knowledge and understanding of the Sinn Féin Republic's military capabilities or lack thereof, wished to avoid renewed armed confrontations. Third, the Irish negotiators had foreseen problems in gaining acceptance for the Treaty but did not envision Civil War. Fourth, there was a basic ideological conflict between the negotiators and Mary MacSwiney. The former wished to end armed conflict through compromise if necessary; the latter was willing to die rather than submit to anything less than the Republic proclaimed by Patrick Pearse.

In late June, the Republicans made their annual pilgrimage to Bodenstown, the gravesite of Wolfe Tone. Here, in front of those she considered true believers, Mary MacSwiney was at her best. Having invoked the names of the martyrs of 1916, 1919 and 1920, for whose cause they continued to struggle, she accused the officers of the Free State of becoming 'ministers of an English king.' She declared her 'undying hate of the British Empire while that empire sought to hold them in bondage,' reiterating her desire for peace, with one important qualifier: 'There could never be real peace while the King of England claimed authority in Ireland, or Irishmen swore allegiance to him.'[117]

Mary MacSwiney had succeeded in gaining the attention and raising the ire of President Cosgrave as he campaigned for re-election. To a crowd gathered in Tipperary he said, 'We are not going to allow people to be led by the nose by persons like Miss MacSwiney,' adding that 'she will obey the laws of this country, or leave it, or go to jail.' When a few women in the audience began to heckle and jeer, holding Republican signs aloft, the President sniped that they 'should have rosaries in their hands or be at home with knitting needles.'[118] Perhaps the President was harbouring the vain hope that Mary MacSwiney would heed the latter portion of his advice and thus remove one of his most nagging, political headaches. The President was not courting the vote of emancipated women at any rate.

The President of the Free State was not the only campaigner to attack Mary MacSwiney. In Balbriggan, George Lyons addressed the Republic issue saying, 'Mr de Valera said the war was finished, but his mind might be changed for him by Bonnie Mary.' He intimated that Mary MacSwiney was responsible for the warlike posture that prevailed: 'We know that she said a short time ago that the arms were only dumped.'[119]

Kevin O'Higgins, perhaps the most aggressive, dynamic speaker in the Cosgrave cabinet, did not speak of Mary MacSwiney directly, but addressed the Republican issue. At a campaign rally in Howth, he said that 'Republicanism was supposed to embody democracy at its highest and most perfect form.' He condemned Irish Republicans who had tried to 'trample to a Republic over the will of the people of the country for which they proposed to gain a Republic.'[120]

In this election campaign, the Republicans once again had to face not only their political opponents but a continuing challenge from the Church. In a letter to the *Irish Times*, Cardinal Logue expressed his concern about the lesser parties that were putting forth candidates, including Labour, Farmers and Independents. He feared that this would split up constituencies to support these particular interests and hence electors might return 'a candidate whose election would not contribute to the general good of the country.' He expressed his conviction that the 'safe-course' was 'to go forward as a body in support of the ministry who have made some mistakes but (had) done wonders during the past year to re-organise the country, establish order, secure peace and lay a solid foundation to build up the future prosperity of the country.'[121]

Despite the speech making and general rabble rousing by politicians, the *Irish Times*, in an editorial, took note of the general mood of the country, 'The people have been apathetic and seem to have lost interest in their own political fortunes.'[122] It may be debated whether the people had lost interest, or had grown weary of the continual process of confrontation and warfare. It had, after all, been more than seven years since the armed uprising of Easter week during which time hopes for a free Ireland had continually been raised, only to be dashed again. This cycle of hope and despair had been accentuated by the continual turmoil brought by physical violence. To many, the appeal of the Treaty, the appeal of an end, was too great to reject. Their apathy came when they realised that even this supposed solution could not be had without more of that which they had tried to end.

While Mary travelled from Longford to New Ross, Kilkenny and Waterford preaching intractability, Eamon de Valera continued to adopt a less aggressive tone. Unlike Mary MacSwiney, he was preparing himself and his supporters to accept political realities. Concerning the upcoming election, for which Mary was working so diligently, Eamon de Valera stated that 'whether or not there will be official Republican candidates is not for the (Republican) government but for the political party to decide.' As if to ease the blow of an assured electoral defeat he added that 'there (was) no chance of fair play for Republicans in the coming elections.' One reason cited was the English threat of war 'which would by itself vitiate any verdict as expressing the real desire of the people.' Added to this were 'a register which is notoriously partial, a rigid press censorship. . . a ruthless campaign of disorganisation of all Republican effort as well as the imprisonment of many thousands of the most active Republican workers.'[123] Eamon de Valera seemed to have written off the election two months before it took place. Through this early statement he hoped to salvage some credibility and respectability for the faltering Republican cause. Mary MacSwiney was more than a little disturbed by such defeatism.

Once again De Valera the pragmatist and MacSwiney the ideologue and optimist, were at odds. De Valera had most certainly given up on military confrontation with the Free State. Speaking in Clare, he said that he had 'never stood for brother's hand being raised against brother's hand.'[124] He had been trying for some months to move towards Republican adoption of a political approach to peace, stating clearly to an American correspondent that 'the war, so far as we are concerned, is now finished.'[125] De Valera understood the increasing unpopularity of the armed civil strife and sought to distance himself from it. In so doing, and by seeking political solutions, he hoped to portray the Republicans as the only well-intentioned survivors of 1916.

Mary MacSwiney cared nothing for this posturing. Her most emotional writing came when she considered surrender: 'Why didn't we die in Kilmainham – Won't some man come out and lead?'[126]

To De Valera she wrote again in early August concerning his suggestion that if the oath were removed they could enter the Dáil. To Mary, this signified 'acceptance of partition, inclusion in the British Empire and many other terms that (she) could not accept.'[127] She understood the problems her attitudes could bring to Sinn Féin, particularly 'the taunts of the Free State' concerning the unresolved disputes among Republicans, but reminded De Valera of one concession she had offered that could have allayed this problem: 'That is why I signified my willingness to go to America so that there would be no need for me either to drop out of things here or to make any statement. You all urged me to stay and help.'[128] Once again, as was her custom, Mary MacSwiney was absolving herself of the responsibility for the dissention that was brewing. It is entirely possible the De Valera did rue the day he did not accept her travel plans. Because De Valera was arrested in Clare in August, the two would not spar again for some months.

Though the government of President Cosgrave was returned to office in the election of August 1923, Sinn Féin succeeded in having forty-four representatives elected, among them Mary MacSwiney from Cork city. There was no question of any of the Sinn Féin deputies taking their seats in the Dáil as such participation would have required an oath of allegiance to the king, a totally unacceptable stipulation. Furthermore, this was a parliament established by the reprehensible Treaty.

Sinn Féin was buoyed by the election returns although their forty-four seats in a House of one hundred and fifty-three hardly gave them a resounding mandate. Partick Rutledge, acting President of Sinn Féin while De Valera remained in prison, called for all available deputies to help organise Sinn Féin 'on a solid and lasting basis,' this requiring that at least one 'cumann' per parish be activated. To help achieve revitalisation Mary MacSwiney became the Sinn Féin publicity director.[129] The post was in recognition of her skills as an orator, her ability to obtain press coverage and her proliferative letter writing.

In October, as many Sinn Féin representatives as possible came together in Dublin for the annual Ard-Fheis (convention), with Mary MacSwiney presiding over the meeting in place of the still imprisoned Eamon de Valera. Here Mary could lighten her rhetoric as she was preaching to those already converted. The meeting had many issues to discuss, including the organisational tasks of recruitment and finance as well as the development of policy statements on the Boundary Commission, volunteer recruits, Irish language and culture, the economy and press relations. Mary dismissed the latter without ceremony saying that 'there was never such an un-national disgraceful Press in any country.'[130]

Mary opened the session with unlikely remarks:

I have already tried to express the deep sense I feel of my inability to preside today, instead of our beloved president. There is nobody but Eamon de Valera himself who can fill the place of Eamon de Valera.

Considering the recent exchanges between the two, the sincerity of these remarks is certainly suspect. Undeniably, De Valera was beloved still, by many of the Sinn Féin delegates. Mary's last sentence was certainly true but perhaps signifies more approval than she actually intended, as she repeatedly strove to present the image of a united front both to those present and to those looking on from outside the convention hall. She continued to believe Eamon de Valera to be the one individual who could best represent Republicans. Although she accepted his leadership position, it in no way signified her acceptance of De Valera's attempts at revisionist Republicanism.

During the Ard-Fheis, Mary wielded the gavel with dexterity and authority, frequently ruling members out of order and then giving herself the final word on an issue. Concerning Ulster, she believed that it should be appealed to on the National aspect rather than on the religious, concluding that 'it was England that put the religious aspect into the heads of those bigoted Orangemen up there.'[131] To the issue of Volunteer recruits she said that they know that physical force is sometimes necessary but it 'must be exercised worthily by men who know themselves to be working in a high and holy cause,' reiterating that the Republic did not want to be represented by 'mere mercenaries or men who merely love a scrap.' She concluded by stating the aim of Sinn Féin: 'It was the great national organisation which in 1917 adopted the Republican Constitution, and would now become the right hand of the government again.'[132]

While using the platform to present her own view of the Irish situation, Mary repeated the often heard phrase that 'England's difficulty is Ireland's opportunity.' The need of maintaining military forces and using physical force when needed and without reluctance was addressed, as well as their combined commitment to a Republic, clear and unequivocal. Her unexpressed aim was to set the movement back on course, her course, not the one being charted by Eamon de Valera.

For those who could not attend the meeting, this speech was printed in pamphlet form and distributed throughout the country. The following year De Valera looked back on this time as an occasion used by 'Miss MacSwiney and others (to) impose their own ideas on the organisation.'[133]

Following the Ard-Fheis it was over the burial of Dennis Barry that Mary MacSwiney was again brought into the public eye. Bishop Cohalan of Cork, as a continuation of his anti-Republicanism, refused to bury the body of the dead hunger-striker in ground consecrated by the Church, the desired final resting place of all Catholics.

The bishop was on record as saying that 'Republicanism in Ireland for the last twelve months has been a wicked, insidious attack on the Church and on the souls of the faithful committee of the Church.'[134] Before the death of Dennis Barry occurred, the bishop had been outspoken in his disapproval of the hunger-strikers, saying bluntly that 'the country (was) being disgraced before the world by the hunger-striking business.' He added that priests should refuse the sacraments to those involved in what he considered suicide. It was because he held this view that he would not sanction Catholic rites of burial for Dennis Barry as Church law clearly forbade the burial of suicide victims in consecrated ground, considering them to have died in a state of mortal sin. The bishop would not be convinced that Dennis Barry gave his life for his country, rather the bishop said that 'he did not give his life at all – he took his own life.'[135]

Mary MacSwiney could not let the bishop's decision go unchallenged. By refusing Dennis Barry a Christian burial was he also saying that Terence MacSwiney died in a state of sin? Mary reminded the bishop that he had officiated at Terry's funeral, and praised him as a martyr for Ireland. She also saw the bishop's action as another clerical rejection of Republicanism, none of which could be let pass, and reiterated her argument that the Church should not issue policy statements concerning political matters.

An editorial in the Republican *Daily Sheet* bore unmistakable resemblance to Mary MacSwiney's prose. It addressed the Bishop of Cork directly: 'When he holds forth as a confessed politician, he is still justifying the ecclesiastical political tyranny to which Republicans have been subjected since their lordships first distinguished between authorised and unauthorised murder.'[136] If these were not Mary's own words, they most certainly were her sentiments.

The bishop raised the MacSwiney ire further with a series of derogatory statements about Mary personally. These untimely and ill-advised remarks were included in his official press release about Dennis Barry. The bishop wrote that there were 'two classes of persons' that bore a heavy responsibility for the activities of the Civil War. The first group, into which he placed Mary MacSwiney, were those 'who had not been Republicans at all, whose plans had misfired, who had suffered a serious loss, and who then discovered in themselves the theory that they had been always the most extreme of the extremes.' He went on that Mary MacSwiney had not only not been a member of Sinn Féin in 1916, but that she, personally, had 'prevented the call from Dublin for a rising to reach the Volunteers of Cork.' Not content with this indictment, the bishop continued that she 'gambled on the life of Terry,' encouraging him to continue the strike 'hoping that in the end the British government would relent.' His final accusation against her was that she had induced nuns in Clifden to keep a bag of money, stolen by Republicans from the Customs House. He alleged that Mary MacSwiney accomplished this under 'false representation,' saying that the bag contained only some papers and souvenirs of Terence MacSwiney.[137]

Mary MacSwiney, already enraged about the circumstances surrounding Dennis Barry's burial, was livid when she read the charges of the bishop concerning herself. The bishop was wrong on all three counts and she was eager to clear up these false accusations. First, she had opposed the 1916 Rising but she did nothing to interfere with the transmission of messages as such an act would have been both dishonest and dangerous. Second, she had not encouraged Terence to maintain his fast, nor would she encourage him to disregard his conscience. Furthermore, she understood she had no say in the matter, hers was a supportive role only. The third charge cast doubts upon her honesty. She had kept the money for a short time, but she would never knowingly deceive anyone about such a serious matter let alone a group of nuns. Because of Mary's record of truth and forthrightness, her personal denials notwithstanding, it would seem unlikely that she deceived the nuns in the manner described by the bishop.

Mary promptly sent copies of her response to the newspaper in Cork. This was not the end of her rebuttal, however. She had been unsure of how to proceed legally in this case, but discovered through her solicitor, Seán Ó hUadhaigh, that one could take a bishop into a civil court only after obtaining ecclesiastical permission, on pain of excommunication. Mary wanted redress but was uncertain if she wanted to proceed in a civil action. While she was considering her possible options, she wrote a letter to the pope, detailing what she considered to be the unconscionable actions of Bishop Cohalan.[138] After consideration, Mary informed her solicitor that she wished to proceed with the matter through the recognised legal channels. In early December, the bishop received a letter from Mary's legal representative stating that proceedings were being instituted against his lordship 'for the false and libellous statements contained in (his) communication re: Dennis Barry in the *Cork Examiner*.' This was the opening salvo in a long legal battle that Mary was fighting as a matter of principle. By February, she was informed that if she wished her case to make any headway, it was necessary that she also have an attorney in Rome. She agreed.

This ecclesiastical wrangling was only a diversion for Mary MacSwiney and her Republican colleagues. As committed as Mary was to seeing the bishop brought to justice, she had also to deal with the political situation in Ireland. The reality of events was grim indeed. Sinn Féin had suffered a political defeat in August, the military defeat of the Republican forces was accomplished, and the general hunger-strike, what many had hoped would be a revitalising tonic for lagging Republicans, had been a dismal failure.

With these discouraging facts before them the TD's of the Second Dáil met in Dublin to plan their future. At this time, they turned their attention to the problem of partition, a matter of seemingly little concern prior to this time. Previously, the Republicans had sought to gain support for their anti-Treaty position by accusing the negotiating team of disloyalty to the Republic of 1916. To shore up their stand, they had turned to condemnation of the oath, which made Irish men and women pledge allegiance to a foreign, oppressing king. The Republicans had engaged in all manner of name-calling, all with the intent of depicting the Free State government as puppets of the British. Now, when none of these strategies had succeeded, the Republican leadership made Ulster and partition their cause.

The meeting of the Second Dáil repudiated partition in principle and also the 'validity of the partitioned government'. In an unusual move, they then turned to 'practical politics in view of the situation created'. One alternative would be to give the whole of Ulster 'complete autonomy for a period mutually determined'. Another option was to allow the six counties a separate government for an agreed period in return for 'proper representation and no gerrymandering of constituencies' as well as 'real freedom from religious persecutions'. If these rather conciliatory, seemingly diplomatic approaches should fail, the TD's recommended a return to their old tactics, calling a complete boycott, rigorously enforced, as to trade, banking interests, etc against all six counties and concerns in the twenty-six counties. This would be accompanied by 'a systematic campaign for the same purpose in America; the same boycott to apply to England as long as Belfast proved recalcitrant.'[139] This was acceptable to the larger body of Sinn Féin and hence became the accepted Republican plan.[140]

While agreeing with the political statement of her colleagues which she had helped formulate, Mary had a much more instinctual answer to the problem. Realising her solution was inappropriate in the political arena but not hesitating to use it when campaigning in the countryside, she said, 'Like it or not, Craig and his government were Irish and if they wanted to be British they could cross the Irish Sea and live in England.' She was equally clear about others who rejected the union of Ireland, saying that the 'Republic was the only lawful government – everybody who dared deny its rights, and who did not give it allegiance would be cleared out.'[141] This type of statement did nothing to enhance her political credibility. It fuelled the arguments of Government leaders who labelled her as an unreasonable trouble maker with no viable plans for Ireland's future, as well as antagonising much of the Protestant, Unionist population of the north. It fuelled criticisms that she was rigid, war-like, and generally dangerous.

As 1923 drew to a close, Mary MacSwiney reflected on the turbulent year just passed. It had been an unhappy, unrewarding twelve months that had seen Republican dreams of electoral or military victory go unrealised. Even if these two goals were too optimistic for some, the desire for a form of legitimisation of the Republican position had also been rejected both by the electorate and those elected.

Mary MacSwiney ruminated about the oath of allegiance, that facet of the Treaty to which she objected so strongly. She remembered that when her brother lay dying in Brixton, the deputy governor came to her saying that if Terence would take only 'one spoonful of food he would be released in two days,' adding that this 'was only a symbol after all, and it would have saved his life.' Now, as the Civil War ended, Mary wrote 'The oath of allegiance is but a symbol too, but one and all they are symbols of surrender, the surrender of the underlying reality – of the principle which distinguishes the souls of fire from the souls of clay.'[142] Her sentiments about the illegality and immorality of the oath remained unchanged and inflexible. In a few years her view would be challenged not from without, as might be expected, but from within the ranks of Republicanism.

Mary also reflected about the Civil War, a black period in any country's history when friendships and families are flayed by guns and resentment. Despite her role in the events just passed, she continued to lay the blame at the door of the Free State and those unfaithful to the profession of 1916. President Cosgrave had, on more than one occasion, accused Mary MacSwiney and her vitriolic rhetoric of sharing a large portion of responsibility for the conflict. Even Eamon de Valera believed Mary to be a much stronger perpetrator of war than he. Mary continued to say that 'the army of the Republic, when attacked, defended itself and the Republic, as it was bound to do.' Concerning her own involvement and responsibility she said, 'The Republican leaders did everything possible to avert this fratricidal strife of surrendering the honour of the nation.' She would never have considered this view short-sighted, but in reality the only concession she had offered those who accepted the Treaty was an opportunity to confess their sins, reject the Treaty and accept Republicanism.

This concept, then, of doing 'everything possible' meant that the Treatyites could be forgiven after confession, rather than being inflicted with eternal Republican damnation.

Some within the Republican party, including Eamon de Valera, realised that some adjustment must be made by Republicans in the future if they were to remain politically viable. Mary MacSwiney was entrenched in the belief that principle was more important than political expediency, rejecting the notion that Republicans claimed 'to be super-patriots,' saying the situation was quite simple: 'They swore to defend the Republic against all enemies foreign and domestic. They meant what they said.'[143]

By the end of the year, the turmoil in most of the countryside had subsided. A memo to the Executive Committee of the Free State government summarised conditions noting that thirteen counties were normal; in another six counties the police force was deemed sufficient for maintaining order; and seven counties (Cork, Leitrim, Galway, Clare, Tipperary, Offaly and Roscommon) still had enough 'armed men' that the 'Civic Guard could not take responsibility for the prevention of crime'. Kevin O'Higgins sought to redress this last situation by adding 1,000 men to the police, who would be 'armed and distributed throughout these disturbed areas for the special purpose of dealing with armed crime.'[144] O'Higgins' activist inclinations were over-ruled and it was decided to forego further use of arms for two more months with the hope that the situation would become defused on its own.

The government had other problems as well with which to deal. Tim Pat Coogan wrote metaphorically that 'the Civil War brought the country to its knees,' citing evidence that 'hundreds of thousands of acres went out of cultivation; of the total population of 2,750,000 in the Free State, 130,000 were unemployed. Damage to Irish property amounted to 30 million pounds and on top of this came the bill for the prosecution of the war.'[145] Added to this was the memory of 665 dead and 3,000 wounded.[146] The task of the government was great. They were charged with the 'highly technical challenge of creating a government, outlining a budget, devising an economic policy; in sum, to give the Irish Free State institutions directions and policies.'[147] This had to be done while a fringe of Republicans led by Mary MacSwiney threw continual verbal darts at the government, hoping to pierce its credibility and legitimacy. Mary, unlike Eamon de Valera, entertained no thoughts of co-operation and vowed to do all in her power to undermine those faithful to the Treaty.

The past two years had proven a time of action and reaction. The Treaty negotiations and subsequent signing had divided the Irish on ideological issues, pitting the pragmatists against the Republican ideologues, with the resultant Civil War from which the government established under the Treaty emerged victorious. It was not a wildly jubilant victory but rather one given reluctantly by the electorate as the most acceptable of two poor alternatives. Nonetheless, there had been a commitment made by the people of the twenty-six counties to the rule of law, even if that law had been established by the British. It was time to turn away from fighting and give all energy to solving the prevailing social and economic ills.

These years had also taken their toll among Republicans. They had lost many of their best and brightest leaders, Harry Boland, Liam Lynch and Erskine Childers among them. While the war against the Free State had been underway, Republicans had maintained a united front. When defeat became inevitable, their encompassing cover proved a thin veneer, and even that had cracks. First, the military was inclined to set its own agenda as had been demonstrated during the seizure of the Four Courts and the general hunger-strike. Second, the leadership was showing signs of increasing differences of opinion. Eamon de Valera, the recognised leader, was gently shifting to make his position more adaptable to the established system while Mary MacSwiney had emerged as the leader of the doctrinaire Republicans, maintaining a basic, no-compromise policy. De Valera was astute enough to recognise this approach as the politics of failure, whereas Mary MacSwiney viewed it as the politics of principle. The two were on a collision course in a struggle for the soul of Sinn Féin.

Mary MacSwiney herself was drained by the experiences of 1922-23. Her hunger-strike had left her physically debilitated, but she was energised psychologically when she considered her two hunger-striking victories over the Free State government. She had been left with new emotional scars from the deaths of her fellow Republicans, in particular Erskine Childers. Efforts to overcome these wounds were made by immersing herself in her work both at school and around the country with her personal zeal and organisational involvement. There remained one nagging problem that no amount of work could blot out, however. Mary was continually disturbed over the changing position of Eamon de Valera, thus keeping all Republicans ideologically pure was her new, added responsibility.

5. The Decline of Sinn Féin, 1924-1927

Following the dispiriting events of the Civil War, 1924 was a time for Republicans to regroup, examine their agenda and set a strategy for the future. With Eamon de Valera still in prison at Arbour Hill, the leadership of the faltering movement was assumed, though never claimed, by Mary MacSwiney who set the course to be followed: continuing to spread Republican propaganda while developing a well rounded political platform. It was hoped that the latter would compensate for the rejection of the former and make Republicanism a more viable political alternative than it had proven in the 1923 elections. Although this was a long range goal, at no time did Mary suggest that Republicans enter into negotiations with the Free State government, preferring to stand alone in righteousness and intractability.

As previously, Mary made frequent speeches wherever and whenever possible, her credo unchanged from Civil War days. In a seemingly paradoxical statement, she told an audience in Dun Laoghaire that Republicans 'were the only apostles of peace in this country' adding that 'nothing was ever settled until it was settled right', a theme begun by her during the Treaty negotiations.[1]

Work with Cumann na mBan also continued, though membership had declined since the Civil War. An official leaflet from the organisation read that members, by 'taking (their) place in the firing line and in every other way helping in the establishment of the Irish Republic' had 're-gained for the women of Ireland the rights that were theirs under the old Gaelic civilisation where sex was no bar to citizenship rights which were long stolen from them under English rule, (and) were guaranteed to them in the Republican Proclamation of Easter Week'.[2] There was a continuing reference in Cumann literature to the concept that women, unlike men, must earn and deserve political rights.

Mary's view of an Irish Republic had prevailed in Cumann na mBan since the previous year. With its membership purged and ideologically pure, she urged her sisters to 'take up the language of Ireland' which would give the women 'an Irish mentality'.[3] Presumably by this Mary meant the women would be in agreement with herself as she was the harbinger of all things Irish and the repository of the only right political ideology.

This commitment to the Irish language and culture was not a new tack as Mary had espoused this since her earliest days of teaching in Irish schools. At St Ita's, she had seen young children become 'quite fluent in speaking, reading and writing Irish' after a few years of intense exposure to the language.[4] She cautioned that teacher fluency was not the only prerequisite, as they must also bring 'the proper atmosphere to the teaching'. This would 'take Ireland and the Irish language for granted' and it would 'be entirely foreign to the apologetic and "God help us" attitude with which (they were) so familiar'. The follow-up, as with most of Mary's arguments, was that this Irish atmosphere was 'incompatible with dominion status, or any other dependent status'.[5] To her, the language issue, as most others, led to the same conclusion: the only logical place in which the Irish language would flourish was an Irish Republic. Her recent experiences in politics, particularly events surrounding the Treaty, solidified her belief that Ireland must be cleansed of all unpure English influences, the language being the most obvious. She herself had sought to immerse herself in Irish heritage, through a study of history, literature and culture, seeing this as the most successful way to achieve an Irish environment. Since 1914, she had become increasingly disenchanted with the British influence in Ireland. While some believed the British had brought governmental organisation and the rule of law to Ireland, Mary contended that they had rooted out the more just and systematic Brehon Laws in attempts to destroy the Irish culture leaving Ireland poor and subservient in the process.

Sinn Féin also felt its obligations heavily in 1924. The organisation saw the necessity of renewed planning, publicity and innovation following its electoral defeats. Mary MacSwiney, because of her knowledge and experience, was placed in charge of an educational lecture series to take place around the country. The topics to be included were citizenship, economics, and 'where we stand now'.[6]

Sinn Féin tried to maintain a shadow government just as it had during the Black and Tan days with particular attention given to finance, health care, education and roads. The conditions for maintenance of such a scheme were deteriorating, however. Attendance at Sinn Féin meetings was declining with the subsequent effect on membership rolls and financial support.[7] It was difficult to go forward with bold new plans when interest lagged and workers and funds were scarce, thus the work of continuing the organisation fell to a few dedicated supporters.

To answer both critics and followers, a constitution was needed which would define clearly policies and goals. Most of 1924 was spent formulating such a document, with the expected debate and bickering over the fine points of wording and syntax. This project was a particular relief to Mary, as her continuing concern was that she and her colleagues must separate themselves from the Free State through an illumination of differences in all phases of government.[8]

A constitution would also address the economic questions that were at issue. Mary reported to a Sinn Féin meeting that she was constantly being asked if they stood 'for peasant proprietorship or communal confiscation'.[9] This Marxist phraseology had abounded since the Russian Revolution, aided by supporters in Ireland including the well known Republican, Peadar O'Donnell. Sinn Féin had to decide 'in detail, the extent to which individual or national ownership shall be applied'.[10] If national ownership of industry and distribution was decided upon, what then would happen with existing businesses?

During a speech to the poitical wing of a workers union in Cork, Mary was asked directly if she were a 'Communist or a Socialist'. Having struggled with these concepts previously, she gave a non-committal reply, stating: 'I am either or both in so far as they do not controvert Christian teaching and common sense and there is no reason why rightly interpreted they should do either.' She readily admitted that the world still consisted of the exploiter and the exploited, hence some form of government intervention was necessary to equalise the distribution of wealth. One remedy to aid governmental decision-making was the concept of Vocational Councils 'where experts would speak at first hand for the needs of the people they represent'.[11]

Mary did not have well-defined economic solutions to Ireland's problems of poverty and unemployment. Rather, she had a vague notion of Christian socialism: an Irish answer to the Sermon on the Mount, where all would be adequately cared for including the poor, the hungry and the imprisoned. Jobs would somehow be provided and native Irish industries would be encouraged. The details of enacting such a policy and the question of how it would be financed were left to others, as Mary was content to set the ideological agenda for Sinn Féin and for Ireland.

Mary's social egalitarianism grew from her own background, her interpretation of the teaching of Jesus combined with a sensitive look at the Irish condition. Though growing up in meagre economic conditions herself, she was aware that many in Ireland lived in desperate poverty both in towns and in the countryside, the distribution of wealth being scandalous. Her childhood and her religious experiences, particularly at Farnboro, had left her with no great longing for material possessions, believing intellectual pursuits and spirituality far more substantive. Nonetheless, she grew to feel that the great disparity in wealth in Ireland had to be adjusted so all might share more equitably.

Throughout the year, she was concerned with the lethargy that seemed to her to prevail in the country confiding to a friend that she dreaded 'slipping into a mere political routine' but to her disappointment 'things seem(ed) to be developing a tendency that way'.[12] To a Sinn Féin group she decried the fact that 'a junta of glorified clerks is being set up in Dublin to contol completely the whole of Local Government in Ireland'[13] while no one was offering solid resistance.

To try to stop the growing air of ennui, Mary spoke publicly as frequently as possible. In a search for new members she told an anti-Treaty meeting in Dublin that 'the Republican party would allow back into its ranks those of the rank and file who had not actually taken part in any executions and who would prove their honesty and sincerity'.[14] How this latter point was to be accomplished was not defined, but it is possible that it meant compliance with the Mary MacSwiney view of an Irish Republic.

She also encouraged a newly released group of former Republican prisoners to join Sinn Féin in order that their time spent at the nation's expense would not be in vain. To give more practical and immediate assistance to the men, she helped form a committee to assist the Unemployment Bureau.[15] In addition, whenever possible, Mary made private, personal appeals to Republicans who were now employers, to reach out to these unemployed victims of the Civil War.

With the unemployment picture so bleak and the housing conditions so desperate, particularly in the Dublin tenements, it was difficult to gain supporters. Perhaps there were many who supported the concept of an Irish Republic but their struggle to make ends meet gave them little time to consider the morality involved in the taking of an oath to the British Commonwealth by the Free State parliamentarians. Margaret O'Driscoll, the sister of Michael Collins, expressed what may have been the view of many: 'No one that knows Dublin will deny that there are hundreds there who would gladly exchange their state of destitution for the rashers and eggs for breakfast supplied to the men and women who are responsible for most of the hardship and struggling of the last eighteen months and for the load of debt that will weigh down this nation for the next two or three generations.'[16]

Mary, however, would not be swayed. While realising that many were suffering because of social inequities, this was not considered a reason to abandon one's principles. Speaking to a gathering in Athlone, she restated her acceptance of violence if necessary for a Republic while castigating the oath: 'A broken bridge is a bad thing but a broken oath is much worse. I would break every bridge in Ireland rather than see one man in Ireland disgrace himself and country by taking an oath of allegiance to Ireland's enemy.'[17]

In July, Eamon de Valera was released from prison, ready to resume the leadership of the Republicans. To his chagrin, however, he found 'the Mary MacSwiney view well established' among his colleagues.[18] *The Leader*, sensing the potential conflict stated, 'Miss MacSwiney's will is to prevail in the Anti-Treaty Party or she will know the reason why.'[19] Mary dismissed this notion as another Unionist attempt to split the Republicans and ferment doubt among supporters. Indeed, with De Valera released, Republicans rejoiced together, for the moment ignoring their ideological differences, in efforts to appear strong and confident.

In August, in a continuing effort to unite authority, members of the Second Dáil met along with those elected in the pact election and the general election of 1923. Mary MacSwiney, as some others, had been elected on all three occasions, but now a decision was necessary on where authority actually resided. Without divisive controversy, it was decided that the Second Dáil, as the direct descendant of 1916 and the parliament established after the declaration of the Republic, was the only legitimate government of Ireland. Hence, it would be the authority to which Republicans were responsible and loyal.[20]

Also to be addressed was the matter of the perception of Republicanism in the United States. P. J. Rutledge had written to some Republican TDs that the situation in America had become 'extremely unsatisfactory' as all efforts there had been turned to short-term fund raising and consequently friendly organisations, in need of re-organisation since the Civil War, had been ignored. He concluded that this could be 'calamitous if allowed to continue'.[21] There was also 'a real danger' from the Clan na Gael, an association formed and controlled by Irish-Americans alone, which was becoming increasingly secretive and 'going its own way'.[22] It was decided to divide the states into three or four large sections and to begin acquiring and updating rolls of groups and their members as a first step to regaining American support.[23]

While these details were being attended and America was the topic of discussion, Mary took the opportunity to criticise President Wilson about his treatment of Ireland. The main point of contention lay with the Fourteen Points and the League of Nations. Mary believed the former to be 'the most magnificent gospel preached for peace of the world since the sermon on the mount', but the president was chastised for not succeeding in carrying out his ideals.[24] Concerning the League, she was less subtle, writing that it was 'a farce' adding that 'it (was) a British preserve' and 'Mr Cosgrave had been admitted to it only as a British subject'.[25]

Having reviewed the troublesome situations, in both Ireland and America, Mary came to a decision. In late November she wrote to a friend: 'A lightning tour from now to May would rake the shekels in if I went out. I feel that it would be good propaganda anyhow.' She then admitted, quite frankly, her importance to the cause: 'After Dev himself I suppose I would have most chance of success.'[26]

With this decision made, she was able to look back on some of the other events that had taken place during the previous months. Personal satisfaction came as Terence's books *Principles of Freedom* and *The Revolutionist* were soon to be published, largely through her efforts with De Valera writing the foreword and Mary the biographical notes. She had been nominated for the Vice-Presidency of Sinn Féin as well as Secretary and Treasurer, positions she was not anxious to assume because of her geographical difficulty of living in Cork while the main group activities were in Dublin. Finally, she had been 'officially forbidden to enter the six counties'.[27] This notification brought its own satisfaction as it recognised her influence and illustrated the fears among the northern Unionist enemy concerning her potential for disestablishing the existing government.

Plans for the second trip to America were quickly laid with departure set for early January, as Mary was anxious to move forward. Before leaving, one more letter was sent to the *Irish Independent* using her now familar pejorative terms toward the government. The letter stated: 'The British have not left in any Irish sense. The Free State soldiers are no more Irish than the "Leinsters" or "Munsters" in spite of the colour of their uniforms.' She also wanted to make a statement about international recognition on which citizens could ruminate in her absence: 'Republicans will continue to denounce the attempt to enrol a portion of Ireland in a League of Nations as a subordinate to England and to pay tens of thousands of pounds for that humiliation to this ancient Nation.'[28]

This time, Mary set sail for America alone with even the modest fanfare that accompanied her last overseas departure absent. During the sea voyage, she considered the questions from Americans that she must be prepared to answer in a convincing manner so that the many Irish-Americans, their Irish allegiance in a quandry, would decide in favour of the Republican movement.

The first question to be answered was why the Republicans had not found the terms of the Treaty acceptable. Peter Golden, an Irish leader in America, informed Mary that after the signing in 1921, the people 'went on more or less a riot of jubilation'. The ensuing war had caused great confusion however, and now 'no one seem(ed) to know what to do or say or think' as they awaited leadership from Ireland.[29]

Regarding the Treaty, Mary always had her stock response ready: the British had made tools of the Irish and left them dependent, subservient and humiliated. For the foreign audience, she would also exploit the actions of Michael Collins to de-mytholigise him in the eyes of his American worshippers saying that 'it was he who persuaded the young men in Dáil Éireann to vote for the Treaty'. She would add, however, that this support was gained only through deceit and outright lies as Collins gave 'his word that there would be no oath of allegiance to England and that the constitution under the Treaty would be Republican whether England liked it or not'.[30] It was hoped that this exposure of the beloved Collins would increase the credibility of Republicans as those who had stood fast in the face of British threats.

The second question that loomed large in Irish-American minds was why the majority Dáil vote concerning the Treaty had not been accepted by both sides. This was well-trod turf to Mary and she was prepared with an answer she hoped would be convincing. Her previous statements were to be reiterated: 'The independence of one's country is one of those fundamental things which it is not lawful to submit to a ballot', and even in light of a majority vote 'the minority would be bound to resist'.[31] She and her colleagues would be presented as the custodians, protecting Ireland's freedom in light of the mistake the majority of the Irish had made in voting away Irish freedom.

The third question required innovative thinking as it concerned why America was not consulted about Republican decisions with regard to the Treaty and a Republican constitution. To this Mary would somehow have to dilute her ready response that the Irish alone were responsible for decisions about their actions in Ireland, a perfectly logical situation in her own mind. Many in the AARIR believed that Eamon de Valera should not have resigned after the Treaty vote. To this, Mary prepared a procedural answer: De Valera was president by national acclamation rather than by election, therefore, he had not in fact resigned. Americans were also concerned that the Irish were interested only in American dollars. The ready response: 'If you believe in our cause why not help financially.'[32] These questions called for a form of sensitive politicking with which Mary was quite unfamiliar or at least had not practiced in Ireland. While in America, however, realising that success depended on assuaging ruffled American feathers, she was able to mute her rhetoric, an exercise in great self-control. Rather than offend her audiences, she contained her emotions, instead vented her bottled rage against the British and the Free State.

A brief explanation about her uncharacteristic behaviour was given in a letter to an American friend: 'I am a most practical, logical, wide-awake, common sense person and a student of history.'[33] If this were the case, Mary's aggressive, pugilistic stance in Ireland was intentionally adopted. There is no evidence to suggest that it was a calculated, pre-planned strategy, rather it seems to have been an intuitive, spontaneous response to the prevailing situation. Her posture in the United States however would seem to have been by design, as it required restraint of her characteristic style.

If suitable answers were made to the anticipated question, Mary could then go on the offensive. She would continue to decry the Free State government as 'just another version of England', the focus of her ire during the previous tour. There would be the usual appeal to patriotism coupled with sentiment for the homeland as Mary came 'to tell the story of Ireland for the past few years and to enlist the moral and financial support of all liberty-loving Americans for Ireland' a country that 'Washington himself declared was identical with his'.[34]

If these arguments proved convincing, a large portion of Irish-Americans would be placed in the Republican column. The Clan na Gael, vociferous though small in numbers, was already supportive but it was towards the undecided members of the AARIR that this new propaganda attack was aimed.[35]

If Mary had hoped for a New York reception to match her previous one, she was sadly disappointed. Her American reception reflected the same apathetic mood that she had observed, and almost despaired of, in Ireland. There were no welcoming bands or parades, no receptions overflowing with supporters and well-wishers, no crowds eager to catch a glimpse of the sister of the martyred mayor, no motorcades to prominent hotels such as the St Regis in New York or the Shoreham in Washington,

DC. Instead, she was greeted by a few faithful, hardworking American supporters who dutifully took her from one meeting place to another. The speeches remained enthusiastic, challenging, often combative, but the size of the crowds were down and their response subdued.

Mary travelled on the train alone, to diminish expenses and spent overnights either with friends or in convents. Her days were filled with morning mass, trains, lunches, meetings, correspondence, newspaper photo sessions, interviews, and 'nuns and priests aplenty'. The schedule remained exhausting but because of the despondency of the gatherings, Mary was not re-energised by the crowds. Rather they drained her completely making it increasingly difficult for her to maintain a mood of vibrancy and optimism. She wrote rather peevishly in her diary: 'I wish committees would not persist in kissing me.'[36]

Rather than the adoring, unquestioning crowds of 1921, people now addressed their visitor with sharp, often accusatory questions which required Mary's best efforts to deflect. This continual defensive battle took its toll, however, and she complained wearily: 'This continual criticism has me nearly worn out.'[37] With her resistance down, she fell victim to a cold and later became ill with a sickness self-diagnosed as 'indigestion fermentation' that left her weak and often listless. To restore her spirit and strength, a short vacation was taken at Coney Island, which proved 'enjoyable and restful'.[38]

Despite the low interest level, the tour continued from coast to coast with stops in Springfield, Rochester, St Paul, Chicago, Cheyenne, Denver, New Orleans, Tacoma, Sacramento and Los Angeles among others. There were occasional moments of hope as in San Francisco when the old title of 'Ireland's Joan of Arc' was re-adopted by the press and she was again labelled 'a valiant and uncompromising champion of justice'.[39]

These occasional spurts of enthusiam were rare as the main thrust of the tour was generally dull and disappointing. Mary wrote frank, forthright letters to De Valera, wanting to keep him realistically appraised of the situation. After two months, she wrote that the 'broader-minded and better-educated people have mostly dropped out (of the AARIR)'.[40] Apparently she did not see this as a repudiation of Republicanism. Later, perhaps in an effort to understand her rejection she wrote: 'Many in America are sore, both for what they consider personal slights and because America was left so entirely without information and guidance after the signing of the Treaty.'[41] In June, after five months of the tour, when the summer heat was again proving bothersome, a most discouraging note was sent: 'Making all allowances for changed conditions and for the readiness with which Americans tire of things, I did not expect to find the apathy quite so bad.'[42]

Combined with the difficulty in attracting supportive crowds, other efforts on behalf of Ireland were also thwarted. Mary applied to attend the 23rd Conference of the Interparliamentary Union in Washington, stating that as a member of Ireland's Second Dáil she was eligible. Her claim was rejected immediately in committee and never put before the whole conference. The concept of the Republic of Ireland was thus refuted at an international level, something not surprising but frustrating to Mary.[43]

The news from home was equally troublesome. In by-elections in which nine seats were at stake, Sinn Féin won only two prompting Mary to write in a letter that she was 'greatly disappointed' and the results had done 'much harm' in the United States where they had 'disheartened the people'. This last remark was qualified with 'not our genuine out and out supporters but the hedgers and doubters with whom nothing succeeds like success'.[44] To her friend, Seán T. O'Kelly, she wrote that the elections, in Mayo in particular, must have been a 'cheat', with some trickery involved as Republicans 'could not have lost Mayo fairly'.[45] Her resilience in refusing to accept Republican rejection remained remarkable.

In the United States, she sought to explain away the defeat by saying that votes were cast under 'clerical and economic duress', adding for emphasis: 'I realise better than you can do what it meant to uneducated country people to be told by a priest that "to vote for the Republican candidate was to vote for the devil".'[46]

More demoralising news came in a letter from Seán T. O'Kelly, this time concerning the annual Republican pilgrimage to Bodenstown where Mary had enjoyed considerable oratorical success in the past. The letter read: 'The crowd was big but there was a marked absence of enthusiasm at any time – even for Dev when he spoke.'[47]

American newspapers, the overwhelming majority of which had been supportive in the past, were now harassing the visitor from Ireland. By papers such as the *New York Times* and *The Beacon Journal* of Akron, Mary was called upon to answer charges of Republican war-mongering. *The Irish Statesman* said Mary was one of a group 'who refused to abide by elections and did their utmost by war to force the majority to submit to them'.[48]

Surrounded by all of these dispiriting events, Republicans became quarrelsome with one another. Mary's offer to remain in the United States and 'take charge' in De Valera's absence had been viewed by him as an effort to usurp his authority which he was guarding more and more jealously. Mary wrote testily in response: 'I should resent very much (this) supposition.'[49]

To accompany this bleak political news, Mary's school, St Ita's, had fallen on financial hard times. As the school was an extension of Mary and her Republicanism, this was not too surprising. The Board of Trustees of St Ita's, under the direction of Professor Stockley, issued a pamphlet stating that if St Ita's was to be secure for all times £25,000 was needed.[50] Fortunately for all concerned 'some friends in the US' made a private collection and raised a substantial amount, enough to ward off closure, for a time at least.[51]

Though throughout the tour Mary said little that was new from statements she had been making since the Civil War, she did make observations concerning American and Irish women. In 1921, she had been most impressed with the vigour of American women but in 1925 she declared quite bluntly, 'They don't seem to be doing much.' She went on to articulate her own view of the role of women saying that 'the women of Ireland... would soon emerge as world leaders in women's rights'. She continued that this did not mean ruling men but rather 'comradeship', adding 'that is the ideal relationship. Women in either the home or politics should not wheedle or coax their way. We Irish women go straight to the point.'[52]

Mary was speaking on behalf of herself and a few female associates who were willing to let their voices be heard in public. The majority of Irish women, however, were not actively involved in either politics or women's rights. The census of 1926 revealed, moreover, that women were almost totally excluded from the professions except for teaching and nursing. There were five female barristers of a total of three hundred and twenty in the Free State; one female architect from one hundred and ninety-nine; and three women solicitors from 1,036. Of the total number of women employed (343,894) over 60% worked in domestic service or agriculture. The only areas where the employment of women was favoured was textile manufacturing, a traditionally low paying occupation. There were also almost 10,000 nuns in Ireland.[53] In the civil service, a woman was forced to resign her position when she married. The legal restrictions on women were severe as they had few property rights, essentially remaining a possession of their husbands; divorce was unavailable for all and in the case of separations, any children were considered as belonging to the father.

The Church, too, gave no encouragement for women to seek reform. The 1920s saw the hierarchy consumed by attempts to eliminate what they perceived as immorality, railing against 'the spirit of worldliness' that had 'crept into the lives of Catholics' creating 'the overmastering desire for amusement and pleasure'. This led to denunciation of 'the grave scandals of modern dances and fashions' as well as 'evil literature and objectionable cinema films'.[54] The Church continued to urge Irish women to emulate the Virgin Mary, particularly with regard to purity and modesty.

When Mary MacSwiney spoke in San Francisco, she spoke of a situation, that, for the most part, did not exist outside of her imagination. There was no organised feminist movement in Ireland addressing women's issues and no overt evidence of female resistance to prevailing conditions.

As Mary prepared to leave the United States, she was realistic about her accomplishments. The money raised was not substantial and the organisational infrastructure remained weak. Many Irish-Americans had decided in favour of accepting the Treaty as 'the Free State propaganda had considerable effect. . . in the US'.[55] Mary's ardent appeals on behalf of a Republic had left them unmoved and she concluded that 'the general apathy in Ireland' was reflected in America. There remained in America, as in Ireland, a number still committed to the principles and promises of 1916 with Mary continuing to give a voice to their position which called for an independent Republic providing national freedom and sovereignty with 'guarantees of religious and civil liberty, equal rights and equal opportunities to all its citizens'.[56] If they began to waver in their conviction they had only to be reminded of her resounding denunciations of all the things tainted by the hand of the British in Ireland, including the Free State government.

Despite the lacklustre quality of the tour which lasted almost a full year, Mary refused to be discouraged. There was no question of her changing her mind about co-operating with the Free State government or of taking her duly elected seat in what she considered the king's parliament. To do so would be a compromise of principle and a rejection of the martyred dead. She was able, nonetheless, to assess the situation of Republicans astutely:

At present the business men have no faith in the ability of our party; Labour is afraid we are too reactionary; Capital fears we are Bolshevist. The young men

– and women – who are Republican, but who are unable to see the vital importance of preserving the continuity of the government established in 1919, are more than half inclined to look upon the elected TDs pretty much as we looked on the Irish Party in 1912-13. They are impatient because they say, 'they are being led nowhere' and 'nothing is being done.'[57]

Mary offered some suggestions to alter this gloomy situation. First, as always, was the necessity of emphasising that the government of the Republic was going to continue its opposition to the Free State until the Republic can 'function again'. She believed that this would allow 'the man with a stake in the country (to) realise that stability without freedom is impossible'.[58] Second, it was imperative that a Republican budget be presented to the Irish people, 'a plan for saving the country financially'. This plan was intended to appeal to both sides of the citizenry.

Upon returning to Ireland, Mary found her proposed plans overshadowed by other serious events that were occupying Republican energy. The first concerned the Free State government which was concluding an amendment to the Articles of Agreement of 1922, the first clause of which revoked the authority of the floundering Boundary Commission and the six counties were signed over to the northern government. The second clause released the Free State from any liability claims arising from the Anglo-Irish War but no mention was made of Ireland's counter-claim, assuming Ireland's liability would exceed any claim. The third clause provided for Irish payment of annual annuities to Britain 'in respect of malicious damage done since the 21st day of January 1919 to property in the area now under the jurisdiction of the parliament and government of the Irish Free State'.[59] This debt was estimated at between £4 and £5 million, to be repaid in a single payment of £150,000 followed by £250,000 for sixty years.[60] The Republicans viewed this as a dismemberment of Ireland coupled with an outrageous payment for the insult.

The second cause for controversy among Republicans was Eamon de Valera who was making noises about the possibility of entering the Free State parliament upon removal of the oath of allegiance. Perhaps for him the reality of the new boundary had been the jolt necessary for realising that Sinn Féin abstentionist policy had become anachronistic. He was anxious to dislodge himself from the mire in which, to his mind, the doctrinaires had trapped themselves seeing no political future in a continuing boycott of the Free State parliament.

The Republican Army caused the third controversy when, in

November 1925, they withdrew their allegiance to the Second Dáil, adding they would be ruled by their own council. The Army leaders may have envisioned the split coming in the political ranks and hence wished to remain un-aligned until the Republican leadership struggle had been resolved. Perhaps, too, the Army leaders believed the De Valera position would prevail, diluting the Republican model to such an extent that it would be unacceptable to them. Lastly, they viewed themselves as a revolutionary, rather than political body.

Mary MacSwiney had gone abroad with the hope of shoring up American support only to return home to find the parent organisation in a state of distrust, confusion and divided loyalties. The movement seemed to be having pieces continually chipped away from its once strong and proud foundation.

Mary and De Valera joined in undeclared battle over a by-election in Laois-Offaly. De Valera 'wanted the election badly' and was in the constituency working from morning until late in the evening.[61] To win under these circumstances would be an illustration of voter-acceptance of his new approach as well as a victory for Republicanism. With an air of innocence, he approached Mary MacSwiney about offering her assistance, saying: 'You know how much I would value your presence in this constituency at the moment' adding that a Republican victory 'would have far-reaching consequences' intimating that this rather indefinite goal was his sole objective.[62]

Mary was not convinced of his sincerity, particularly as she was hearing more and more rumours about De Valera's possible compromise, thus refusing to lend her help in the by-election. Instead, she continued to make speeches denouncing the Free State parliament and those who had entered or sought to do so. Again, De Valera wrote: 'I certainly do not understand about your speeches being "no compromise".'[63] This came just a few short weeks after 'he announced publicly that he would personally be prepared to enter the Dáil, if he could do so without having to take the oath'.[64]

When the election took place, De Valera's candidate was defeated by the candidate for Cumann na nGaedheal, the party of the Free State government. Mary MacSwiney could feel that this was in effect a moral victory for Republicans of her persuasion as De Valera had failed to be convincing despite his new approach. What may have happened was confusion and resultant abstention among Republican voters.

De Valera was now convinced that Republicans had to choose between his more moderate approach and the abstentionist politics of Mary

MacSwiney. In a statement to his colleagues, he wrote that he wanted 'to be let free' to try his new approach as it was 'the best way to kill apathy'.[65] For this purpose a special Sinn Féin Ard-Fheis was called and convened in Dublin during March 1926.

When the convention was convened, De Valera presented a resolution that if the oath were removed, elected members should take their seats in the Free State parliament. Before a vote could be taken, Father O'Flanagan, Vice-President of Sinn Féin, 'introduced an amendment to prohibit representatives of the party from entering "into any usurping legislature set up by English law in Ireland"'.[66] This amendment was passed by 223 votes to 218. Later, De Valera's amended resolution was defeated 179 to 177 with 85 abstentions.[67] The effort by De Valera to enter into a form of parliamentary dialogue with the government had been rejected and so, to his surprise, had De Valera himself.

Once again Mary MacSwiney had a victory, but it was joyless. Because the vote was so close, it could only mean future dissent and possible splits within the Republican movement. This moral victory for principle would perhaps cost the doctrinaire Republicans their political lives. In an effort to avoid this, and to provide onlookers with some sense of cohesion, Eamon de Valera and Mary MacSwiney stood together on the podium vowing to continue their fight for Ireland. The two also issued 'a joint message to "Ireland's friends abroad" that 'whilst differing in policy we are united in our determination to break the alien power'.[68] This must have been an act of will for both, as De Valera and Mary harboured mutual distrust and suspicion. Neither, however, was yet willing to cast aside the other's support completely.

This semblance of unity was short lived as by the end of the month De Valera resigned from Sinn Féin and was going forward with plans for his new party, Fianna Fáil, as a vehicle for his 'new departure'. In a final effort at reconciliation, the Republican factions met together once more. De Valera now took an antagonistic stand, stating, to Mary's chagrin, that the Second Dáil should be delegated to some 'mythical region' where it would 'claim no right, nor try to exercise any'.[69]

Mary and her ideological colleagues were dismayed by this attitude but still wished to consider the possibility of some form of unity although one friend, Brian O'Higgins, dissented calling it 'mock unity'.[70] The MacSwiney faction would agree to a coalition Executive Cabinet if De Valera would agree that if his party won a majority in the general election an All-Ireland parliament would be summoned admitting 'immediately all those from the north who would attend' and to 'ignore the Free State constitution and frame an Irish one.' Added to this, they must not enter 'the Free State parliament under an oath-bound Ministry', and recognise the assembly of Dáil Éireann.[71]

Mary was asking De Valera to wage an election and if victorious revert to the Republic, something Sinn Féin had been trying to accomplish since the signing of the Treaty. The only compromise offered was an unspoken one: if De Valera agreed to this consideration, Mary would refrain from denouncing him as a collaborator during the election campaign. This time it was her turn at innocence as she wrote, 'Honestly, I cannot see why that should have annoyed them' adding 'Dev was as nasty as he could be'. She admitted a small amount of culpability: 'I suppose I fight harder for what I believe in than others do and perhaps less tactfully.'[72] What she would not admit was that efforts toward reconciliation were totally one-sided; De Valera would do the electoral work, Mary and her followers would reap the rewards in victory, hardly a situation De Valera could accept. Mary emerged with her principles intact but Sinn Féin shattered.

Mary feared that with this 'new departure' they would 'have the Treaty debate all over again'. Furthermore, she believed that 'the policy now adopted by Fianna Fáil seem(ed) to be that which we refused four years ago. . . If that was not proper policy for Republicans in 1922, how can it be right in 1926?'[73] The final outcome, she predicted, would be most disastrous as 'Dev will be left high and dry and a few faithful and honourable souls left high and dry with him, while the Free State will be stabilised by a large accession of oath bound deputies.' All this would result from a position by De Valera that was 'wrong in principle'.[74]

De Valera and his supporters left Sinn Féin completely after no suitable agreement could be reached. In the course of six months, the doctrinaires had their ranks greatly depleted, first by the withdrawal of the IRA and now by Fianna Fáil. The policy of 'no compromise' was being held together but by fewer and fewer reflecting their overall divergence from the politics of the mainstream.

As the split became wider, Mary began to speak publicly about De Valera and his policy. To the *Irish World* she wrote: 'I have no doubt he means well, but then so did 90% of those who passed the Treaty.'[75] She began lumping De Valera with those who were unfaithful to the men and women of 1916, making him an unworthy leader for the Irish. Her disappointment and annoyance were real and heartfelt as she believed 'he behaved rottenly'.[76] Nonetheless, she had known him for many years and now worried privately about his financial condition. He had been paid a small salary as president of Sinn Féin, enough to provide modestly for his growing family but now, his income gone, Mary was concerned for his material well-being.[77] This concern was not revealed publicly, however, and onlookers saw only a hardliner whose only emotions seemed spent on behalf of the Republic and not in worry over personal matters. Perhaps if Mary had let some of her worries and concerns be seen more openly, she would have been viewed more sympathetically rather than as one given to harsh moral judgments and condemnations. She seemed to have felt that such expressions would have been interpreted as weakness, a perception, however inaccurate, enhanced because she was a woman not wanting to give male critics any opportunity to seize upon what may have been considered a female vulnerability. No doubt she was continually mindful of Ireland's past when the British seized upon Irish indecision and weakness. Similarly, Irish efforts at compromise had repeatedly come to naught, breeding Irish frustration and humiliation. Mary could avoid all these pitfalls by remaining firm, strong and most importantly, non-compromising.

The Republicans were badly shaken when Sinn Féin met again in the autumn for the annual Ard-Fheis. J. J. O'Kelly had complained in a letter to Mary that De Valera had left the organisation 'demoralised and penniless' with little hope for making 'much headway under such circumstances'.[78] Seán Buckley added to this note of pessimism writing that 'the ordinary Republicans were practically unanimous. . . in favour of the President (De Valera)', going on to show the self-doubt that continued to plague the movement: 'Why should we constitute ourselves into a sort of ecclesiastical council to pronounce ex cathedra a dogma which we know perfectly well a lot of our own people will not agree to.'[79] He reflected the growing mood to discard the non-compromise policies of the past and move towards conciliation. Frank Gallagher wrote to Mary as one who had been on hunger-strike for the Republic in 1924 but now found De Valera's proposals acceptable. He believed that the 'rank and file of the Sinn Féin club members (were). . . profoundly dissatisfied with the old policy'. He reported: 'People are jumpy after their seven years of turmoil, terror and death. (They) will oppose a war policy.'[80]

Mary heard and understood what was being said but did not accept the real or implied recommendations. She continued to believe with the unwavering faith of past martyrs, that one had to continue to have loyalty in order to be saved. Her Republicanism was religious in tone and quality, believing that to deny one aspect was to deny all and thus condemn oneself to damnation. There were no half-truths or half-principles – to equivocate was to deny.

Her answer to critics came during the Ard-Fheis. While prominent members Austin Stack and Daithí Ó Donnchada were dispirited by the depletion of their ranks by the split and emigration,[81] Mary forced enthusiasm and decreed that the Sinn Féin position would not be compromised and would, in fact, become more steadfast. These actions were reminiscent of her return to Ireland after the death of her mother, at which time she took control of the family, buoyed their spirits and showed by word and example that the MacSwineys would not succumb. Under her guidance the future policy was set. Realising their present weakness, Sinn Féin would not contest the next election in the twenty-six counties; instead the cumann were to be 'thoroughly re-organised for an intensive scheme of educational work'. In the future 'attendance at classes and the study of Irish' would be compulsory; there would be 'obligatory support of Irish manufacture'. These were felt to be the conditions that would best safeguard 'the inalienable right of the nation to its sovereignty and integrity; the de jure position of the existing Republic' and 'the non-co-operation of the citizens of the Republic in the subordinate and humiliating position in which English law' had placed Ireland.[82] To assert herself and her beliefs in the face of mounting adversity, Mary offered one final resolution: 'No member of Sinn Féin may make use of the Free State or northern courts for civil actions until he or she has first tried to obtain a settlement by Republican arbitration.'[83] The motion was passed without opposition or amendment.

Mary's answer to De Valera was to move Sinn Féin into an even more intransigent political position and to demonstrate for all to see what a true Republican was. Her intention was to highlight differences, rather than to move towards reconciliation.

At this time, Mary and Sinn Féin, realising their poor bargaining position, were to act as the watch dogs of the Republic. They would remain ideologues in a world of pragmatists, continuing to lead by example, criticising and prodding but not participating and thus, through their self-imposed exclusion, remaining pure.

This left Mary open to charges that she was hindering the development of Ireland through her constant criticism and general negativism. Kevin O'Higgins asked: 'Does the unity of Ireland lie along the road of Anglophobia or doctrinaire Republicanism?' He concluded that those who would answer yes, passed a sentence on their country of 'endless strife and bitterness'. He added that they had in 'their public life today men and women, particularly women, whose driving force was hate.' It was a 'hatred to the idea of there being any prevailing co-operation between this state and the people and government of Great Britain'. He concluded: 'To talk about eternal hostility to Great Britain and accomplishing the unity of Ireland, was to talk of two conflicting ideals.'[84] The majority of the Irish people had now reluctantly accepted the truth of this remark. Mary MacSwiney, to whom the comments were aimed, did not.

Although this governmental attack may have been expected, from within the Republican movement feelings against Mary MacSwiney and her ideological brothers and sisters ran high. Countess Markievicz denounced the 'self-righteous fools' and 'unlogical persons' who said 'they stand for principle and for the honour of the Republic and prefer to do nothing but shout continually "the Republic lives"', adding 'I think the ordinary man and woman in the street will agree with us'.[85]

Dorothy Macardle, a De Valera supporter, addressed Mary directly in a personal letter in which she began by calling Mary 'a formidable champion' and one who would 'do a great deal to keep the controversy decent and fair'. Eventually the attack was made as the letter continued, 'I wish your sense of our moral inferiority did not come out so plainly in spite of yourself.'[86]

Mary was also criticised by Frank Aiken who was touring the United States. He wrote in friendship and as one who believed he understood her inflexibility:

You are a hard, proud woman. . . You love Ireland as few have ever loved her. In your heart you love the men and women who serve her and sympathise with them in all their trials. But you don't show it – few know it. Most of them think that you look upon them not as friends to be helped but as potential enemies to be distrusted. . . They think you look upon it as a crime to possess the weakness inherent in human nature.[87]

The letter was not received well, the recipient's first response being: 'Why can you people not let the government position alone.' Upon reflection, however, Mary became more philosophical: 'I suppose one's national faith must be something like one's religious faith – a gift.'[88] She saw herself, as her critic had reminded her, as being among the favoured few for having been chosen for this gift. Though she had once stated that God was not on the side of those most heavily manned and armed, her religious analogies suggest that she claimed to have Him on the side of radical Republicanism.

The Irish press in the United States, largely converted to De Valeraism, sniped at Mary as well. *The Irish World* immediately supported De Valera, the editor urging the Republicans to 'get together and fight as one'. He went on: 'Why should not Mary MacSwiney and her colleagues back the anti-oath movement to the limit and with a united front sweep this Free State abortion out of existence'.[89] An editorial in the *Irish Statesman* said that Mary made any 'paragraph in which her name is mentioned, a peg upon which to hang an exhaustive, if not convincing, exposition of the origin, development and future of anti-Treatyism'.[90] These criticisms from various sides indicate that many were growing weary of Mary and the seemingly unworkable alternatives she offered.

This attitude by the press was reflective of the mood in the United States. Already the Clan na Gael, the group Mary expected to be most responsive to her position, were 'unanimous in their support for the (Republican) Army'.[91] When the split with De Valera came, reactions among the Irish-American population were mixed, support existing for each side with others asking the two to reach a compromise agreement and unite against the Free State government.[92] As divisions widened in Ireland, American groups grew tired of the bickering, many unsure of the ideological issues involved. One association president wrote: 'The majority of our people here believe that you should not concentrate on technicalities'.[93] The movement in America had divided again as it had over the Treaty, but this time the American doctrinaire Republican militants had joined in spirit with the IRA rather than with what remained of Sinn Féin. Perhaps they saw the party singing its political swan song, as their promised revitalisation had never occurred. American groups which had reluctantly supported the Free State, now accepted De Valera's proposed alternative as a stepping stone to Irish independence.

Mary reflected on this political turmoil while continually troubled with family problems. Sister-in-law Muriel, never emotionally stable, had left Ireland in a fit of pique, vowing never to return – the memories too intense and the associated sorrow too great. In addition, she felt continual pressure to be brave and courageous as a constant tribute to the memory of her dead husband. Taking her young daughter with her, she had fled to the continent. Mary, as godmother and co-legal guardian of the child, worried continually and wrote a barrage of begging letters to Muriel in Germany urging them both to return at least for a visit. Muriel refused to correspond and the only communications were through friends and acquaintances abroad.[94] Brother Seán, drinking and jobless, was also a drain both emotionally and financially on his oldest sister who urged him to emigrate to Canada in an effort to pull his life together saying: 'We can have no more of the present regime.'[95] With her life in this generally unsettled state, the new year of 1927 was greeted with neither joy nor anticipation.

Elections were to be held in June, 1927 and Fianna Fáil was preparing to contest them as energetically as possible. Because the economic picture in the country continued on its unchanged, abysmal course, they believed the Free State government vulnerable in the light of its laissez-faire policies which seemed to offer little hope to the Irish poor.

Despite the decision from the previous autumn, Sinn Féin was uncertain of the best policy to pursue with regard to the elections. Mary MacSwiney, in a spirit of political depression, believed that Sinn Féin should husband its fast diminishing financial resources, not contest the election and spend the money on a broad programme of national education about the 'futility of compromise'.[96] Other members of the organisation were of a different mind. Count Plunkett, having known of Mary's position for some time, urged her to reconsider as he believed taking part in the electoral process was 'one of the few means' left to Republicans to show that their 'movement (was) alive and that (they were) fighting to secure Ireland's independence'.[97] Some believed that failure to contest would be misunderstood as a sign of defeat that might 'dishearten and discourage supporters'.[98] In a meeting of the Sinn Féin executive, this latter view prevailed; preparations were begun to select suitable candidates and Mary MacSwiney ran again in Cork.

During pre-election events, at the prompting of the Joint Conference of Sinn Féin and Fianna Fáil delegates, meetings were organised between the 'Chairman and Vice-Chairman of Sinn Féin, the Chairman and Vice-Chairman of Fianna Fáil (and) the Chairman and Vice-Chairman of the Army Council', the purpose being to adopt 'proposals for unity or co-operation in the coming election'. If this was impossible, a policy should be secured concerning the course to be followed should the combined Republicans win a majority in the elections.[99]

The news that this process was being attempted was met with enthusiasm by Republicans around the country. Father O'Reilly, representing those 'in remote parts of the country' wrote to Mary: 'Here we are – ready to work and able to get the people's votes to turn out the present crowd if only our leaders will allow.'[100] He continued: 'We want to see independence in our day and we see a good chance of it if we are not prevented by our leaders.'[101] Another letter came from Michael Domhnaill of Kerry who described the poverty and famine rampant in his county. Emotionally, he implored the leaders: 'Settle your differences (otherwise) – the Passing of the Gael will become an accomplished fact if the hirelings of His Majesty get another lease of office.'[102]

Mary received these letters with reservation, feeling they were accusatory in tone. She answered them in the press writing: 'While many appeals have been made to me personally to help bring about this unity, there seems to be a general belief that I am one of the chief obstacles in the path. Perhaps I am – to a false unity.'[103] She continued to lend only a deaf ear to any type of emotional appeal that would call for a compromise in principle. It mattered little that those in the economically depressed west of Ireland were asking for only a small shift in the Republican position in order that they might vote their conscience. Her attitude held little relevance for many ordinary Irish men and women, who continued to harbour the desire for a free country so typical in rural areas[104] but failed to understand the esoteric appeals of Mary MacSwiney. Her idealism was viewed as nit picking stubbornness which only served to isolate her cause.

In dealing with Fianna Fáil, Mary was unshakeable, stating firmly and clearly that the Republican position, as she defined it, had to be safeguarded. This would involve 'Fianna Fáil giving up the most dangerous part of their policy – that is, to go into the Free State parliament as a minority if they can do so without taking the oath'.[105] Understanding De Valera's popular appeal, she urged 'to bind all energies to remove the barrier which makes a reunion of Republican forces impossible'. If he would do so the majority position, her position, would be safeguarded, 'the people would respond and we should have a landslide as in 1918'. Realising this may have been overly optimistic, she concluded: 'It is worth a trial and it is the only way.'[106]

De Valera was being asked to throw over the party he had just created and return to the unsuccessful Republican politics of the past, hardly an appealing offer although as a politician, he coveted the votes, however humble the number, that Sinn Féin would draw. He answered Mary in the abrupt tone now familiar in their correspondence: 'What you call the "minority" position of Fianna Fáil is an essential part of the whole programme and to give it up would be to cripple the policy as a whole.' Looking realistically at their differences and by now realising Mary MacSwiney was immovable, he concluded: 'As convinced that I am right as you are that you are right, I feel that we can only agree to differ.'[107]

Despite all efforts at unity, the lines were too sharply drawn and the personalities too embedded in their positions for it to succeed. The *Irish*

Statesman, never a proponent of Mary MacSwiney's policies, recognised her influence in an editorial that ended rather prophetically: 'Miss MacSwiney will have a hard job to keep the courage of her faithful few screwed to the sticking point, but I imagine her influence, though less potent than it was, is still strong enough to veto a pact with Mr de Valera.'[108]

While the discussions over unity were in progress, Mary accepted an invitation to address a Republican group in Glasgow, the organisers having arranged a concert, the receipts from which would go to Sinn Féin. This proved a powerful drawing card to Mary who was reluctant to take time from the campaign but understood the need to replenish Republican revenues. The trip was not without incident. During the train ride to Larne, from where a ferry would be boarded for Scotland, as Mary sat reading, awaiting the train's departure from the Belfast station, she was served with an order forbidding her to be in Northern Ireland. She calmly took the offending order and dropped it out of an open window. Sergeant Kelly, not amused but reluctant to create a scene, retrieved it, put it beside her on the seat and left the train. On the return trip, she was again met at Belfast station by the sergeant who asked her if she were going directly to Dublin. When she refused to answer the queries of the 'enemy agent', he arrested her. The officer in charge, perhaps realising that this could prove a tactical error, rather than taking her to the police station, chose to escort her to the border in the company of several other police officers. Mary's reputation had served her well and the police, giving a rare display of discretion so often lacking in such encounters, chose not to pursue the matter that could well prove an embarrassment while elevating Mary's prestige in the eyes of her follow-ers. This was but a small triumph for her, however, considering the outlook for the coming elections.[109]

The election results gave Sinn Féin no cause for rejoicing. The Free State government obtained forty-six seats, Fianna Fáil forty-four, Labour twenty-two, Farmer's Party eleven, National League eight, Sinn Féin five, Independents fourteen, Independent Republicans two.[110] The Republicans had gained some supporters through Fianna Fáil as in 1923 Sinn Féin had forty-four seats, but the gains were not overwhelming. It was to the other parties of special interest, Labour and Farmers, that the voters had turned to seek a solution to their economic doldrums. The Republican voters had shown their disenchantment with past policies and swung to De Valera, hopeful that his new approach would be successful. In this surge away from extremism, Mary MacSwiney suffered her first electoral defeat.

Her sadness was not so much for herself as for the rejection of her ideals by the Irish people. She wrote bitterly to Hannah Sheehy-Skeffinton: 'What the Free Staters were not able to do in 1922 or 1923 and what they would not have been able to do in 1927 has been accomplished by Fianna Fáil in Cork city.'[111] To her supporters she explained the loss: 'It is clear that the minds of many of the people have been confused owing to the recent split in the Republican ranks and that the issues involved in the new policy have not been understood.' She offered as proof the observation that the 'seats lost by uncompromising Republicans have been taken by Fianna Fáil candidates.' It could not be admitted that perhaps the public had understood and decided to accept De Valera's plan.[112]

In the midst of all this disappointment, Maud Gonne MacBride sent words of encouragement: 'I am very disappointed that you were not elected. Your clear brain and unfailing courage are so necessary – elected or not you will always be one of the contributors of our nation.'[113] Mary accepted this assessment and would continue, despite the defeat, to consider herself a contributor when many others would see her as a detractor.

The election results were a torment but worse was to come when in August De Valera and his Fianna Fáil delegates entered the Free State parliament. After all efforts to enter without taking the oath had been refuted, they took the oath but declared it meant nothing. De Valera would never be forgiven by Mary MacSwiney for what she believed was his ultimate unprincipled act. He had joined the enemy and now must be regarded as one of them. She summed up her attitude succinctly: 'I have no use for Eamon de Valera or his compromise and I despise him for his conduct of recent years.'[114]

The ranks of Sinn Féin had slowly been whittled away since the signing of the Treaty in 1922. This movement to Fianna Fáil represented the largest block of support to be lost at one time. What remained of the doctrinaire Republicans? It was a small core group that was now, with all waverers gone, united in spirit and belief. In their political isolation, they believed that their numbers could diminish no further as anyone having stayed with them to this juncture was firmly committed and equally determined. It was perhaps the only ray of light in the cloud filled sky.

Mary reviewed the situation and wrote grimly: 'It is a tragedy that Irish people have been taught to look upon the natural demand for their country's freedom as abnormal and unattainable.' She concluded with words that a frustrated mother might use with her recalcitrant adolescent: 'This is but a temporary phase.'[115] She exhorted her followers in Cork to 'keep together' adding 'it is a great cause we are privileged to serve, too great to be easily won'.[116]

6. The Battle for Republicanism – Sinn Féin versus Fianna Fáil, 1927-1932

'Our biggest danger is our own discouragement and it is the hardest enemy to overcome.'[1] This was Mary's summary of the Irish situation in 1927, one that had been deteriorating gradually for the doctrinaire Republicans since 1923 and had become particularly dismal. Their support was diminishing at a great rate, as many realised the ineffectiveness of continued intransigence.

Mary MacSwiney would never accept this defeatist interpretation of her no compromise policy. The principles involved in maintaining the Republic had not changed for her nor would she attempt to adapt them to changing circumstances. In her mind, Irish conditions had remained constant: Ireland was still subjugated by an alien invader, though now it was couched in the guise of the Free State government.

Hope that the remaining members of Sinn Féin would form a cohesive unit went unrealised as those still committed to Mary's concept of Republicanism began a round of disputes and squabbling. Peader O'Donnell, the Marxist contributor to *An Phoblact* sought to demonstrate that the root of Ireland's problems lay in the class struggle. He began his offensive gradually, well aware of the air of cynicism that would greet such suggestions in Catholic Ireland, where the clergy continually harped on the evils of godless Communism, by questioning the viability of Sinn Féin: 'The inertia that kept Sinn Féin contesting elections as its only activity has sent the organisation staggering out into the wilderness.'[2] He went on to attack the Second Dáil: 'There is no feeling among Republicans that the surviving faithful members of the Second Dáil have any plan of campaign around which it has sought to collect representatives.'[3] Believing that ordinary citizens could not be blamed for disregarding this government as the people were 'not capable of clearing their minds of the de facto government and giving allegiance to the de jure',[4] he suggested a 'revolutionary effort' was necessary whereby the capitalist forces that hold the Irish 'in thrall' would be overthrown,[5] the land returned to its rightful owners and peace and equality reign in Ireland.

His solution to Ireland's problems was as narrowly focused as Mary's: O'Donnell believing economic re-organisation was the sole answer while Mary reiterated the all encompassing benefits of a Republic. Neither considered that Ireland had an integrated problem of religion, economics and unfulfilled Nationalistic longings.

Mary was quick to respond that Irish 'troubles (arose) not so much from private ownership of land as from foreign ownership',[6] ridiculing O'Donnell's organisational plans as 'even more nebulous than were those of the bluffers of 1921'.[7] Her belief was strong that a movement founded only on 'class consciousness' could 'never effect the removal of the foreigner' and would succeed only in 'forever betraying the national revolution which alone (could) secure for every citizen of Ireland what (was) rightly his due'.[8] There was a continual refusal to accept O'Donnell's assessment that Ireland's woes had an economic base as she was locked into her own view that the imperialistic British were the perpetrators of all evil:

In Ireland our national enemies and our economc enemies are one and the same class. If all the workers of Ireland were true to the nation, if they realised that they are the nation – for there are few, if any, of the real Irish among the idle rich – and that the economic freedom and social justice for which we long can only be attained in a free Ireland, then bending all their energies to wiping out the national enemy, they would find that Ireland was theirs to mould it in the spirit of justice – equal opportunities for all citizens, privileges for none.[9]

The ideals expressed were good ones and few could fault Mary for her hopes for Ireland. The practicalities of implementation remained serious, however, with those within the government believing that they were engaged in the most suitable plan for a solution. To them and to many other Nationalists, some action was better than continual musings about the magical powers of an Irish Republic that would wondrously turn all Irishmen and women into co-operative, just souls filled with selfless zeal in creating the utopian, Republican state of Ireland.

Mary had been struggling too long against the British and those West Briton Irish with 'slave minds' to accept a Marxist interpretation of Ireland's woes. She accepted the concept of social equality but rejected Marx' denial of the importance of national boundaries and 'national seclusion'. There was also an aura of godlessness about it that Mary accurately perceived as being unacceptable to the Irish people: rather, Ireland needed 'a true Christian democracy'[10] not compromised by English restraints or affiliations. Mary accurately assessed Ireland's long association with Nationalism, understanding that a union of Irish workers with those of Britain would ever be a strained one at best and most unlikely at any rate. Her failure came in not understanding that Nationalist aspirations among most of the Irish had been met, at least tentatively, by the terms of the Treaty. Dissatisfaction would occur if there was a failure to move towards more complete independence as Michael Collins had indicated with his 'stepping-stone' analogy.

Ideological wrangling carried on over a period of months between Mary and Peadar O'Donnell, receiving little attention either within Republican circles or without. To the majority of the Irish people, neither position seemed particularly relevant as perhaps the longevity of the discussion, particularly of the national question, had rendered the point almost moot.

Discussion among Republicans soon deteriorated from the reasonably lofty ideological plane to flinging mud at a personal level. It was suggested in a Sinn Féin meeting that perhaps work within the movement should be distributed according to gender; the men would be active in Sinn Féin while the women would be confined to Cumann na mBan. Just as the sexes were divided by the seating arrangements in some country churches, so too would the Republicans be separated. Unlike the churches, however, where despite segregated seating, all joined in the same worship service, women would be excluded from the decision-making process within the Republican movement. Mary saw the attack as directed at herself as she was by far the most visible female member of the Republican hierarchy. She wrote an angry letter to her old friend J. J. O'Kelly, denouncing him for his lack of loyalty and general short-sightedness. Unaccustomed to being the recipient of Mary's wrath, he sought to make light of the situation and to shift responsibility to unnamed others by writing: 'The idea (of separation) crossed my mind when writing you and was but the expression of views that have frequently dropped from well-meaning colleagues. I naturally foresaw that you would think it reactionary.'[11] He did not admit to finding the concept reactionary himself.

Mary suspected that the effort to exclude women from Sinn Féin may well have been an effort to remove her alone from a prominent position. The most likely candidate among the Sinn Féin leaders to have begun such a plan was Father O'Flanagan. Though he was as committed to the Republican concept as was Mary, the two had a long-standing mistrust of one another, perhaps each coveting the other's authority. This was the first time that a direct attempt had been made to exclude women from the movement. De Valera had shown some reluctance in dealing with women but had never dismissed them as unable to perform in the political arena. Astute politician that he was, he made use of them when it was advantageous, such as with Mary's first American tour.

Mary did not limit her ire to her colleagues in Sinn Féin but took her case to the people. At a rowdy, enthusiastic reception by 3,000 people at Belmullet she addressed the issue directly: 'Some people were alarmed nowadays to have women in the Irish movement, but wasn't the truth told by women just as good as the truth told by a man?' The cheering approval of the audience provided a positive response.[12] Judiciously, Mary did not refer to her previous contention, that, in an Irish Republic, women would be equal with men, this seeming less than likely when Sinn Féin was already trying to segregate the sexes. The proposed advantage to women of a Republic was already in danger of falling victim to sexism with perhaps an undercurrent of misogyny.

Although the issue was dropped, it had its desired effect for Mary MacSwiney withdrew her name from nomination for Vice-President of the Standing Committee of Sinn Féin, much to the delight of certain members. She had served for two years and in review felt that her presence had not been beneficial and 'a complete change' was necessary to infuse new life and diffuse old tensions. Mary could not refrain from teasing her detractors as she departed, observing that 'it was comic' to 'sense the fright that took possession of certain people. . . lest. . . I might be persuaded to withdraw my resignation'.[13] Although she would continue to work diligently for the cause she happily extracted herself from the bag of squabbling cats that the Standing Committee had become, believing the problems to be solved were too burdensome, the issues too big and the cause too great to allow oneself to become enmeshed in a battle of personalities.

Although it would never have been Mary MacSwiney's intention, by removing herself from the Standing Committee of Sinn Féin, she left this decision-making body in male hands, as some of its members had intended. She would continue her active role but without benefit of a title, thus reaffirming this role for women in the society generally.

Perhaps in a subconscious effort to prove the viability of the women's efforts, Mary initiated new direction for Cumann na mBan. She organised a protest march to Mountjoy Jail where five Republican women, led by Máire Comerford, were hunger-striking to obtain political prisoner status. The situation was resolved favourably for the involved women when their demands were met and they were permitted to receive 'letters, parcels and visits and have free association with each other all day'.[14] The government would not label the status of the women as that of political prisoners, but in fact, their treatment was what was expected by those in that category. Republican women still seemed adept at coercing the Free State government through hunger-strikes, a precedent established by Mary in 1922. This episode, combined with the recently exhibited Sinn Féin attitude towards women, illustrated the continual cleavage in equality of the sexes, with women being considered weaker beings needing special work and treatment.

Cumann na mBan was channelling much energy into the Prisoners' Defence League, for which Mary worked tirelessly. The women also began a more sinister operation with the publication of a broadsheet entitled *Ghosts*, its objective being to harass jurors involved in the trials of Republican prisoners, often listing their names and insinuating violence against them if the prisoners were found guilty.[15]

As the situation for Sinn Féin continued to disintegrate, Mary hastened the proceeding by rejecting potential supporters. Peadar O'Donnell's appeal for a broader based organisation was viewed as an unpatriotic effort to dilute the truth and thus unworthy of the cause. At the Ard-Fheis of 1928, Mary moved that the members of Sinn Féin, 'while in complete agreement with the ideals of the Gaelic League and Gaelic Athletic Association' could not attend or join in their functions because 'murderers of Republicans or their servants' were permitted to take part.[16] This type of rejection only served to alienate many who had a genuine love for Ireland or Irish culture on the basis that their political solution to Ireland's plight differed from that of Mary MacSwiney. Her denunciations were both elitist and offensive to those who had risked much during the Anglo-Irish war and believed that their present actions were in the best interests of Ireland. It also robbed Sinn Féin of any moderating influence, leaving it radical and extreme just as Mary intended.

There were also Republicans, in seemingly good standing, questioned concerning their bona fides. Art O'Connor, President of Dáil Éireann, was asked to resign because he had begun practicing law in Free State court rooms. He believed Mary had begun the move for his dismissal and hence forward he was unceasingly hostile to her. Mary's logic was simple and not surprising: it was not possible for a true Republican to practice law in the courts of the heathen, imperialist invaders.[17] This continual 'more Republican than thou' mentality served to foster her reputation for moral superiority, witch hunting for non-believers and set ideals that only the martyred dead had reached.

There was the continuing power struggle with the Republican Army to be attended as well. Mary chided Army leaders for demanding 'unquestioning obedience', assuring them that this was most certainly not forthcoming. To Sinn Féin headquarters she wrote: 'Surely it ought to be possible to find agreement and co-operation on the basis of co-equality and mutual help between the civil and military arms of the Republic.'[18] This plea for co-operation was ironic indeed, as Mary had shown repeatedly that the only co-operation she would countenance would be the effort of others to succumb to her doctrine of Republicanism. Rather than seeking co-operatiom from the Army, she sought their submission.

In November and December of 1928, another attempt was made to reconcile the disjointed Republican factions with the formation of 'Comhairle na Poblachta' an organisation intended to 'exercise a co-ordinating and directive influence in Republican efforts'.[19] Members of all shades of Republicanism, the Army, Sinn Féin, the Second Dáil, Cumann na mBan and the Republican left, met together. The Free State government noted the presence in Dublin of the delegates and described them as 'the extreme militant element', including Mary MacSwiney, Seán MacBride, Maud Gonne, Count Plunkett and Frank Ryan. A government report noted that 'the delegates, whilst in the city, were kept under observation'. These public officials seemed more concerned than necessary as those assembled, despite their title, remained unable to co-operate as each faction continued to believe that they should be in the ascendant position. Of course, Mary MacSwiney voiced her unchanged opinion that the Second Dáil remained the legitimate government of Ireland, hence it was in charge. J. Bowyer Bell labelled this new organisation 'a paper tiger, which after a promising start decayed leaving the individual organisations to go their appointed ways'.[20]

The one positive accomplishment to appear out of this period of dissention was the long awaited Constitution of the Irish Republic, unveiled in January 1929. Mary had been 'honoured with the task of framing the draft constitution' and had done so carefully and conscientiously to establish 'Liberty, Equality and Justice for all citizens of the Republic'. The document included provisions for 'free universities for the capable; pensions, health insurance, unemployment compensation, a national housing scheme, subdivision of big ranches, nationalisation of transport, shipping and banks'. Land would belong to the government but held in trust by the user who could also will it to an heir. No food was to be exported until the home population was provided for and a National Economic Council would be formed to act in an advisory capacity 'on all matters dealing with the individual interests and economic development of the country.' Basic freedoms were guaranteed such as freedom of conscience, free assembly, free expression and the inviolability of the home. Despite differences with the hierarchy, Mary, through the constitution, took 'cognisance of the fact that the population of Ireland (was) predominantly Catholic', hence 'no legislation which (was) definitely anti-Catholic (could) be provided for'. Equal facilities and endowments were to be provided for schools of all religious denominations 'but no child shall be obliged to attend religious instruction contrary to the wishes and beliefs of his or her parents'. This was the limit of toleration, however, as 'no provision (was) made for godless schools'. Mary's egalitarian ideals did not extend to atheists or those who might wish to limit religious instruction to the home.[21]

The remaining seventeen members of the Second Dáil met in the Rotunda in Dublin to review the draft constitution. In the evening, about 150 members of the public also assembled while Cumann na mBan Volunteers stood guard at the doors. Mary addressed the gathering, saying it was for them to find solutions to Ireland's problems, suggesting a new beginning could be made through this constitution. The audience was particularly receptive to the details of the defence forces intended to secure the island against hostile invasion by air or sea.

The *Irish Times*, Anglo-Irish in outlook, reported the meeting in a particularly patronising tone, beginning with the headline 'Miss MacSwiney's Dáil in Session' and referring to the deliberation body as the 'only Simon Pure Dáil Éireann'. The whole proceeding was reported with an air of the ridiculousness of this event particularly that the participants 'professed to regard the proceedings seriously' and proceeded with 'the utmost gravity'.[22]

This cynical, sometimes bemused, attitude towards the Second Dáil illustrated the prevailing air of superiority held by some government supporters. This, combined with Mary MacSwiney's belief in the moral transcendence of Republicans, aggravated hostile feelings and national tensions. Mary felt compelled to respond to what she termed these 'would-be insults' and wrote angrily to the editor of the *Irish Times*. She was particularly indignant over the appellation 'Miss MacSwiney's Dáil' and snapped: 'I wonder if there are people silly enough to imagine that they will weaken the allegiance of loyal citizens of the Republic by calling them "Miss MacSwiney's followers". It is too absurd.' She concluded: 'The caption is of a piece with the anti-Republican mentality which hopes to cast ridicule on the government of the Republic by the puerile practice of labelling it with the name of an individual.'[23]

Perhaps because of her problems with Sinn Féin, Mary was particularly defensive about the Second Dáil, seeing it as the last bastion of true Republicanism. Any effort to demean this institution was seen not only as a personal attack but as a tasteless, unforgivable stomping on the graves of Ireland's heroes.

J. Bowyer Bell, describing the Second Dáil, wrote that it 'still functioned but on such a high plane of moral righteousness that few could see the point. To the cynical it seemed only to provide a platform for the shrill lecturing of Mary MacSwiney and the disgruntled rumbling of J. J. O'Kelly'.[24]

Aside from the slight verbal skirmishing in the press, the consitutional convention, so long in the making, generally went unnoticied with crowds small and public attention scant throughout the proceedings.

Although efforts to keep the Republican movement afloat were continuous, these brought little reward. It was a time for 'quiet building, slow grouping, dreary plodding, looking inward for inspiration, not outward for loud cheers'.[25] But Republicans had been hearing these same instructions since 1924 and to no apparent avail as their cause continued to meet with persistent rejection. The belief by some that this apparently unsuccessful strategy should be changed to one of active militancy was beginning to penetrate Republican consciousness.

Movement in any direction was slow as Ireland continued to suffer extreme economic hardship. *An Phoblacht* described the situation of 'human misery of the native Irish starving on their own middens'. There were three cases reported to the Clare Board of Health of families starving in that county. Extra carriages had to be put on the trains leaving Clare for Cobh to accommodate the huge number of young people seeking to emigrate.[26]

For those remaining in Ireland, the devastating conditions were worsened for Republicans when the government instituted a new wave of repressive measures against them. Republicans, when harassed, were urged to sign an undertaking not to work against the government. Mary, 'fully conscious of the terrible economic pressure that help(ed) the Free Staters make so many do things that should not be done', was regretful because this made it easier 'for the enemy to segregate and concentrate on those who will not sign'. In an effort to do what she could for her faithful followers, a scolding letter was written to the head of the Ford factory in Cork urging him to cease passing over the names of known Republicans on the Labour Exchange lists.[27]

Mary's personal life was intruded upon as well by government agents of the CID. Six men came to her house, went through the books and papers in her desk and then methodically searched the house for arms. Mary, never wishing to give satisfaction by appearing anxious or alarmed, kept busy in the kitchen 'making cakes' for some expected guests, believing she had got the best of them, 'making them feel ashamed' by her silence.[28] It may have been even more disconcerting to the young men if she had set forth on them with one of her fierce harangues.

Meetings and gatherings at which she spoke were also under surveillance, as a meeting in Cooraclare 'was subjected to continuous interruption by a party of CID'. Intimidation of this sort only provoked Mary and at Kilkenny she stated again that there had been a ceasefire 'but there was no surrender'. To antagonise government observers she declared: 'The men that had been fighting were getting ready to fight again and would fight again if the Irish people attempted to turn down the Irish Republic.'[29] Republicans were responding to the government by turning to a renewed acceptance of violence.

While continuing this seemingly necessary public display of bravado, in private Mary was somewhat more realistic about the outcome of her political pursuits. To friends she wrote that 'people who have been working for many years have perhaps got tired and a bit hopeless'. She retained her faith in the people of Ireland, however, believing 'their hearts are with us, they believe that ours is the only right way but they are not yet ready to make any more sacrifices (or) to risk anything', concluding that 'poverty (was) largely the cause of the lethargy'.[30] Indeed, the economically deprived state of so many Irish people was burdensome enough without becoming politically active. Mary had to continue to believe this otherwise her work would be meaningless and purposeless.

She retained her belief that support would be regained through education but realised, regretfully, that there was now a whole generation of young people to whom the Second Dáil was unknown.[31] To remedy this untoward situation, a scheme for the education of the young in patriotic teaching was drafted, to be implemented through Sinn Féin. The programme would include weekly meetings of story telling, ballad singing, Irish conversation classes, games, dancing, plays, excursions and 'stories of great men'.[32] She was encouraged in these efforts by Brian O'Higgins of Sinn Féin who wrote encouragingly that such plans and Mary's continuing lecture series would 'stir hidden memories' and 'again awaken national consciousness in the young people'.[33]

This high value on education also necessitated that Scoil Ita and other schools of its type be fostered and supported as schools were 'becoming more and more shoneen'.[34] Mary's school, however, continued to face financial problems. The number of students had remained constant at about fifty over the past several years. The tuition was £8 per year per child with a teaching staff of one principal and three assistants with one more needed. Because the school directors did not recognise the Free State, no government endowment was available, making continual outside donations necessary. To this end, Mary was encouraged to write a letter to Archbishop Mannix of Australia, now a De Valera supporter, beseeching him to lay partisanship aside for a moment and ask members of his diocese, so many of whom had Irish roots, to support her school in the interest of maintaining Irish culture and language. A report of the condition of the school justified the need for its continuance as it provided the right atmosphere in which 'to kill that un-Irish mentality'. The great value of St Ita's, as described by its founder, was that 'it had succeeded in turning out pupils who (were) as naturally Irish as American children are American'.

Mary also proudly noted the scholastic successes of her former pupils: 'Some are Doctors, one is completing her studies in Law, several are successful teachers, some are developing into successful business women and some are married.'[35] Among these students, advanced education was being encouraged at a time when the presence of women in prestigious professions was rare. It is noteworthy, too, that women had a choice to make between a career or marriage. Without flouting all of society's norms regarding female education, Mary encouraged her female students to do all of which they were capable in the area of education, gender notwithstanding.

Although Mary believed that women were perfectly capable of operating in the political arena, as she had done for many years, she maintained traditional moral values for Irishwomen. This was perhaps an outgrowth of the Victorian concept of woman as the purveyor and upholder of morality within the home, values that had been internalised in her childhood home. Mary had become particularly disturbed with the portrayal of a morally lax young woman in Peadar O'Donnell's most recent novel, *The Knife*. As an illustration of his respect for Mary's insights and opinions, despite their differing ideological orientation, he had sought her comments on the draft of the book. Mary, as always, was fascinated by his use of language and facility with words. She was not as fascinated by the character of Nora, the antithesis of all Mary hoped to find in Irish womanhood. She urged her friend to change the book, writing, 'An Irish girl would not, I think, speak so.'[36] Mary was illustrating her naïvety regarding human relationships in Ireland. Though her political experiences were many, her personal experiences had been few as everyone Irish was thought to be as morally sound as she herself. In her moral shortsightedness, she would not have questioned the feasibility of Nora if the character were English and Protestant. Mary was concerned that the characterisation would project a poor image to the outside world and giving bad example was a sin against which Catholics had long been warned. Mary cherished the ideal of the hardworking, virtuous Irishwoman devoted to God and family and willing to sacrifice all for Ireland.

Her own experience, or lack thereof, had brought about her view of morality and purity. From before the time of her birth, the Irish clergy had looked suspiciously upon marriage, seeing it as a lesser calling than celibacy, a concept reinforced by Mary's education with the nuns. Throughout her years at school young girls were continually urged to emulate the Virgin Mary particularly with regard to sexual purity, ideas reiterated in the MacSwiney home. Later, the saints whom she admired both with regard to their teaching and their daily lives, tended towards asceticism, a practice she thought worthy of adopting. For Mary, sexual expression was sublimated into religious practices and later politics. It remained, as well, that she was given charge of the family, necessitating pursuance of a career. As she pointed out to her own students many years later, a woman could have marriage or a career, the two not being compatible. Finally, to please her bother Terence, for whose approval she continually strove long after his death, she tried to fulfil his expectations for Irish womanhood.

She continued to ignore feminist issues that were being raised. Helen Moloney, a socialist activist and voice for working women's rights, urged support for the plight of women in the work force contending that they were 'unorganised and exploited', used by unconscionable men to replace working men at cheaper rate. She believed that all women workers were held suspect as possible rivals by men but domestic servants in particular were given 'a most degraded social position'. It would not be until 'men revise their ideas towards women workers' that women could be organised into unions.[37]

Mary did not take up the fight in this struggle for equality but chose to once again hide behind the banner of the Republic, which, when implemented, would somehow magically cure these problems, by the resultant social co-operation. This position was particularly suspect after the movement in Sinn Féin to organise work activities according to sex.

The paper, *An Phoblacht*, that carried the appeals of Helen Moloney illustrated the general insensitivity to the plight of women. While Helen urged equality of opportunity, the paper carried a column entitled 'For the Woman of the House' which encouraged women to work for the Republic not on an equal basis with men but rather in the traditional role of a co-operative, supportive assistant. The column concluded with recipes for producing better oatcakes and baked herring as well as other household hints. As a sop to women who may have sought more, Brian O'Higgins, in an appeal to sentimentality, wrote in a poem that 'the only school in Éireann is an Irish mother's knee'.[38] Home, hearth and motherhood were the concepts deemed most fitting for Irish women.

At Scoil Ita, Mary's pace was unrelenting as she taught six hours a day with one break of half an hour, leaving her, by day's end, 'naturally fagged'.[39] This effort was happily made to preserve, what Mary believed her school to be, 'a national asset'. There was no motive for personal gain, as she concerned herself little with material accumulation, desiring only enough money to have the school continue and she and Annie to survive. For her part, Mary made do with two dresses, one for everyday and one for Sunday, not from any belief in self-deprivation but because that was all that was necessary.[40]

The continuing downward spiral of Republican political fortunes was beginning to take its toll on Mary. There were fewer and fewer even within the movement who were capable of meeting her criteria for Republican purity. After her falling out with the Sinn Féin Standing Committee, she complained of becoming 'more and more appalled at the want of moral courage and the personal bias so evident in our own ranks' and wondered if it would end 'by rejoicing the hearts of our enemies by bringing us really to sixes and sevens'.[41] This caused her to view the Second Dáil as the 'symbol of great truth'[42] and seemingly the only group left that contained her ideological equals as their ranks became more and more elitist.

There was also a growing realisation by Mary that only by taking up the gun could Republican objectives be met, putting aside for the time that this would demand co-operation with the Army with whom relations over authority had been strained for some time. Her writing illustrated this: 'We must all see the importance of strengthening the Army so that it may be fit to undertake the task that will assuredly be placed on it'.[43] The leadership conflict was not addressed but she assumed that those in charge of the Army would heed 'the lawful government of Ireland'.[44] It is questionable whether this was said out of naivety or hopefulness, but, realising Mary was never dull in such matters and was well aware of Republican inner working, the latter is most likely.

Mary had never shied from accepting violence as the only alternative in some instances. To a group of fishermen in Cork and Kerry, who were being continually hampered by foreign poachers in steam trawlers, she said the answer was 'patrol boats, properly armed and the guns would soon be talking to the poachers'.[45] Perhaps this was an effort to gain support as well as foreshadowing future events, while keeping the Free State government aware that Republicanism was still a threat.

This mood was demonstrated further in a half-joking note to a friend in America concerned with the propaganda effect of President Cosgrave's tour. Mary's letter read: 'I am very disappointed that with all the young men in America at present, that a tarring and feathering operation or something equivalent could not be carried.'[46]

Pent-up frustration was beginning to make her temper shorter and her tongue sharper. When questioned about the Ultimate Financial Settlement arranged by the Free State government, she labelled it the work of 'Blythe and his co-worms'.[47] The acceptance of Fianna Fáil in the United States was explained away as 'De Valera worship, pure and simple' and American 'muddled thinking'.[48] The one occasion on which this rhetoric was stifled was in a lengthy letter to the Pope, written in objection to the Free State government's appointment of a Vatican representative in which Mary made 'formal protest. . . on the grounds that Mr Bewley, the representative of the King of England on behalf of the Irish Free State does not represent Ireland or the people of Ireland'.[49]

As the decades changed, Mary's political isolation continued to grow. The people of Ireland looked for a solution to their continuing economic slide, now made worse by a growing world recession. Emigration seemed to be the only solution that many could devise particularly among those from eighteen to thirty of whom over 450,000 had left from Ireland since 1922. Frank Gallagher estimated that about 70% of the 'old IRA had emigrated'. This depletion in the work force still left '100,000 unemployed. . . involving at least 400,000 people in dire distress'.[50] Though some may have admired Mary's fixation with the principles of Republicanism, it provided no relief from their immediate problems.

It had been hoped that the new constitution would provide incentive for renewed support of the Second Dáil. Even this met with problems, however, as both the money necessary for publication and a printer to undertake the task were difficult to secure. Because the government had been stepping up its harassment of Republicans, there was no printing firm in Ireland who would publish the document, printing finally being done in the United States.[51] Mary had submitted the document to *An Phoblacht* believing that at least the salient features of the constitution would be printed in this Republican paper. The editors were of another mind, however, as Frank Ryan and Peadar O'Donnell, the two most responsible for the paper's content, were committed to Marxism. The MacSwiney constitution was not far reaching enough in its national-isation schemes for their taste, hence unacceptable for publication. The editors responded to Mary's queries concerning the absence of discussion of the draft constitution with a second point of rejection: 'We do not admit the claims of surviving members of the Second Dáil Éireann that they constitute the government of the Irish Republic.'[52] This direct rejec-tion, though it had been hinted at in the paper for some months, was another in a series of blows to Mary that was compounded when the Army council agreed with the position of the paper.[53]

During this time an attempt was made by some to press forward with Marxist ideology within the Republican camp and then for Ireland, partly through the formation of Saor Éire. It developed as a response to the economic crisis, the government's inability to deal with it despite efforts such as the Shannon Scheme and the Electricity Supply Board, as well as the Free State government's over-reaction to dissenting groups. The hierarchy of the Catholic Church, always suspicious of Socialism in any form lest it reduce the authority of the Church in the area of education and lessen its influence over government policy, also became entwined in what became Ireland's 'Red Scare'.[54]

Mary MacSwiney, no stranger to clerical criticism and after eight years still pursuing a court case against Bishop Cohalan, found herself in a rather tenuous position during this controversy over Communism. As a Catholic, she sought a religious Ireland in which the Church was recognised as having a special place; as a Republican, she objected to the continual negative response given to the intentions of herself and her colleagues by the hierarchy.

First, she came to what she believed to be the aid of Saor Éire: 'I am no protagonist of Saor Éire, because I believe it is a bad national policy to divide the people of Ireland on a class basis, but I know these men, most of them are excellent practising Catholics and not one single one of my acquaintance would stand for an anti-Christian state or for a materialistic regime with its fanatical hatred of God.' Concluding that they did 'stand against the present iniquitous social system', she reminded the Irish hierarchy that it was long past time that they insist that the 'principles of social justice laid down in the encyclical of Pope Leo XIII. . . would help to end for all time. . . the twin evils of Capitalism and Communism.'[55]

Mary had unwittingly illustrated the difficulty inherent in attempting to bring Marxism to Ireland. Despite the realisation by many, particularly Republicans that the hierarchy was an unmitigated nuisance, most remained 'excellent practising Catholics' and could not reject what had become an intrinsic aspect of their lives. For centuries in Ireland, the maintenance of the Catholic religion had been a means of tantalising the British overlords; it was the one political statement that the Irish had never ceased to make despite the Penal Laws and all other forms of personal oppression instituted by the British. It kept them Irish when all British energy was being exerted to make them English. The Catholic religion was too firmly entrenched in the Irish psyche to fall victim to economic arguments. The people of Ireland had survived through centuries of poverty, many believing that religion had given them the moral and physical strength to carry on and continue to tweak the nose of British authority. What Marx saw as an opiate, the Irish saw as a spiritual bond of unity that remained an important part of the struggle. Although the hierarchy had continually let their people down by currying favour with British authority, often in order to secure some small concession for maintenance of their own place, enough of the clergy remained allied to the population that generalised anti-clericalism was avoided. The people also found in themselves enough belief in and reverence for Catholic doctrine to look beyond the perceived errors of those in positions of Church authority. The actions of the hierarchy were ignored or overlooked when they fell too far from personal convictions.

Mary MacSwiney exemplified this model except she did not let what she considered unacceptable behaviour by the hierarchy go unchallenged, defying them continually with her participation in Republican affairs. When in prison she had made an issue of reception of the sacraments in defiance of hierarchical orders, attempting to make a mockery of their position by flouting both her Republicanism and her Catholicism. Now, she was coming to what she believe to be the aid of her friends in Saor Éire by proclaiming for them their steadfastness with Catholicism.

Lest she appear to be fraternising with her long time opponents in the hierarchy, she again began to question Church decisions. She was particularly disturbed by the Eucharistic Congress planned for Ireland in 1932, addressing a letter to the Pope, which began with a long diatribe against British injustice in Ireland and continued by urging the Pope to postpone plans until 'a united Ireland could fittingly join in that great celebration'. It was her considered opinion that, to avoid Republican demonstrations during the Congress, the government of the Free State would perpetrate further outrages 'against those who had courage and patriotism enough to refuse to sell their national birthright under a threat of immediate and terrible war'.[56]

When these words fell on deaf ears, Mary, understanding the Congress would go on as scheduled, tried for a lesser victory. This time her letter went to the Papal Nuncio in which the proposed presence at the Congress of Cardinal Bourne, Archbishop of Westminster, as the papal representative was objected to. Mary wrote that his presence 'would give great pain to many' as he was 'well known to be unfriendly to the national ideals' for which Republicans stood.[57]

These requests were both rejected, probably not to anyone's surprise. It was the gesture that was important, however, and the message was once again delivered that one could question Church decisions. Mary questioned and challenged for the sake of the Republic but just as her concept of Republicanism went largely unheeded the authority of the Catholic Church went largely unchallenged. It remained then and now the most powerful influence in Ireland.

Criticism of Mary's supposed anti-clericalism was readily available. The *Cork Examiner* printed a letter to the editor from a 'Catholic Irishman' that accused her of being so obsessed with 'her mythical Republic' that she viewed all her political opponents as 'so many recruits to the legion of Lucifer'. The writer concluded that she was 'doing one woman's part to discredit, in the eyes of the populace, the teaching authority' of the Irish bishops.[58] Such anonymously written items only served to annoy Mary who believed if one had any courage or honesty these written offerings would be signed. The editors of the *Catholic Mind*, easily identifiable, added chauvinistically that 'the lack of Catholic spirit and due reverence for our pastors will eventually bring us to the level of Spain and Mexico'.[59]

While openly critical of the Church's political policy, Mary was a ready adherent of its moral position. Throughout the 1920s the Church had been at war with immorality albeit in the form of Saturday night dances or seemingly sensuous movies arriving from abroad. The government of the Free State accepted and reflected this supposedly high moral sense in part to maintain a more compliant population as well as to placate Church leaders who would return the favour when called upon, as so recently exemplified with the Joint Pastoral.

An illustration of the government's concern with moral values came with the issuance of letters patent for both the Abbey and Peacock Theatres in Dublin. These theatres were directed to be 'instrumental in the promotion of virtue and instruction of human life' and were ordered to omit 'any expression or passage or gesture offensive to decency, piety or good manners'. Further, there would be 'no profanity or impropriety of language. . . permitted on the stage' as well as no 'indecency of dress, dance or gesture'.[60]

Mary found no problem in accepting this sort of regulation and even joined in the spirit with an attack on the 'floods of immorality poured into this country from England' to the 'detriment of the religion and morals of the rising generation'. She added that the government of the Republic would not tolerate this 'new invasion of Ireland' because 'being free as well as Catholic, they would scorn the cant that pretends it is broad-minded to admit every unclean thing'. To withhold 'pagan poison' was not to restrict 'intellectual freedom'. She was particularly incensed by the birth control teachings of Dr Marie Stopes whose words were 'not suitable mental food for Irish Catholic and Christian girls'.[61]

Mary willingly accepted Church teaching about faith and morals, but not about political issues in which she believed the Church had no place; the irony being that she long had urged Churchmen to proclaim from the pulpit against the British occupation of Ireland and now against those she considered their agents, the Free State government. Her own personal piety is not in question but Mary reacted to the Church in the same way she did to political associates, both were acceptable when they agreed with her personal beliefs but rejected at any sign of a differing opinion.

The Joint Pastoral letter had been followed quickly by the passage of a new coercion bill by the Free State, the former having been intended by Cosgrave to ease the reaction to the latter. The government, already wary of a Communist threat, had been told by an informant, having attended a Republican Army battalion meeting in Tipperary, that rifles would be arriving soon and a new offensive would begin around Christmas.[62] Under these new repressive measures, *An Phoblacht* was 'adjudged by the Military Tribunal to be subversive and was ceased'.[63] Frank Ryan and thirty-one other Republicans were then rounded up and imprisoned for various lengths of time for their alleged, often real, anti-government activities. Mary referred to the arrests as 'sanctimonious humbug about law and order'.[64] The government, sensing the rising popularity of Fianna

Fáil, in the midst of declining economic conditions, was trying to maintain social control, enhance their own credibility and regain popular support.

Amid growing criticism, it was hoped that the 'Statute of Westminster', passed by the British parliament in 1931, would also illustrate the Free State government's commitment to an independent, if not Republican, Ireland. The statute 'acknowledged co-equality between Britain and the dominions and the right of dominion Parliaments to repeal or amend Westminster legislation affecting them'.[65] Mary was firm in her renunciation and wished to alert the Irish to its treachery calling it 'arrant humbug, a sham to lull again the restlessness of the people. . . awakening to the fact that the Treaty and the unfree state. . . are not. . . a stepping stone to freedom and prosperity'.[66] Mary was not alone in her criticism as the *Cork Examiner* called it a sop to the Irish because England was having difficulty in the far east, adding that perhaps the British would want to recruit in Ireland.[67]

While Mary was making only verbal forays against the Free State government, Eamon de Valera was making concrete gains for Fianna Fáil. The economic situation combined with the inertia of the Cosgrave regime drove many to seek solutions through De Valera. There were also those who continued to wish for a free, separate Ireland and dismissed such Free State accomplishments as the Statute of Westminster as inconsequential. To the majority of the Irish who sought a Republic, De Valera was their one realistic, remaining hope. Even Mary admitted that her own organisation had lost public credibility and saw many changing to support her former colleague 'less with real hope of success than dread that if he fails there is not longer any hope'.[68] She also contended that American opinion had been confused when De Valera while on tour, had made 'out and out Republican speeches'.[69] Though she viewed his tactics as deceptive and dishonest, the public now flocked to his side, spurred on by his promise to eliminate the oath of allegiance as well as payment of land annuities and to repeal the Public Safety Act. Those caught up in their dire financial situation and the emotion of the moment asked few questions concerning Fianna Fáil's plans for Irish economic stability.[70]

When elections were called in early 1932, De Valera had all his pieces in place and became increasingly confident of victory. Some formerly doctrinaire Republicans also supported Fianna Fáil, using the argument from Treaty days that a De Valera victory would be a stepping stone to a Republic. De Valera supporters made an emotional appeal contending that by not voting for Fianna Fáil, Republicans who had refused to compromise would remain in prison. Sinn Féin responded predictably that their organisation could not solicit votes for any candidate, who, despite what he may profess or promise, 'before he can even be nominated, must make a public declaration that, if elected he will swear an oath of allegiance to the King of England'.[71] Mary MacSwiney agreed and went on to offer the prediction that if elected and despite lofty promises, before long De Valera would be throwing Republicans into prison.

Despite Sinn Féin's abstention and Mary's dire predictions, Fianna Fáil won the election and after a peaceful, orderly transition of power, Eamon de Valera became the new leader of the Irish government. Peadar O'Donnell viewed the results pragmatically for Republicans: 'To put Fianna Fáil in was the only way to put the Cosgrave gang out. Fianna Fáil was the flail to thrash the pious and illustrious William and Co.'[72]

It had been hoped, by some, that the parties of the left would make a credible showing considering the publicity wrought by the government's ban on such organisations as Saor Éire and the dialogue in the Republican press. Expectations went unfulfilled, however, as the Communist Party garnered less than 1000 votes and James Larkin, the illustrious Irish labour leader and organiser, was not re-elected by Dublin workers.[73]

This response by the electorate illustrated that despite the desperate economic environment, Marxist arguments held little appeal for Irish voters, while appeals to Nationalism, such as those made by De Valera, continued to be attractive. The Irish had not lost the Nationalist aspirations that they had demonstrated during the Sinn Féin election of 1918 but were no longer willing to pursue their dream through political radicalism and violence. Ronan Fanning argues in *Independent Ireland* that as a long conquered nation, the Irish sought and cherished cultural separateness from the British.[74] Though this was clearly the case, a ceiling had been placed on the price that the majority of the Irish were willing to pay.

For Mary and her colleagues, the election was an illustration of the lifelessness of their programme, now only reacting to opposing forces rather than initiating action. Their song had been sung unchanged and repeated for so long, that the Irish public seemed immune to its preaching and name calling, preferring to hear more activist solutions to Ireland's problems. Sinn Féin was based on negativism – not sitting in the Free State parliament, not seeking solutions through compromise while continually calling God's wrath upon those who defied their methods. The few positive approaches – the programme of education and the Constitution of the Second Dáil, proved too little too late and provided no answers to immediate problems of economic stagnation, emigration and increased demand for de facto independence.

7. Solitude in Intransigence, 1932-1942

Mary MacSwiney went about her work ever hopeful of changing Irish behaviour with regard to the Republic. Each year she looked forward to Easter as a time to commemorate and celebrate the events of 1916 and perhaps rekindle the spirit that had ignited her small nation not so many years ago. By 1932, however, she was hampered in her enthusiasm by a continuing battle with ill-health. Her hunger-strikes had exacted a toll not only from the government but from Mary's digestive system as well. This was combined with a heart ailment of undetermined origin that in turn brought kidney dysfunction. At age sixty, poor health was doing what opponents had long sought to do without success, curtail the activities of Mary MacSwiney. Reluctantly, she turned down an offer to address the Easter Commemoration in Belfast, consideration having been given both to her health and the order prohibiting her entry to Northern Ireland. Her answer was given after an opinion was sent from Sinn Féin headquarters urging her to decline for the same reasons.[1] Perhaps their interest was not so much in consideration of her physical well being as in having her removed from a Republican leadership position.

To many, Mary remained the authoritative voice of Republicanism. Her presence or advice continued to be sought after as exemplified by Killarney Republicans who wrote to ask her views on 'the wisdom or otherwise, of having the Sinn Féin Publicity Bureau re-established in Killarney'.[2] She took the short journey to Mallow to serve as the featured speaker in the town's Easter commemoration.[3] There, after the band had played, she beseeched all to join again the Republican organisations of which their community had such a long history. Later, in June, she delivered the opening speech in Bodenstown for the Wolfe Tone commemoration.[4] In order to distance themselves from organisations such as Fianna Fáil who tried to don the mantle of Republicanism but were held as compromisers by the doctrinaires, the 'true Republican pilgrimage' took place a week after the official commemoration.[5] Mary was also active in a new committee formed in Cork to find work for unemployed

Republicans while continuing her endeavours on behalf of the Prisoner's Relief Association. Later in the year, she was asked to assist with the upcoming demonstrations in honour of the sixty-fifth anniversary of the Manchester Martyrs to be held in late November.[6]

While her physical activities were more restrained than in previous years, Mary's pen found no rest. She led a resistance movement against the Eucharistic Congress, a huge international Catholic event, coveted by ecclesiastical authorities and a product of long involved planning, scheduled to be held in Dublin. It was entirely unlikely that it woud be influenced by a small group of disaffected Republicans. Nonetheless, Mary continued her challenge. Upon realising that the occasion would be held despite her resistance, she focused her attention on particular areas of concern. The first was her request to Cardinal MacRory that all military displays be eliminated, there to be no official recognition given to the representative of the king and that the ceremonies be free from 'all glorification of the Free State.'[7] Her second objection was to the papal honours due to be bestowed on William Cosgrave during the ceremonies. The pope was informed that this recipient was both a traitor to and murderer of his fellow countrymen and to so honour him would give 'grave offence to a very great number of Irishmen and make papal honours a laughing stock' in Ireland.[8] The Vatican was presumably able to identify Mary's talent for over-statement as her requests went unheeded.

The change in Mary's physical activity level seemed to leave her time for ferreting out British inspired flaws in Irish society. The Boy Scouts, or the 'Baden-Powell Organisation', was attacked for implanting in young Irish minds the 'English pagan idea of Honour' in place of 'guidance of conscience and respect for Catholic principles'.[9] As in the case of the Eucharistic Congress, her criticisms and suggestions were not regarded seriously, instead these diatribes only gave her enemies more ammunition to indict her as a petty, bitter and resentful loser.

A criticism from Mary viewed as less trivial was her repeated warnings to De Valera concerning his proposed negotiations with the British. De Valera intended that these talks be used to put an end to the land annuities issue which had been a campaign promise and perhaps, to establish new trade agreements. Just as Mary had warned against the Treaty negotiations in 1921, she again attributed only the vilest of motives to the British. A personal appeal was sent to De Valera, which in itself was a concession as Mary had shunned his very name after he took the oath of allegiance in 1927. Now, five years later, she wrote a personal, sincere letter warning him about British treachery to which she believed he was blind: 'I greatly fear that there is something more sinister afoot. The only thing the English want is a further split'. She added that some within his party advocated the necessity of British capital in Ireland and closer relations with their best customer, concepts which differed widely from the Republican point of view.[10] The new leader, awash in the glow of his election victory and confident in his ability to handle the British, paid no heed to these admonitions. Mary's influence, as her health, was on the wane.

One of the few positive notes of the year occurred when Máire Óg, Terence MacSwiney's daughter, came to live in Cork with her two aunts, Mary and Annie. As an infant, she had been taken to the continent by her mother who had then resisted all requests to return to Ireland despite the fact that Mary held joint custody of the child. Máire Óg had spent her early years in Germany, but in 1932, at age fourteen, she chose to return to Ireland in the hope of a more stable family environment. The newspapers sensationalised her return with stories that Mary had gone to Germany secretly and kidnapped her niece. In actuality, the events were much more mundane, as Máire Óg had written to her aunt asking if she could be brought to Cork, a transfer carried out openly without a trace of the surreptitiousness suggested by the press. Mary was overjoyed to have Máire Óg with her. After initial adjustments by the child to a new language and a new culture, the two developed a close affection and respect for one another.[11]

While De Valera was planning conferences with the British, Mary floated a trial balloon before her colleagues in the Second Dáil, believing the time was auspicious for a presentation to the Irish people of the contrasts between themselves and Fianna Fáil, high-lighting the latter's lack of a true Republican concept. Mary's plan was as close as she would ever come to a compromise as she advocated, or at least presented for consideration, three main points. The first was the acceptance of dominion status for all of Ireland 'with a Senate along the lines of the Council of Ireland of the 1920 Act'; second, the oath was to be reworded accepting the King as Head and the only link binding the members of the Commonwealth together; third, the complete removal of all customs barriers between England and Ireland, Ireland being the thirty-two counties. This was to serve as a preparation for a united English and Irish effort to get Empire Free Trade at the upcoming Commonwealth conference in Ottawa.[12]

These concepts are notable for various reasons. First, it is the first time Mary had indicated that she would accept any type of association, however vague, loose and non-committal with the English monarchy. Second, she had begun to consider the importance of economic issues for the future of Ireland, something she had always considered secondary and not worthy of a sacrifice of principles. Third, she continued to under-estimate the strength of Unionist resistance in the north still believing that if the British withdrew from the north all Irish people would be united in peace and harmony. Fourth, her own principles were left intact as Ireland would be a Republic within the Commonwealth, with no actual allegiance sworn to the King but having the advantage of favourable trade agreements. (This arrangement is similar to the agreement reached with India in 1948.) In sending these proposals she wrote 'that as guardians of the Republican position it is up to us to be alive and wide awake and to put our spoke in before further mischief is done'.[13] With these suggestions, Mary was moving away from the fierce Republican rhetoric that had been a part of her image for so long. As she had long advocated, an effort was being made to present the people of Ireland with concrete proposals and possible solutions to their national problems. The proposals would bring a free, united Irish Republic and economic advantages at the price of remaining under the same kingly umbrella as the British. To Mary, never having been given to any form of compromise, this was one which could be entered upon without straining the principles of 1916.

It is unclear why Mary chose this time to show a degree of compromise in agreeing to accept a loose commonwealth association under the British monarch. Perhaps her decision was due to a confluence of realisations including the election of Eamon de Valera which seemed to seal the tomb of politically doctrinaire Republicans, the continuing lessening of their numbers, the lack of compliance of the IRA to the Second Dáil, all precipitated by her growing ill-health as a reminder of her own mortality. Perhaps if there was compromising to be done, she could keep it to a minimum in order to retain the Republic and it would be done on Mary's terms, not leaving it for the less ardent to negotiate after her death. Though she would have preferred no association with Britain, she could console herself and salve her conscience with the belief that the power of the monarch was limited, the British politicians would be kept out of Irish affairs and Ireland could gain from preferred trading partner status with Britain. Mary, having repeatedly demonstrated her belief in her own infallibility and purity regarding Republican decisions, may have felt that her statements would be accepted by those who still considered themselves loyal adherents to the Second Dáil. Perhaps too, for a brief, fleeting moment she understood that she had adopted the politics of failure and if Ireland was to have any hope of peace and unity some movement on her part was necessary.

The members of the Second Dáil were receptive to the proposals but by now they were but a small, fringe group, still accepted as true Republicans but viewed by most within and without the movement, as the aged, often eccentric, old guard. Their influence along with their prestige was minimal. Although Republicans were greatly splintered, for the moment the Socialist left and the Army were more in the limelight with Sinn Féin struggling to maintain a voice. Mary was continuing to do what she believed to be best for Ireland but now, few were listening. She had reiterated her plea for an Irish Republic continually over the last fifteen years. In 1932, when her ideas had undergone a change, however slight, her audience, after a continuing diminution, had gone.

Republican dissension continued to fester when, in February 1933, the Army Convention decided to release its members from the restriction that prevented them from taking part in national elections, deciding that the most effective way to oppose Cosgrave's candidates was to support Fianna Fáil. Lest Republicans be too outraged by such a suggestion, their statement added that the Army did 'not in any way commit . . . to acceptance of Fianna Fáil policy' as it was 'not Republican' and 'its economic policy (would) not bring social justice in the long term'.[14] Despite this disclaimer, this was a victory for Eamon de Valera as he could feel reasonably secure about a large block of Republican votes. The split was deepened when the Army failed to consult with Sinn Féin about the Easter commemoration. Brian O'Higgins, as a leading officer in the latter, felt piqued over being ignored and shared his annoyance with his friend Mary MacSwiney.[15] The Army was continually manoeuvring to assure its own ascendancy over Republicans.

There was also continuing controversy within the Army about the degree of acceptance of Marxism. The Communist elements strength had peaked in the early 1930s and was beginning to decline by 1933. Although the Army had cut itself off from the Second Dáil and pursued an independent path, Mary continued to give advice to all with the optimisic hope that at some point Republican unity would again recur. This unity, by now in need of a miracle, would of course be under the leadership of the Second Dáil.

To preserve the facade of Republican unity, Mary defended the IRA through an abundance of letters to the editors of various publications.

She felt the need to do so was particularly acute as the clergy were continuing their assault, the Bishop of Galway stating emphatically that the IRA was allied with Communism and anyone joining was a sham Catholic.[16] Bishop Cohalan of Cork had reiterated that the aims and objectives of the IRA embodied Communistic principles.[17]

As a mother might come to the protection of her offspring, Mary, in unsolicited remarks, tried to rescue the reputation of the Army, writing:

No section of the Republican movement is Communist, though every section of it calls aloud for a Christian social system to replace the Pagan Capitalism which has brought the world to the verge of ruin and is the direct cause of Communism. In this demand for a complete revolution of the social system, Republicans are but preaching the recent Encyclical of Pope Pius XI – Republicans are as strong and as effective opponents of an anti-God campaign as any section in Ireland or out of it.[18]

In private, Mary uged IRA leader Moss Twomey to clear the air about Communism in the Army, telling him that the enemies of the Republic, unknown to him, had 'been inspiring policies which would tend to split' the Republicans.[19] In another written appeal she again assumed her motherly position and included a letter she had written, that he might issue in order to better state the Army's position. Though her influence was disappearing, she still exhibited controlling behaviour in Republican matters. The national issue was strongly identified: when the connection with England was completely broken there was to be 'national ownership of the national resources' so that an influx of foreign capital could be prevented. There was also the inclusion of the Army's belief in Christian social justice in which it would be 'impossible for any man to exploit his fellow man'.[20] Eager to maintain this link with Republican social-economic policy and Catholicism, Mary said: 'No one is entitled to own a surplus until everyone has enough. That is not Communism, it is just the doctrine of St Augustine and St Thomas. It is good Catholic teaching.'[21]

As the year progressed, Mary became embroiled in a dispute with Cumann na mBan leaders during an executive convention held in Dublin, in June 1933 presided over by Eithne Ní Chumhaill. One of the issues slated for discussion was the question of continuing allegiance to the Republic through the Second Dáil or to the Republic alone. The discussion was intense and heated as speakers rose to support one view or the other. Mary MacSwiney was thunderstruck by the challenge made to the credibility of the Second Dáil, believing it an intrinsic aspect of

Ireland's past, necessary for the continuance of true Republicanism, as well as being the de jure government of Ireland, to which all owed allegiance. Those in disagreement argued that 'to ask young girls and women to render allegiance to a government which does not and cannot function is simply taxing their powers of credibility beyond reason'.[22] When the vote finally came, Mary MacSwiney and her followers were defeated by twenty-six votes to seven with two abstentions.[23] A change was made in the constitution so that members gave allegiance to the Republic alone, not the Second Dáil because 'it had become evident that to confine membership so, was to isolate ourselves from the growing generation and to make progress towards our goal impossible'.[24]

Mary was filled with profound sadness when the results of the vote were announced as this rejection of the old guard was unbelievable to her. She immediately announced her resignation from the organisation. Despite a unanimous appeal issued by the members that she stay on, Mary left the hall and another large group became her former colleagues.[25] Upon departing, she announced: 'You allowed youngsters of two months standing in Cumann na mBan a vote to decide issues that the majority of them know nothing about.'[26] Her resignation and exit were accompanied by Síghle Ní Geanin and Eibhlín Ní Trobraide.[27]

Mary claimed that the Second Dáil had been repudiated to enable the organisation to move closer to Fianna Fáil, believing that most of the new branches were 'composed of ardent De Valeraites'. It was her conviction that this (or any) was 'no time to show a sign of compromise and thus lower the ideal in the minds of the country generally'. She went on to predict doom for the organisation as 'no recruits (bought) at such a price (would) be worth having'.[28]

Although this disassociation from Cumann na mBan was difficult, Mary did not waver for a moment over her decision, though with her refusal to adapt to a different generation she was becoming more and more of a solitary figure. Her belief remained that principles and truths were constant and people should accommodate to them rather than vice versa. A continuing point of dispute concerned who should be the arbiter of these Republican truths and principles, Mary remaining convinced that she was one of the chosen few responsible.

The return trip to Cork was long and dispiriting but at her home one supportive letter awaited. Kathleen O'Moore of Drumcondra wrote: 'I have heard you spoken of as "The steel anchor of the Republic." Again I heard the remark made "If our men were only one-half as straight, honest and uncompromising as Mary MacSwiney, we should have had the Republic long ago".[29] Mary could only agree with the latter statement but now she believed that women had to be included with men on lists of those who had disappointed the Republic.

Despite her quick withdrawal from the meeting hall, Mary would not leave the organisation too quietly. In Cork, she succeeded in having her entire branch withdraw from the main organisation, asking her allies in other areas to do likewise. She was also hopeful of having a general convention called, at which time the issue could be voted on again. Defiant activism was her typical response to rejection.

Unfortunately for her, neither of these plans met with success. Scattered members withdrew but the branches generally accepted the constitutional change. The special convention idea also brought a negative response, even from Mary's ideological colleagues. Eibhlin Ní Trobraide wrote from Dublin that it was 'absolutely out of the question' as most of the executive did not believe in 'Dáil Éireann, and would boycott such a plan'. It was even reported that some members who had resigned were starting to go back to their branches.

With the immediate flurry of activity over, the supporters of the Second Dáil, now extremely few in number (about fifteen in Dublin) departed but left the main body of the organisation intact. Those set adrift made a very loose commitment to meet again in the autumn to review their situation, a rather inglorious conclusion to an originally defiant protest.[30]

Nora Connolly, the daughter of James, chose this time to write in *An Phoblacht* about her father's view of women. He believed that 'women in a movement, must not, as a matter of course, be the drudges. . . performing its arduous, inglorious and thankless tasks' under the supervision and domination of men. If women were not given an equal voice in policy making the movement would be destroyed and it would serve as 'a conscious, deliberate aid to the continued demoralisation and degradation of the race.' She went on to write that in 1933 'progressive and revolutionary women (had) no voice in the council of the revolutionary movement.' Women were 'showing that "damnable patience" and (were) content to be the drudges of the movement'.[31] It was inferred that Cumann na mBan contained these 'drudges' and that Mary MacSwiney, one of the few women who sought an active role in Republican decision-making was being eased out of her role. Though Mary had found no problem in the role of Cumann na mBan as an auxiliary organisation, she did not believe that women were incapable of taking their place in the vanguard of Republicanism. Her efforts to do so had not gone unchallenged as she now found herself out of Cumann na mBan and on the periphery of Sinn Féin.

At the annual autumn meeting of Sinn Féin, the membership became embroiled in controversy once again. The point of disagreement was the right of members to receive pensions or take jobs from the Free State government. Mary was firmly opposed to allowing Republicans such latitude and had long urged the orgainisation to make 'a statement to the country on the meaning and limitations of allegiance to the government of the Republic'.[32] She believed that such actions would give credibility and legitimacy to the Free State government and weaken the Republican position in the eyes of onlookers. To her it was particularly inane that some who upheld the right to take jobs with the Free State also forbade members to buy Gaelic League and Vincent de Paul flags through contributions on their flag days.

The situation came to a head because Father O'Flanagan, who was standing for the presidency of Sinn Féin, had taken a position especially created for him by the Free State. It was not one that had been advertised as would usually be the case with a civil service position.

His acceptance of the job was particularly offensive as there were many members who were 'very down and out financially', were eligible for pensions yet refused them because it was seen as 'not compatible with uncompromising Republicanism'. Mary concluded that there was 'considerable cynicism and bitterness that people in high places (could) be so accommodating while the small fry (were) expected to be so much more drastic with themselves and their principles'.[33]

Although Mary had stated that 'more than sixty per cent' of the members agreed with her position, her count proved overly optimistic. When the vote was taken, the resolution passed allowing Father O'Flanagan to be President despite his job with the Free State.

This was one more defeat for Mary. Her first reaction, as confided to friends, was to leave the organisation. After serious consideration of the matter and through the encouragement of her allies, especially J. J. O'Kelly, she decided to stay on.[34] This decision was made in part because of the growing popularity of De Valera and the perceived need to maintain a united front against him. Mary's stature was still such that she believed her resignation would 'do further harm' when 'real Republicanism' was already in a 'very difficult position'.[35] To maintain unity, she had retained an uneasy alliance with her old sparring partner, Father O'Flanagan.

While the issue of jobs, pensions and loyalties were fresh in Mary's mind, she was becoming involved with a new women's organisation,

Mná na Poblachta, under the leadership of Nodlaig Ní Brugha and Eibhlín Ní Trobraide. Directed particularly at those women who had left Cumann na mBan the previous spring, its aims included: 'Organising and training the women and girls of Ireland for the purpose of breaking the connection with England by every right means in our power, helping the government of the Republic in the exercise of its functions as the lawful government of All Ireland and securing for the Republic international recognition.'[36]

Mary had been involved in the early organisational meeting but following the Sinn Féin Ard-Fheis and the reconsideration of the issues raised, she declined from joining the new women's group. This refusal was due in part to a difference in opinion with Eibhlín over the Father O'Flanagan issue. Eibhlín had written to Mary quite unequivocally: 'I cannot see your point of view with reference to Father O'Flanagan's position', confessing to have given the matter a good deal of thought but failing to reach Mary's conclusion that his job indicated unfaithfulness to Dáil Éireann.[37] She questioned how the priest's position differed from other civil servants such as postal employees, teachers or income tax officials. To illustrate sensitivity to the issue, however, in the proposed women's organisation, members would not be allowed to participate in Free State elections because this meant one was 'voluntarily helping, although unconscientiously perhaps, to maintain the "Treaty" position'.[38]

Mary responded that she did not lump civil servants in the same category with Father O'Flanagan for whom a special job had been created, believing that 'civil servants got their posts by competitive examination' hence Republicans were 'quite entitled to hold them' providing no oath of allegiance was involved.[39] Although believing that voting should not be allowed, she contended that there were other acts which she considered 'at least equally compromising – even more harmful in a way because they give more bad example'.[40] The position of Father O'Flanagan was one such action under fire but taking of pensions also fell into this category chiefly due to the impression given that one's principles were for sale. While realising that many had been forced to accept jobs or pensions through economic hardship, these people 'should not be pushed into or permitted to stand for positions of honour which (would) compromise the Republican organisation'. She concluded that it was 'farcical to strain at one wrong and swallow another.'[41]

This refusal to join Mná na Poblachta was in part due to Mary's remaining fit of pique from the Ard-Fheis and her further annoyance that Eibhlín did not agree with her. Perhaps too there was the lingering belief that to start out in an organisation with ideological differences already identified was courting disaster. The last years had provided enough disappointments, no need to go begging for more. This episode also illustrated Mary's continuing belief in her own Republican infallibility and complete unwillingness to concede to another's point of view, having become suspicious of any organisation in which there was even a remote chance of disagreement. Although not necessarily considering herself a better person than her detractors, she certainly considered herself a better Republican.

Following the Ard-Fheis of 1933, Mary remained disgruntled about the state of Sinn Féin leadership but kept busy preaching her doctrine of no compromise. When the issue of De Valera's economic policy was raised, Mary reiterated that the current economic war could only be settled one way, 'the way of freedom, freedom from any connection whatever with the British empire'.[42] Irish citizens were encouraged to suppport her view when she entreated a crowd at the Town Hall in Cobh: 'No man may let down his task until he either loses his life or the cause is won.'[43]

As her suggestions made to the Second Dáil about compromise had gone largely unheeded, Mary resumed her previous position concerning Irish involvement with the British empire. Her momentary flirtation with compromise, having not met with success, was discarded forever. One can imagine that Mary may have at times chastised herself about her weakness though done for Ireland as she had never failed to point up such conduct in others. Perhaps her mind had not changed completely but her speech was for public consumption with every opportunity taken to cast aspersions upon the traitor De Valera by pointing out his continual consorting with the enemy British.

When not attacking De Valera, some of her strongest words were used in response to Eoin O'Duffy's Blueshirts, a right wing organisation formed in response to their perceived threat of Communism. Mary said that a 'Republican government would put O'Duffy on trial for high treason',[44] adding on another occasion that 'if there was a greater scoundrel in the country she for one would not care to meet him'.[45] To put this issue in a Catholic perspective, she told her audiences and readers that 'the Pope's encyclical (was) as much a negation of Fascism as it (was) of Communism' neither system being compatible 'with the individual freedom which (was) a natural human right'.[46]

De Valera was also indicted for his actions in issuing a new coercion act by which he allegedly dealt more severely with Republicans than with Blueshirts 'who were supporting England' under the direction of O'Duffy and MacDermot, 'the real enemies of the country'.[47]

Throughout the year there was the continuing, though seemingly vain, hope that Republicans could achieve some form of unity. Mary, now placing all trust in the Second Dáil, realised that their numbers were dwindling and wondered what was to be done when they diminshed further.[48] A joint conference of the Second Dáil, the Army and Sinn Féin was held during May of 1934 at which time the belief was verbalised again that if the three could join together under one constitution, pledging loyalty and mutual support, there would be a 'reawakening of interest at home and abroad' combined with increased 'moral and material support'.[49] The efforts made at reconciliation were again rather half-hearted with the usual result, talk without action.

As the days passed, Mary looked forward with some misgiving to the upcoming Sinn Féin Ard-Fheis. At a personal level her feeling about Father O'Flanagan remained unchanged and she continued to reject his involvement with the Free State government. These thoughts were foremost as she travelled to Dublin for the autumn convention of 1934.

When it came time for the election of the president, Mary's fears were realised with the re-election of Father O'Flanagan. It had been her hope that during the year that had passed, the membership would have had sufficient time to re-think and conclude that a continuation of his presidency was inconsistent with Republican ideals. Unfortunately for her, her speeches and writing of the last year had not succeeded in changing the allegiance of the majority at the convention.

Following the vote, Mary felt duty bound to resign from the organisation. Her statement of the reasons for her resignation was clear and blunt: it was due to 'the decision of two consecutive Ard-Fheis that a person who holds a job or a pension from the Free State may be president of Sinn Féin'. Her conclusion was similarly clear: 'While such a decision holds good I hold Sinn Féin false.'[50]

In another letter she brooded further over the state of affairs. Two issues were recognised: first, that it was unfair to exclude from Sinn Féin ' all the young people who (were) entering the civil service in the ordinary course and without any consciousness of wrong doing'; second, 'that self-preservation being the first law of nature, one could not expect Republicans to starve'. There was a third issue that could not be overlooked subsequent to the leaders advocating the use of Free State courts and taking jobs and pensions from these usurpers: that after these things were accomplished, it was 'about time for those who believ(ed) in no compromise and who (could) not purchase ease and comfort. . . at such a price to let Sinn Féin go to destruction in its own way'.[51]

Some at the convention labelled the resignation a reaction to petty jealousy, believing Mary lusted after the presidency and begrudged it to Father O'Flanagan. Although she had an open dislike for the man, he was not the first person in the movement with whom she had a personality clash. The charge of jealousy was petty in itself as Mary had illustrated her unwavering commitment to principle since her early days of political involvement.

Caitlín Bean Brugha, a long-time friend and widow of a martyred Republican, realised this and immediately came to the defence of her colleague. She chided the Standing Committee of Sinn Féin for tolerating such unworthy suggestions saying it was 'inconceivable that petty motives should be ascribed to her (Mary) by those who (had) worked with her and who have been so well aware of her selfless devotion to the Republic'. Mary was defended as 'the symbol of Ireland unconquered', one who had 'given all her life and her great ability to the Cause of Freedom'.[52]

Mary, of course, was just as firm in her commitment not to compromise over her resignation as she was not to compromise over the Republic. Though her decision was firm and irrevocable, this did not release her from the sorrow and disappointment she felt in resigning after such a long union. In a personal letter to a friend she confided: 'The whole business saddened me more than I can say – a great organisation irretrievably compromised to justify the weakness of one individual.'[53]

Mary left the convention room and Dublin, alone both physically and ideologically. Since the Civil War of 1922-3, she had been gradually hiving off a place for herself and her doctrinaire companions. The Civil War had brought the first great split, followed by the defection of the Army from Sinn Féin, De Valera and his Fianna Fáil supporters departed in 1926, as did Sáor Éire and the extreme left in 1932; Mary left Cumann na mBan in 1933 and finally Sinn Féin in 1934. The only friends left to her were the dwindling number of members of the Second Dáil. In her continuing effort to keep the Republican movement pure, undefiled and united, Mary had succeeded only in seeing it splintered into a multitude of organisations none of whom were willing to defer any longer to her. Just as she had given an example of intransigence after her brother's death, now those around her, former colleagues, were exhibiting this same characteristic. Her adherence to principle or her stubbornness, depending on one's point of view, had left the Republican movement split just as Ireland was split. The prospect of reuniting either remained extremely remote.

Her hope for one Ireland, united and free from bonds of servitude with England, was as unlikely now as at any time since the Anglo-Irish war. As De Valera endeavoured to manoeuvre the twenty-six counties away from England, Britain tightened her economic and psychological grip on the six northern counties.

An Phoblacht, in a review of the problems within the Republican move-ment, said that it had been 'cursed with an exaggeration of individualism' coupled with 'an absence of cohesion (and) an unexpressed distrust in leadership'.[54] Although Mary had never sought personal glorification within the movement, she had shown a consistent mistrust in the views and efforts of others and hence fits the description provided by the Republican press.

Mary was reminded of the seeming futility of her efforts when reading the Cumann na mBan column in *An Phoblacht*. Movement leaders recognised in an accepting way that their members were scarcely likely to 'excel as air pilots and machine gunners' but were capable of doing 'a giant's part' in 'arousing resistance to the. . . iniquitous social system'.[55] It was also reported that the organisation was larger than at any time since 1921-22 with over fifty new branches having been formed during the last months of 1933, after the withdrawal of Mary MacSwiney.[56] Perhaps her exit had left many with the perception that the group had been de-radicalised and was no longer just an ineffectual Republican voice crying out in the Free State wilderness. With the ideal of a Republic no longer linked with the archaic, arcane and meaningless Second Dáil, the women saw it as a more viable organisation as it could now work with De Valera towards their mutually declared Republican goal. To Mary, it was but one more rejection of her beliefs and ideals, as Irish women seemed to be saying that her principles were too extreme and unrealistic in the practical world around them. Their Nationalistic sen-timents were still present but sought to be exercised in a more workable environment.

When Mary returned to Cork, she took up her own lonely vigil as guardian of the Republic. Unlike the revitalisation within Cumann na mBan after her resignation, Sinn Féin failed to do the same. Most male Republican energy was being funnelled into the IRA. Following a period of negotiation by the Army after the Civil War, there was now a more forceful return to the old ways with the gun being taken up again.

Efforts at unity continued as always but the Army was emerging as the leader as they wanted 'to control everything and everyone in any organisation with which they (were) connected'.[57] Sinn Féin, recognising their growing impotence, sought to strike a deal putting themselves in charge of civilian activity with the Army restricted to military operations under a banner of unity.[58] As it was hard for leaders of Sinn Féin to forget that 'for years (the Army Council) had been disparaging Sinn Féin up and down the country',[59] any co-operation was tenuous at best. Mary, hardly in a frame of mind to pass equitable judgment, declared that Sinn Féin was 'not a virile organisation now nor (did) it seem likely to become one'.[60] The leaders of the Army, on the other hand, were exuding a new confidence. Moss Twomey wrote an optimistic letter to Mary stating: 'I am very hopeful that the Republican movement is going to gather great strength very rapidly.'[61]

Although Mary wished always to keep a keen eye and a critical tongue on all Republican activities, she was limited in her efforts by a severe bout of ill health. During the summer of 1935, her heart condition became life threatening, so much so that she began to reflect on her past life in the manner of one about to give it up. The conclusion reached was stated modestly when she wrote that hers had been 'a full and busy life'.[62]

Mary's time had not come, however, and during her recovery period she had an opportunity to study current events. Her conclusions were in keeping with those of the IRA leaders: Ireland could only gain its freedom through armed forces, in part because Fianna Fáil had continued to do the work of the British in Ireland.

There was also the rumbling of another European war to be considered. On this issue Mary showed no hesitancy, stating that in such circumstances Ireland should declare its neutrality and most assuredly 'Irish lads should not enlist in the British army'.[63] Anyone who went to fight for England, either at home or abroad 'should be deprived of Irish citizenship forever'.[64]

While Mary was regaining strength, Fianna Fáil provided a cause against which she could rally support. Under De Valera's direction the government had begun a new series of repressive measures against Republicans as they recognised the potential threat about which Moss Twomey had prophesied so optimistically. The formation of a new Republican organisation, Cumann Poblachta na h-Éireann, had spurred the government's already aroused interest. This group saw partition as Ireland's most pressing problem and hence would be attacking De Valera from a direction with which he had few problems in the past.[65] In consequence, during late 1934, *An Phoblacht*, seen as an organ of the IRA, began having more and more articles censored until finally in June 1935 it was suppressed altogether. The IRA had escalated military activity and had been involved in various shooting incidents and at least two killings. The government reacted with a Coercion Bill with the IRA being declared an illegal organisation.[66]

This government attack on Republicans brought Mary into the debate. There was a personal reason added as her brother Seán had been arrested and spent eleven days on hunger-strike in Arbour Hill without charges being brought against him.[67]

Eamon de Valera allowed himself to become involved in a private and then a newspaper debate with Mary MacSwiney over the IRA issue. First, she had baited him in a series of private letters saying that this 'new Fianna Fáil mentality' was the 'outcome of compromise and surrender'.[68] Later she asked: 'Are you going to do what is right and just or become a second murder gang, like the Cosgrave-Mulcahy ministry?'[69] Sufficiently incensed by these accusations, De Valera returned, 'Are you not aware that defenceless citizens have been murdered in the most cowardly manner?' continuing, that there must be some authority to prevent and punish murder.[70] Mary would not accept that the IRA was responsible and accused De Valera of further demoralising the people by infiltrating the IRA with spies. That said, she hit full stride, responding: 'The cheap, impertinent, insincere letter I have received from you makes me alter my view point of the depth of unworthiness of which you are capable.'[71]

De Valera, never one to accept criticism or insults graciously, went to the press and accused Mary of sanctioning killing and other life threatening acts of terrorists. The answer to this came at a Republican meeting where she said she did 'not stand for shooting anybody but if any man was shot by the IRA it was for being a spy'.[72] De Valera, speaking in Galway, claimed that her condonation and justification must be an encouragement to those (terrorists) and their associates to plan and commit more'. He justified infiltrators on the grounds that the government had the right to try and know the actions of any subversive group committed to Civil War.[73]

Mary replied that she was denouncing the terms and use of the Coercion Act which De Valera had himself denounced 'with at least equal vehemence in the Free State parliament in 1931'. She was doing it 'for exactly the same reasons and in exactly the same circumstances'.[74]

The two concluded their debate with a final round of insults. Mary claimed that De Valera had chosen 'the ignoble course of permitting himself to be made England's tool'.[75] Her protagonist responded through the editorial page of his newspaper *The Irish Press*, that Mary MacSwiney was 'obsessed by delusions. . . pitiable to see in a person of her intelligence and intellect'.[76] Mary wished that she could 'win the sweep' then 'spare £500 to start a sane Republican paper'.[77]

De Valera had the final word in this confrontation when Fianna Fáil candidates won by-elections in Galway and Wexford. Mary's answer was unconvincing as she denied these victories indicated that the public generally approved the policy of coercion but rather that voters had been deceived into believing that 'Fianna Fáil Republican speeches really meant fidelity to the Republic'.[78]

The elections did indicate a further polarisation of loyalties within Irish society. On one side were the followers of De Valera, a loyal and growing majority who saw him as a leader moving them away from Britain and gradually asserting Irish Nationalism. On the other side were the radical Republicans with the IRA, committed to militarism and violence, as the emerging leader. As De Valera seemed to be satisfying the Nationalist aspirations of the majority, the radicals illustrated a growing concern for the issue of Irish unity, hoping that would attract interest and followers.

The enactment of the Coercion Bill gave new vibrancy to the Republican Prisoners' Committee of which Mary was a chief spokesperson, a position not relinquished since the Civil War. She reiterated her charges that prisoners were being 'kept in deadly silence', that normal purchasing privileges had been removed, exercise denied and they were 'locked up for twenty-four hours at a time'. The blame for all this mistreatment was attributed to Eamon de Valera. To a large group meeting in Dublin, Mary said that she once believed that De Valera 'would rather put his hand in the fire than stand for the coercion of any Republicans' but, unfortunately, she now came before them and spoke 'with a sad heart'.[79] The President of the Free State was depicted as imprisoning his former colleagues with vigour and enthusiasm.

The President was challenged by Mary on other fronts as well. As he strove to encourage new industry and economic advantage for Ireland, Mary pointed up that such efforts only served British imperialism. Regarding the airport to be built at Shannon, people were reminded that the British would have 51% of the shares and it 'would inevitably be used for war'. So too, the new oil refinery in Dublin and the munitions factory in Connaught would 'insure that Ireland will be involved in

England's wars'.[80]

De Valera's dramatic declaration of a new constitution for Ireland also went unappreciated by Republicans. De Valera saw the document as a giant leap away from the British yoke and one of which all Irish people could be proud.

Mary saw it in directly contrary terms believing that what it secured was 'the control of the King of England and subordination of Ireland to his Britannic Majesty'. She went on in a disgusted tone: 'How those nations must laugh at "Éire's" claim to nationhood – this "sovereign, independent democratic" Éire – when every representative she sends abroad is appointed by the King of England and Irish citizens have no status in other countries except as his subjects.'[81] She took no joy in the special position of the Roman Catholic Church, instead believed it was a 'subversion of the Republic of Ireland'.[82]

Other critics of the new constitution cited its lack of any new initiatives into social policy in light of recent encyclicals. One detractor wrote that the new document illustrated De Valera's 'inability to come out of the eighteenth century' and was 'a great disappointment'.[83]

Women's groups were infuriated, one writer saying it was not a return to the Middle Ages, it was 'something quite different and much worse'. She continued that under the new constitution women's opportunity for earning, her civil rights, status and 'her whole position as a citizen' were jeopardised by the women's clause. This clause referred to woman's special role in the home and in particular 'that women and children shall not be forced by economic necessity to enter avocations unsuited to their sex, age or strength'.[84]

Characteristically, Mary MacSwiney had expressed no particular enmity over these issues. She retained her single-mindedness with regard to the Republic and the effect on it of the new constitution. There was no wish to have her argument diluted by raising feminist issues. With her basic acceptance of women in the home influencing her as well, she was most concerned that the constitution was 'all treason, since it is not the Republic' adding rather dejectedly: 'It is all very sad.'[85]

Mary continued to make pronouncements on other issues as well. The Spanish Civil War was gaining much attention in Ireland, men having been dispatched to fight on both sides. Mary was unimpressed with either case saying that she would 'not lift a finger to help to foist on any unfortunate country either Communism or Fascism' as she had 'profound contempt for both'. Those eager to bear arms in Spain were reminded that 'Spain sent no volunteers to help (the Irish) when (they) were fighting the Black and Tans'. All Irishmen were encouraged to 'stay at home and take the mote out of their own eyes before trying to work on the beam in their neighbour's'.[86]

Republican organisations, noting that Mary MacSwiney could still gain press attention and even raise the hackles of the President on occasion, courted her to consider rejoining them. From Sinn Féin, in need of vigour and enthusiasm, came a letter telling Mary that her 'right place' was 'in the ranks of Sinn Féin' and this was 'the wish of many in Sinn Féin'.[87] The writer of the letter showed little understanding of Mary's character if it was seriously thought that she would reconsider membership unless Sinn Féin recanted the statements that had brought her resignation.

Similarly, Cumann na mBan sent an invitation asking Mary to once again participate in their proceedings. The reply was snappy and direct saying that as long as the organisation sought to secure pensions from and thus recognise the government of the Free State, Mary considered them 'guilty of treason to the Republic'. Consequently, she felt justified in assuming that their invitation was sent 'by mistake'.[88]

The Second Dáil continued to be the one body held true and dear but she reluctantly recognised its depleting ranks and influence due to 'treachery, secession and. . . death', its active membership having been reduced to seven. A rather disheartening note was sent to J. J. O'Kelly in which she admitted that none of the seven were 'getting younger or stronger' nor were they following the Dáil resolution concerning the number of meetings to be held, this generally being left to herself and Sceilig 'to see what (they) could do'.[89]

Mary had been made painfully aware of her own poor health when she was told in January of 1938 that she might need to undergo surgery for the removal of cataracts. As her vision continued to worsen, she made 'novena after novena to Lourdes'.[90] This condition was an added burden on her failing heart. She hardly feared death but believed suitable provisions regarding the future of the Republic had to be made.

The remaining members of the Second Dáil came together to decide what provisions to make for what they still believed to be the legally constituted government of the Republic of Ireland. Mary recognised that Sinn Féin retained 'value from the point of view of continuity' but believed 'it was hopeless to expect the rank and file of the people. . . to join an organisation which stands on the position of 1919'. She suggested that all who believed in 'complete separation from the British Empire' should be joined in a blanket organisation and then 'gradually brought to see the importance of maintaining the 1919 position'.[91] The group she believed most capable of carrying out this task was the IRA, the only Republican group that continued to maintain its vitality.

At one of their last official statements, the Executive Council of Dáil Éireann repudiated 'the misleading agreements signed in London' by De Valera and his associates in April of 1938. Foremost among the reasons cited was the failure of the negotiations to discuss the problem of Irish partition. Second, they repudiated the payment of £20 million to England, believing it was Ireland that required restitution; third, they denied that Ireland had any obligation to assure the English government that it would not 'permit its territory to be used as a basis of attack against Britain' while England used Irish territory and territorial waters 'as a basis of attack on her own enemies and otherwise contrive(d) to involve (Ireland) in her wars'; fourth, the Taoiseach (President) had no authority to discriminate in England's favour for the Rynanna air bases or oil refinery; last, they repudiated common citizenship with the British Empire, a most unsavoury conclusion to the offensive negotiations.[92]

The proud, still defiant but ageing members of the Second Dáil met in mid-1938. The snickers of some onlookers who mocked their air of solemnity, did not go unnoticed but they held to their trust believing it sacred, a gift from the martyred Irish dead that gave them strength to accommodate the mocking looks of non-believers.

With Mary's encouragement, a decision was reached and a formal statement issued in which the surviving members of the Second Dáil transferred their authority to the Irish Republican Army, believing that they would 'carry their task to victory in the spirit of the men who proclaimed and established the Republic'.[93] It was a sad realisation for the ageing Dáil members but it showed an acceptance of reality that had been lacking in their actions for many years. Their power and influence had become anachronistic, their only benefit being derived from the inspirations still provided to their few followers. By others embued with a different form of optimism, they were viewed as a continuing stumbling block to Republican unity and consequent victory.

In their defence, they had remained the voice of 1916 and had not let those around them, whether in or out of the movement, forget the ideas that the early leaders had espoused. Mary MacSwiney, in particular, had been the watchdog of all Republican activities, quickly pointing out ideological errors to those she felt had strayed. As De Valera himself had once admitted, she had remained his conscience.

For Mary personally, this decision ended her co-operation in organised Republican activities. Contrary to her belief that it was only through organisational effort that Republicanism would prevail, she was now completely divorced from such endeavours. Her best efforts had been given always but gradually they had been rejected. When the rejection was becoming clear, Mary departed from one group after another claiming ideological differences.

As the door closed on this last organisational involvement, it did not keep out the sound of Mary's continued recriminations against the activities of the state. The coming of war, which she believed inevitable, caused her to issue continual advice, insisting that Ireland remain neutral and eliminate 'the humbug that makes a virtue of Irishmen supporting every cause England favours'. In her truth, the converse was more accurate.[94] Ireland's defence system 'should be directed to the protection of that neutrality against all outsiders including England'.[95]

The partition issue was also expanded upon. Eamon de Valera was putting forth the argument that the unambiguous acceptance of the British Empire was a means of getting the north to accept unity. Mary saw this as an argument of 'slave-minded Irishmen who persisted in thinking the British Empire sacrosanct',[96] maintaining that the real issue was the recognition of the Republic in which there was no border.[97] Mary's personal belief was that the current anti-partition talk among the British was because they wanted Ireland as 'one unit for defence purposes' and as soon as the current crisis passed England would 'let her poor tools in the six counties down as easily as she let puppet state Czechoslovakia down a few weeks ago'.[98] The old slogan was rejuvenated that England's difficulty was Ireland's opportunity.

During the last months of 1938, Mary gave all energy to increasing Irish awareness of the inherent dangers in becoming involved in England's war. Letters were written and public lectures given including one in Cork City Hall with Mary MacSwiney the featured speaker.[99] On every possible occasion, she pointed to the Fianna Fáil leadership as ever increasing the bonds of Empire, citing such examples as British airmen using and testing Irish airports; the improvement of Irish ports: De Valera receiving athletes from Britain and Northern Ireland as one united; finally 'banquets wasted' on American Ambassdor to England Joseph Kennedy who Mary referred to as British Ambassador Kennedy because his efforts were aimed 'to fool the Irish in America into withdrawing their opposition to an Anglo-American alliance'.[100]

When the Second World War broke out in Europe, Mary felt great relief when Eamon de Valera maintained Irish neutrality often despite great pressure and intimidation from the governments of the allies. It would be impossible to measure the influence that Mary's words had on the decision, but she personally rested more comfortably knowing her best effort had been given. After many years of disagreement, she and De Valera had found some common ground.

As the war in Europe was beginning, the IRA seized the opportunity to bring more confusion to the British with the initiation of a bombing campaign in England. These events had not taken Mary by surprise. As a mark of respect for her long work on behalf of the Republic, Seán Russell, the IRA leader, had travelled to Cork to explain the campaign, its plans and ramifications to her. He spread the maps out on her desk, indicating where the attacks would come. Mary hesitated with her approval momentarily fearing for the innocent lives that would be lost. This was war, however, the Irish had made their blood sacrifices over many generations, and now the battle-ground was to shift locations. The Army leader left Belgrave Square with Mary's approval, blessing and fervent hope that the Republic would prevail.[101]

The explanation for this approval was made clear:

I am no advocate of shooting if it can be avoided; again I remind you that Republicans did not initiate or desire the horrible war forced on them in June 1922. But while Ireland has young men, Mr Frank Aiken or any successor of his will get recruits to stand for full freedom of Ireland and no shams. They know little of Irish history who think otherwise.[102]

Despite Irish neutrality, the war years brought extensive censorship to the Irish press. J. J. O'Kelly fretted because Republicans were unable to 'get a line into the Irish press and private printing fees were prohibitive'.[103] Republican activities were severely curtailed, an example coming in Cork when people were not allowed into City Hall to sign a clemency petition for Tomás MacCurtain and known Republican activists were once again being rounded up and detained. Mary's letters to newspaper editors were either rejected or severely censored when she continued to question the motivations of De Valera and his government.[104]

By 1940, her health, even more than government watchdogs, was curtailing her activities. Medical advice was rest for her diseased heart and kidneys and although she wished otherwise, loss of physical energy imposed its own restrictions. Annie MacSwiney confided to J. J. O'Kelly the difficulty in trying to limit her older sister's activity. He responded: 'It is Máire's very nature to respond in every fibre of her being to every throb of the national travail.'[105]

Ill health claimed Mary's life slowly as she spent most of 1941 struggling on a day-to-day basis. Throughout the time her mind remained clear, she followed the condition of the state as closely as possible but now her support was limited mostly to prayer.

Mary MacSwiney died in her home on 8 March 1942. At her bedside were sister Annie, niece Máire Óg and a priest to give her Extreme Unction. Even on her death bed she retained the spunk and spirit that had characterised her life. While the priest sought to initiate her into a third order of a religious community, she shook her head violently and made motions to her family. Máire Óg stepped forward and after some consultation with her dying aunt, told the priest that Mary was already a Third Order Benedictine so there was no need to repeat the investiture. This final battle won, after so many lost, Mary MacSwiney died.[106]

Conclusion

After a funeral mass at St Patrick's Church attended by only family members and a few close friends, Mary MacSwiney was buried in St Joseph's Cemetery, Cork. The private ceremony was a response to Mary's request that she be given a quiet burial, devoid of public displays, the lone exception to her directive being a brief oration given at the grave by Brian O'Higgins. In what she believed would be her sister's wish, Annie MacSwiney declined Eamon de Valera's request that his representative be present. To respect her desire for simplicity, the tombstone erected bears only Mary's name and dates, in contrast to the much grander monument nearby in Terence's memory. Even in death, Mary wished to remain in the shadow of her brother, claiming only reflected recognition.[1]

Although an elaborate funeral ceremony and procession were lacking, Mary was eulogised in letters written by friends and in national and international press statements. Long time friend, J. J. O'Kelly, wrote concisely: 'There is no finer groundwork for the true story of the Republican movement than Mary's life.'[2] Professor Stockley, another friend, supporter and confidant, recognised his colleague's dedication to the Republic: 'They never fail who are in a great cause.'[3] The *Cork Examiner*, long unsympathetic to Republican issues, carried a lengthy obituary detailing Mary's life concluding in summary: 'Two great traits marked her personality. The first was her sincerity in all she did and said, and the second her steadfast adherence to her ideals. Because of these she was admired as much by her political opponents as by those who followed her cause.'[4] The paper may have been reaching for praise with the words about Mary's opponents, but was following to an exemplary degree the Irish custom of only speaking well of the dead.

The Irish World in New York, long converted to De Valerism, nostalgically recalled the woman it had supported in the early 1920s: 'Mary MacSwiney hated sham and openly dared the tyrant. She believed in logic and never departed from principle to accommodate expediency.' The article praised her as one who 'possessed a brilliant mind' while being 'brave (and) inflexible in truth'.[5] The *New York Times* carried a lengthy obituary, detailing Mary's efforts on behalf of the Republic, with emphasis on her American tours. By contrast, *The Times* of London ran a scant three lines in which the passing of a Republican activist was noted. Mary would not have been surprised by this lack of interest from the paper in which she had been so frequently denounced, as had her brother Terence, and their mutual mission. Many who knew or cared little for Mary's theories on Ireland, remembered at least her remarkable speaking abilities. A friend recounted the words of Countess Markievicz: 'I spoke for an hour and a quarter without difficulty. I'll keep adding to my speech from day to day and when I get back to Madison Square Garden I'll be able to speak for two hours and rival Mary MacSwiney.'[6]

Others remembered her more as a teacher than as a political activist – a teacher who sought to correct the untruths she perceived the British and Irish West Britons had perpetrated upon her countrymen for centuries. She taught Ireland's cultural heritage, exalting the Gaelic language as well as the justice of the ancient Brehon Laws. She was not limited to the Ireland of long ago, however, illustrating her topical interests with her refusal to recognise the 1921 partition. During a geography examination written by Free State officers, she changed a question that read 'Name the counties that border Norther Ireland' to 'Name the counties that border the province of Ulster'. The corrected question was returned to the examiners with a note explaining that 'the children of Scoil Ita would never be taught the geography of their country after the insolent Act of an alien Parliament'.[7] Throughout her many years of teaching it is unestimable how many had their consciousness raised concerning Nationalist issues by Mary MacSwiney.

Mary's influence on the role of women in Ireland went beyond providing formal education for her students. Those sent to her were encouraged to pursue careers in male dominated fields as Mary took pride in the number of St Ita's graduates entering medical and law schools. To illustrate women's ability to participate in the world outside the home and to compete successfully, she led by example. Though her teaching career was one traditionally engaged in by women, upon entering the world of politics she was in a situation unfamiliar to most Irish women. Here she functioned well and authoritatively, never shirking responsibility while becoming one of the most important voices in Sinn Féin. Her continual speechmaking and proliferative letter writing, made her a public figure of influence.

Beyond this, the signals she sent were somewhat mixed. She maintained the conviction that any woman could achieve whatever she desired on the basis of hard work and perseverance, a perception that did a disservice to future generations of Irish women. By refusing to acknowledge both legal and social barriers to the advancement of women, Mary gave credence to the misconception that there was no need for a feminist movement in Ireland, a belief she reiterated in 1921. She failed to take into account the legal subordination of women in such areas as pensions, jobs, reproductive issues, property rights, divorce and child custody as well as the discrimination prevalent in education and entry into prestigious professions. In her own life she had followed the career path she desired, consequently believing that any other woman could do the same. There was no sensitivity to the plight of women less determined, intelligent, or single-minded than she, or that it took special women to obtain that which was available to ordinary men. She also accepted the traditional role of women as home makers and child care providers, following the lead of celebrated feminist John Stuart Mill, who believed women naturally suited to such assignments. This acceptance occurred in Mary's personal life, as she took up housekeeping tasks in deference to her brothers and in public life with Cumann na mBan. Though believing their denotation as 'camp-followers' to be scurrilous, nonetheless she accepted unquestioningly the supportive role of the women's organisation. Mary had never spent time considering the specific roles assigned to each task, believing she held the grander view that each should serve Ireland in whatever task was asked or was at hand. The grander view proved to be detrimental to future generations of Irish feminists as they had to wage continual battle to reverse these stereotypical images legitimised by an activist such as Mary MacSwiney. Women continued to be viewed as those who carry out men's orders, tending to the 'less important' housekeeping details, thus freeing men's time to pursue the affairs of state, business and the larger world outside the home.

Mary had chosen to channel her attention away from women's rights issues in favour of Nationalism. One might speculate that if she had gone on in the women's movement her consciousness would have been sufficiently raised to include a broader spectrum of women's rights. Although not totally improbable, this seems unlikely, as she never challenged the Catholic Church's pronouncements concerning women and continually placed women's issues as secondary to Nationalist aspirations. Considering the manner in which her mind persevered on most matters once she had committed herself, it seem unlikely that she would have adopted a full slate of feminist concerns.

Mary's dedication to and predictions about the Republic remain notable and prophetic. Though the Republic of Ireland was declared in 1948, this would not have appeased her as it still lacked the six northern counties. In 1940 she wrote: 'Mr de Valera said that partition was the only main issue left between Ireland and England. That is false. The issue of independence is more important and as the greater, it includes the less.'[8] The present situation of violence in Northern Ireland gives credence to her prediction that compromising would only bode ill for Ireland while her insistence that an issue was not settled until it is settled completely is borne out daily in the streets of Belfast and Derry. One might conjecture that if her views had prevailed in 1921, before Ireland was divided, a long term settlement, agreeable to all could have been achieved. It may have involved a prolongation of the Anglo-Irish war but may well have been settled within years, rather than stretching into decades as has been the case. Though many believed, both then and now that concessions were necessary, Mary looked at the situation in historical perspective, realising that all efforts at compromise by the Irish had led to their continued subjugation.

Though Mary's dream of a Republic for all of Ireland has not come to pass, she influenced to some immeasurable degree the direction taken by the leaders of the Free State. Though certainly not representative of a majority of Irish citizens, her constant criticism of those in power and her continual challenge to them to recognise the Republic of 1916 kept this issue before the public and the public's elected representatives. De Valera referred to Mary as his conscience, others labelled her the conscience of Republicanism, while still others attributed to her this role for all of Ireland. While having no ambition to secure meaningless titles, Mary was concerned with the effects she could produce among her opponents. Government leaders knew that she would remain a thorn in their sides, constantly prodding, harping and nagging them towards fulfilment of her Republican dream. Her high public profile, coupled with the respect her family had gained through their sacrifices for Ireland, did not go unnoticed or unappreciated even if many grew weary of Mary's perpetual rantings. Government leaders, including Cosgrave, De Valera, O'Higgins and Mulcahy, did not ignore the challenges she presented but rather engaged in verbal skirmishes, perhaps understanding that to ignore her would lessen their own credibility but through such attention giving further legitimacy to her cause. Mary's never ending criticisms of the government helped at least to keep those in power continuing to pursue a more independent Ireland.

Some people believe that Mary MacSwiney left a further legacy to her countrymen – one of intolerance and militarism under the banner of no compromise. Seen in retrospect, hers may have been the best posture to assume in 1921, to hold out for a free, united Ireland but it has turned out to be counter-productive over time. Once a divided Ireland was recognised by the international community and by many Irish themselves, the 'no compromise' doctrine fuelled a policy of hatred in Northern Ireland, becoming so entrenched that neither side believes it can make meaningful concessions without suffering rejection of principles, or forgetting their martyred dead. Subsequently, all efforts at reaching a political solution to Ireland's problems have come to naught, as the art of politics recognises the need for compromise. As late as November 1983, in Northern Ireland, Sinn Féin reiterated its policy not to take their seats in the British parliament when elected. Mary MacSwiney would have applauded this reaffirmation of her long held belief that any co-operation with the British government was to the detriment of Ireland. Today such intransigence produces more sectarian hatred and violence, underscoring the need for mutual compromise if a solution is to be found and peace established.

In the United States, Mary's legacy lives on among the small but vocal and financially supportive followers of Sinn Féin and the IRA. Just as in Ireland, the majority of Irish-Americans followed the path of Republican moderation blazed by Eamon de Valera. Similarly, as Mary MacSwiney retained influence over a small, hard core group of doctrinaire Republicans in Ireland, this was repeated in the United States. She was the first person so committed to tour so successfully in America, with the result that her name and her message were long remembered by a small but solid corps of believers. Following Mary's last tour, her message was reiterated primarily by members of the IRA, many notable and persuasive orators in their own right, who built on the foundations she had laid. Just as during the tour of 1921, Irish sympathisers continue to give large sums of money to be used at the discretion of the radical Republican leadership. Then, as now, in many cases this financial generosity has been accompanied by an incomplete knowledge or understanding of the issues involved, being given in a sentimental spirit of national pride in the ancestral homeland. Then, as now, all guilt and responsibility is removed from Irish shoulders and placed firmly and squarely on those of the British. This assuaging of guilt, clearing of one's Nationalist conscience through monetary gifts and rejection of responsibility were the appeals of Mary MacSwiney in 1921 and 1925 and are echoed today by her ideological descendants.

Mary's interaction with the Church retained elements of a love-hate relationship. Because the hierarchy had continually scorned Republicanism, Mary was repeatedly at odds with Catholic leaders, insisting that they stay in the pulpit and out of politics, saying: 'We are willing to be your most obedient subjects when you interpret the law of God but we will defy you when you seek to impose the law of England on us.'[9] She had fought a long, complicated court battle against Bishop Cohalan for his attempts to discredit her character, finally dropping the suit in 1932 on advice from her attorney who reported that they had reached an ecclesiastical stone wall. In agreeing to go no further, Mary remained fierce, commenting to the Apostolic Nuncio in Dublin: 'I wish to state definitely that I do not willingly submit to the suppression of (the case).'[10] Mary's challenges to the hierarchy generally went the way of her challenges to the Free State and then to De Valera, few taking up her cause. Though she gave an example of questioning, the general mood of the Irish towards the hierarchy has remained one of docility with their teachings being generally heeded as exemplified in the mother and child health care issue of the early 1950s, the constitutional amendment referendum on abortion in 1983, and the divorce referendum in 1986.

With regard to religious teachings of the Church, Mary was unwavering in faith to the point of being offensive to Irish Protestants. Her attitude, denoting the superiority of Catholicism, was and remains a popular force which leads northern Protestants to fear the consequences of popery should all Ireland be united. As in other matters, Mary subscribed to unity on her own Catholic terms, hardly a mind set conducive to co-operation or tolerance.

Mary's personality, as with her contributions to Ireland, was complex and sometimes even contradictory. To those who knew her personally, she was a warm, loving woman full of good humour and intelligence. She spent her life giving of herself to others, her family, her students, her Ireland, with no hint of personal scandal being found in her life, her closets being strangely bare of skeletons. The early dedication of her life to God seems to have excluded from her future any type of sexual relationship with men. Though no formal vow was taken, celibacy was her chosen path, or perhaps the only path that she saw, thus, while having many men among her friends and colleagues, she thought of them, as her niece reported, 'only from the neck up'.[11] Mary subscribed fully to the Church's teaching regarding female purity and morality, being an extreme moral conservative perhaps as a fitting counter-balance to her political views. This moral rigidity was a suitable outcome of the Victorian era into which she was born and the Irish-Catholic environment in which she was raised. Perhaps her moral and political beliefs both serve to illustrate her intolerance for half-measures, her inability to waver from strict literal interpretations and her disgust of situational ethics. Her actions and responses were comparatively easy and predictable as she saw things clearly in terms of black and white, right and wrong, with no possibility for various shades of colour or interpretation. Such tunnel vision did not make her life easy but it certainly eased decision-making while giving her complete confidence in the rightness of her responses.

Most assuredly, a strong directive for her activism came from her brother Terence whose death, she believed, had left her responsible for fulfilling his dream. Hers was the notion that if the dream went unfulfilled somehow the memory of Terence and his heroic death on hunger-strike would be lessened. As upon many others who died for Ireland such as Patrick Pearse and Erskine Childers, Mary bestowed instant sainthood, making them grander in death than in life, thus providing heroes for Irish Republicans to emulate. Because of her brother's example and Pearse's call for a blood sacrifice if Ireland was to be free, Mary spent much of her life trying to achieve martyrdom, physically through hunger-strikes, ideologically through continual disregard of government directives. Though Mary's life ended without her Republican dream being realised, she died having realised the words of Terence: 'She was bereft and she was then found marvellously true.'[12]

Notes

Introduction
1. Ernest Gellner, *Nations and Nationalism*, Cornell University Press, 1982, p. 1.

1. From Suffragist to Nationalist
1. Interview with Máire Brugha, Terence MacSwiney's only child.
2. University College, Dublin Archives, MacSwiney Papers, P48a/3, letter.
3. P48a/300(2), personal notes.
4. Lawrence J. McCaffrey, *The Irish Question, 1800-1922*, University of Kentucky Press, Lexington, 1968, p. 130.
5. C. Butler, *Benedictine Manachism*, London, 1919, pp. 76 and 90.
6. *New Catholic Encyclopedia*, McGraw-Hill, New York, 1967, Vols. 2, 10, 14.
7. Carlton Younger, *Arthur Griffith*, Gill and Macmillan, Dublin 1981, p. 23.
8. See McCaffrey, *op.cit.* and F. S. L. Lyons, *Ireland Since the Famine*, London, 1973.
9. See Moirin Chavasse, for the most thorough biography of Terence MacSwiney.
10. P48a/462, memoir.
11. *Irish Citizen*, 11 July 1914.
12. *Ibid.*
13. *Irish Citizen*, 2 August 1913; see also Mary Daly, *Social and Economic History of Ireland Since 1800*, Dublin, 1981.
14. *Irish Citizen*, 20 March 1915.
15. *Irish Citizen*, 20 Feb. 1915.
16. *Irish Citizen*, 17 Jan. 1914.
17. *Irish Citizen*, 4 July 1914.
18. P48a/300(2). See also George Dangerfield, *The Strange Death of Liberal England*, Granada, London, 1983; *The Damnable Question*, Constable, London, 1976, p. 33.
19. *Irish Citizen*, 23 May 1914.
20. *Irish Citizen*, 9 May, 1914.
21. P48a/300(2).
22. *Irish Citizen*, 11 April 1914.
23. *Irish Citizen*, 2 May 1914.
24. *Irish Citizen*, 2 May 1914.
25. *Irish Citizen*, 23 May 1914.
26. P48a/300a.
27. *Ibid.*

28. P48a/300(2).
29. Margaret Ward, *Unmanageable Revolutionaries*, Brandon, Co. Kerry, 1983, p. 95.
30. P48a/8(2).
31. P48a/8(260) and P48a/8(12).
32. P48a/14.
33. P48a/8(12) – Cumann na mBan leaflet.
34. See James Plunkett, *Farewell Companions*, Arrow, London, 1977.
35. *Irish Citizen*, 14 Nov. 1914.
36. *Irish Citizen*, 21 Nov. 1914 – Mary's letter to the editor.
37. *Irish Citizen*, 21 Nov. 1914.
38. *Ibid.*
39. Statement from the leadership of the Volunteers as quoted in F. X. Martin, *The Irish Volunteers, 1913-1915*, James Duffy and Co., 1963, p. 154.
40. P48a/300(2)
41. David Fitzpatrick, *Politics and Irish Life*, Gill and Macmillan, Dublin, 1977, appendix.
42. *Ibid.*, p. 94.
43. Dorothy Macardle, *The Irish Republic*, Corgi, London, 1968, p. 123.
44. *Ibid.*
45. Quoted in Macardle, p. 128.
46. *Irish Citizen*, 25 July 1914.
47. *Irish Citizen*, 11 April 1914.
48. Interview with Mrs Tyrrell.
49. See Frank O'Connor, *An Only Child*.
50. P48a/300(2).
51. W. Allison Phillips, *The Revolution in Ireland*, London, 1926, p. 86.
52. *Ibid.*, p. 88.
53. Fitzgerald, p. 109.
54. Terence MacSwiney, *Principles of Freedom*, Kennikat Press, Port Washington, New York, 1970, p. 118. First published, 1921.

2. *Martyrdoms, 1916-1920*
1. Fitzpatrick, p. 7.
2. Macardle, p. 133.
3. Macardle, p. 135
4. Maureen Wall, 'The Plans and Countermand, the Country and Dublin' in *The Making of 1916*, K. Nowlan, ed., Stationery Office, Dublin, 1969, p. 204.
5. Interview with Mrs Brugha.
6. Interview in the *Washington Times*, 11 Dec. 1920.
7. Chavasse, p. 50.
8. Chavasse, p. 59.
9. Chavasse, pp. 60-1.
10. P48a/462.
11. P48a/462.

12. *Ibid.*
13. Retold by Mrs Maura Tyrrell who, as a student, was present during the arrest.
14. P48a/191.
15. Chavasse. pp. 64-68.
16. P48a/7(i).
17. P48a/74.
18. P48a/74
19. P48a/7(2).
20. *Ibid.*
21. P48a/74
22. P48a/78
23. *Ibid.*
24. P48a/7.
25. P48a/25(4).
26. P48a/25(3).
27. *Cork Free Press*, 29 July 1916.
28. P48a/27, letter to Bishop Cohalan.
29. Mrs Tyrrell and Mrs Brugha.
30. Retold by Mrs Tyrrell.
31. *Principles of Freedom*, p. 116.
32. P. 117
33. P48a/2(38).
34. P48a/31, Christmas Programme from St Ita's, 1916.
35. 48a/336.
36. P48a/368.
37. Lil Conlon, *Cumann na mBan and the Women of Ireland*, Kilkenny 1969, p. 37.
38. Macardle, p. 203.
39. Ronald McNeill, *Ulster's Stand for Union*, London, 1922, pp. 259-9.
40. Quoted in Macardle, p. 204.
41. Lil Conlon, p.59.
42. *Ibid.*, p. 64.
43. Jenny Wyse-Power, 'The Political Influence of Women in Modern Ireland,' in *Voices of Ireland*, William Fitzgerald, ed., Dublin, 1924, p. 159.
44. Quoted in Fitzpatrick, p. 30.
45. Interview with Mrs Tyrrell.
46. Conlon, p. 78.
47. Pamphlet, NLR, *Ireland Today*, Report by the Society of Friends, 5 Oct. 1920.
48. University College, Dublin, Archives, Richard Mulcahy Papers. P7/C/100 from lecture notes.
49. P48a/283, A Brief Report of the Work Done by the Agriculture Department, /Dáil Éireann 1919-20.
50. P48a/467.
51. Society of Friends Pamphlet.
52. Chavasse, p. 123 and Mrs Brugha.

53. Quoted in Chavasse, p. 130.
54. Chavasse, p. 145.
55. Chavasse, p. 145.
56. The most thorough treatment of the hunger-strike is that of Moirin Chavasse, *op. cit.*, as well as the hunger-strike file in the MacSwiney collection, University College, Dublin Archives.
57. Interview with Cathal Brugha.
58. *Cork Examiner*, 10 Sept. 1920.
59. P48a/110/1.
60. *New York Call*, 6 Sept. 1920.
61. P48a/436.
62. P48B/431. The letter was signed by Muriel, Mary and Annie MacSwiney but the draft is in Mary's handwriting.
63. Terence MacSwiney, pp. 20-1.
64. Bishop Cohalan, 1922; retold by Mrs Brugha.
65. Mary's response to Bishop Cohalan; Mrs Brugha.
66. P48B/429.
67. P48B/433.
68. P48B/433 re Short see *Hansard's Parliamentary Debates.* 20 Oct. 1920, p. 1052.
69. Interview with Mrs Brugha.
70. P48B/466(4), a draft lecture Mary delivered on *The Principles of Freedom.*

3. *The First American Tour, 1920-1921*

1. *Irish Times*, 26 Nov. 1920.
2. *New York Tribune*, 5 Dec. 1920.
3. Pamphlet, NLI, Hannah Sheehy Skeffington, *Impression of Sinn Féin in America.* Dublin, 1919.
4. *New York Tribune*, 5 Dec. 1920
5. P48b/449.
6. *New York World*, 8 Dec. 1920.
7. *New York Post*, 8 Dec. 1920.
8. *New York Times*, 9 Dec. 1920.
9. *New York Evening Post*, 8 Dec. 1920. See also the *Interim Report of the Committee on Conditions in Ireland – 1921.*
10. *New York Times*, 9 Dec. 1920.
11. *Washington Star*, 20 Dec. 1920.
12. *New York American*, 13 Dec. 1920.
13. See Patrick MacCartan, *With de Valera in America*, Dublin, 1932.
14. R. M. Fox, *Rebel Irishwomen*, Talbot Press, Dublin and Cork, 1935, pp. 66-67.
15. *New York Times*, 20 Dec. 1920.
16. *Boston Globe*, 20 Dec. 1920.
17. *Ibid.*
18. P48a/192(3).
19. P48a/192(5).

20. *Ibid.*
21. P48a/115(47)
22. P48a/292, copy of Bond Certificate of 2nd loan 26 August 1921.
23. P48a/115(3).
24. *Ibid.*
25. *Ibid.*
26. *Ibid.*
27. *Ibid.*
28. P48a/162-3, draft speech intended for publication.
29. P48a/171.
30. 17 March 1921.
31. 27 Feb. 1921.
32. 12 March 1921.
33. *San Francisco Examiner*, 11/12 March 1921.
34. P48a/115(14), cable to Father Peter Yorke.
35. P4358a/115(7), letter from Mary to O'Mara, 15 Feb. 1921.
36. P48a/9(5)
37. P48a/115(6), letter to Harry Boland, Feb. 1921.
38. P48a/9.
39. *Washington Times*, 11 Dec. 1920.
40. P48a/115(17).
41. P48a/115(7)
42. P48a/162-3.
43. P48a/225(47), letter of 20 July 1921.
44. P48a/115(3).
45. P48a/115(6).
46. P48a/9(5).
47. P48a/9(5).
48. *Ibid.*
49. *Ibid.*
50. *Ibid.*
51. P48a/398(21).
52. *Irish World*, 30 July 1921.

4. *The Civil War Years*

1. Quoted in Macardle, pp. 427-8.
2. Macardle, p. 431.
3. Macardle, p. 436.
4. For the best description see Macardle, parts 9 and 10. Much of the actual correspondence is cited.
5. P48a/300(5).
6. *Ibid.*
7. P48a/234(7).
8. P48a/9(7).
9. P48a/419(5) and interview with Mrs Brugha.

10. P48a/301.
11. Seán Cronin, *The McGarrity Papers*, Tralee, 1972, p. 111.
12. P48a/448(4).
13. P48a/239(6).
14. *Ibid.*
15. P48a/234(21).
16. P48a/448(19).
17. P48a/234(20).
18. P48a/300(5).
19. P48a/37(7).
20. P48a/300(5).
21. P48a/448(19).
22. P48a/226(6), letter to Joseph Scott in Los Angeles, 27 March 1922.
23. P48a/448(4).
24. Debate of Treaty, p. 110. Official Report, *Debate on the Treaty Between Great Britain and Ireland*, Dublin, 1922.
25. P48a/60(50). Letter to Anne MacSwiney.
26. Macardle, p. 567.
27. P48a/60(50).
28. *Debate on the Treaty*, pp. 110-111.
29. P48a/290(2).
30. P48a/416.
31. P48a/301, undated memoir.
32. P48a/441.
33. *Irish Independent*, 6 Feb. 1922.
34. Macardle, p. 598.
35. P48a/235(5).
36. P48a/400(12).
37. *Poblacht na h-Éireann*, 22 May 1922, letter signed by Margaret Pearse, Kathleen Clarke, Mary MacSwiney, Catherine O'Callaghan and Eithne Inglis.
38. P48a/448(6) – handwritten note for submission to the press.
39. P48a/419(2).
40. P48a/234 11/1.
41. P48a/441.
42. P48a/448(19).
43. P48a/113.
44. *Ibid.*
45. P48a/204 – copy of the sermon in unidentified newspaper clip.
46. *Cork Examiner*, Aug. 1922.
47. P48a/448(6).
48. *Irish Times*, 11 Oct. 1922.
49. State Paper Office, Dublin (SPO) S.1369/9.
50. *Morning Post*, 28 Oct. 1922.
51. Macardle, p. 737.
52. *Irish Independent*, 4 Nov. 1922.

53. *Irish Independent*, 6 Nov. 1922.
54. Letter from Mary to *Irish Independent*, 25 Nov. 1922.
55. *Poblacht na h-Éireann*, 7 Nov. 1922.
56. *Cork Examiner*, 13 Nov. 1922.
57. *Irish Times*, 9 Nov. 1922.
58. *Irish Times*, 20 Nov. 1922.
59. *Irish Independent*, 13 Nov. 1922.
60. *Irish Times*, 9, 18 Nov. 1922. *The Nation*, 21 Nov. 1922.
61. State Paper Office S.1369/9.
62. See State Paper Office S.1369/9.
63. State Paper Office S.1369/9 from Jamaica Council AARIR.
64. *Irish Independent*, 23 Nov. 1922.
65. *Irish Times*, 18, 25 Nov. 1922.
66. *Irish Times*, 21 Nov. 1922.
67. Mulcahy Papers, University College, Dublin Archives, P7a/179.
68. *Irish Independent*, 17, 25 Nov. 1922 and State Paper Office S.1394.
69. State Paper Office S.1369/9.
70. *Poblacht na h-Éireann*, 21 Nov. 1922.
71. State Paper Office S.1369/9.
72. *Ibid.*
73. *Ibid.*
74. *Ibid.*
75. *Irish Times*, 24 Nov. 1922.
76. *Irish Times*, 24 Nov. 1922.
77. *Irish Times*, 30 Nov. 1922.
78. National Library of Ireland, NLI, *Ghosts of Kilmainham*, Kilmainham Jail Restoration Society, 1963.
79. *Republican War Bulletin*, 2 December 1922.
80. *Irish Independent*, 26 April 1923.
81. *Irish Independent*, 28 Nov. 1922.
82. *Irish Times*, 23 Nov. 1922.
83. *Catholic Herald*, 2 Dec. 1922.
84. S. 1369/9.
85. *Ibid.*
86. P48a/417.
87. Interview with Mrs Brugha.
88. P48a/402(47) – draft of letter to the *Irish Press*.
89. *Irish Times*, 12 March 1922.
90. From letters between DeValera and Mary MacSwiney in the possession of Cathal Brugha.
91. *Ibid.*
92. *Ibid.*
93. See T. Ryle Dwyer. *De Valera's Darkest Hour*, Dublin, 1982, p. 136 and letters of Cathal Brugha.
94. *Ibid.*

95. S.1369/9.
96. S.1369/9.
97. *Ibid.*
98. *Ibid.*
99. *Ibid.*
100. *Irish Independent*, 24 April 1923.
101. Archbishop Byrne Papers, Holy Cross College, Dublin 172/2/54.
102. *Irish Catholic Directory* for 1923, p. 554.
103. Lily O'Brennan Papers, UCD Archives, P13/53.
104. *Ibid.*, P13/58.
105. *Irish Independent*, 3 May 1923 and Terence de Vere White, *Kevin O'Higgins*, Dublin, 1948, p. 182.
106. O'Brennan, P13/62.
107. *Irish Independent*, 1 May 1923.
108. *Irish Independent*, 2 May 1923.
109. Macardle, p. 774.
110. See Macardle, pp. 774-8.
111. Letter from De Valera to Mary MacSwiney, 9 May 1923, in the possession of Cathal Brugha.
112. Dwyer, *op. cit.*, p. 138.
113. Dwyer, *op. cit.*, p. 110.
114. Unidentified clip P7/b/224.
115. *Ibid.*
116. *Ibid.*
117. P7/B/224.
118. *Irish Times*, 23 Aug. 1923.
119. *Irish Times*, 23 July 1923.
120. *Irish Times*, 30 July 1923.
121. *Irish Times*, 11 Aug. 1923.
122. *Irish Times*, 30 July 1923.
123. P7/B/228, unidentified clip from 18 June 1923.
124. *Irish Independent*, 16 Nov. 1923.
125. Dwyer, p. 144.
126. P48a/448(20).
127. P48a/39(2).
128. P48a/39(2), To De Valera, 5 Aug. 1923.
129. P48a/236(11) note from Sinn Féin H.Q.
130. P48a/70 – address to Ard-Fheis.
131. P48a/70.
132. *Ibid.*
133. *Historical Studies X*, London, T. O'Neill, *Irish Republicanism, 1922-27*, p.161.
134. *Irish Independent*, 29 Nov. 1923.
135. Unidentified clip. P48a/231.
136. *Daily Sheet*, 14 Nov. 1923.

137. Clip from *Cork Examiner*, undated, P48a/231.
138. P48a/197(5).
139. P48a/290(24), TD's meeting outline.
140. P48a/426(1).
141. *Freeman's Journal*, 29 Jan. 1924.
142. P48a/427.
143. Letter to the editor, *Irish Independent*, 17 July 1923.
144. State Paper Office. Executive Council Minutes, 30 Nov. 1923, G2/3.
145. T. P. Coogan, *Ireland Since the Rising*, Pall Mall Press, London, 1966, p. 47.
146. *Ibid.*
147. J. Bowyer Bell, *The Secret Army*, Anthony Bland Ltd., London, 1970, p. 41.

5. *The Decline of Sinn Féin, 1924-1927*

1. *Irish Independent*, 8 March 1924.
2. P48a/21 – leaflet.
3. P48a/8(29).
4. Letter to the editor, The *Irish Statesman*, 7 Feb 1925.
5. *Ibid.*
6. P48a/406(7).
7. P48a/290 44 – Sinn Féin report and Peter Pyne, 'The Politics of Parliamentary Abstentionism: Ireland's Four Sinn Féin Parties, 1905-1926', in *Journal of Commonwealth Comparative Politics*, Vol. 12, no. 2 (1974), pp. 206-227. Pyne states that income had gone from £26,000 in 1923 to £17,000 in 1924-5. Also although the number of cumainn had risen to over 1000 in 1924 from 700 in 1923, 'almost a third of the 1,025 branches existing in June were unable to raise the affiliation fee by the time of the Ard-Fheis at the end of the year. Thus by November 1924 the party was slightly weaker in terms of the number of affiliated cumainn than it had been a year previously.'
8. P48a/290(44) – letter to Sinn Féin.
9. P48a/290(44).
10. P48a/299/23 – criticisms on draft constitution.
11. Draft of speech – P48a/299(27).
12. Copy of a letter to Seán, probably O'Kelly, P48a/228(4/2).
13. P48a/72/1.
14. *Irish Independent*, 12 March 1924.
15. *Irish Independent*, 8 March 1924.
16. Unidentified newspaper clip, Mulcahy Papers, P7/B/228.
17. P48a/405(1).
18. T. O'Neill, 'Irish Republicanism 1922-27', *Historical Studies X*. London: p. 158.
19. *The Leader*, 26 July 1924.
20. P48a/290(44) – notes from meeting of Second Dáil.
21. P48a/134.

22. P48a/134.
23. *Ibid.*
24. P48a/134(42) – letter to Ms Inness, Philadelphia.
25. Letter to Editor, *Irish Independent*, 18 Sept. 1923.
26. P48a/118(4)/1.
27. Notification – P48a/237(28).
28. *Irish Independent*, 1 Jan. 1925.
29. Letter from Peter Golden, 18 Jan. 1925, P48a/116(2)1.
30. Letter to editor, *New York Evening World*, 10 Sept. 1925.
31. Unidentified newspaper clip, P48a/189, folder 4, 1925 tour.
32. Letter to Joseph Scott in Los Angeles, P48a/121(15).
33. *Ibid.*
34. P48a/167, draft of 1925 speech.
35. Letter to Mary from Liam[?], 29 April 1925.
36. Diary in MacSwiney collection.
37. *Ibid.*
38. *Ibid.*
39. P48a/189, unidentified newspaper clip.
40. Letter to De Valera, 3 March 1925. P48a/119(47).
41. To De Valera, 24 April 1925. P48a/120(20).
42. To De Valera, 6 June 1925. P48a/120(44).
43. P48a/121(16)/7.
44. Letter to Sinn Féin, not for publication, 17 April 1925, P48a/397(11).
45. P48a/119(38).
46. To editor, *The Irish Statesman*, 19 Sept. 1925.
47. P48a/12111(18) – 9 July 1925.
48. The *Irish Statesman*, 19 Sept. 1925.
49. Letter to Seán O'Kelly, P48a/12111(18)/6.
50. P48a/34.
51. P48a/25(20).
52. *San Francisco Examiner*, 15 March 1925.
53. Official Census of Irish Free State, 1926.
54. *I.C.D.* – 1926 (for 1925), p. 558. From the Bishop's Lenten Pastoral.
55. Letter from Mary to the President, 19 Oct. 1925, P48a/238(3).
56. Proclamation of the Republic, quoted in full in Macardle, *op. cit.*, p. 155.
57. P48a/238(3).
58. *Ibid.*
59. Financial Agreement, 1925. Printed in full in Macardle, appendix 31.
60. Macardle, p. 812.
61. Letter from Eamonn Donnelly to Mary, 7 Feb. 1926, P48a/42(11).
62. Letter from De Valera to Mary, 10 Feb. 1926. P48a/42(13).
63. *Ibid.*
64. T. R. Dwyer, p. 155.
65. P48a/82(1).
66. Dwyer, p. 157.

67. *Ibid.*
68. Longford and O'Neill, *Eamon de Valera*, p. 242.
69. T. Ryle Dwyer, p. 157.
70. Letter to Mary, 29 March 1926, P48a/42(25).
71. Letter from Mary to Seán T. O'Kelly, 8 June 1926, P48a/136(10).
72. *Ibid.*
73. To editor, *Irish Independent*, 6 June 1926.
74. Letter to Dorothy Macardle, 26 April 1926, P48a/371(1).
75. Told to *Irish World*, 12 Sept. 1926.
76. Letter to brother Seán, 29 March 1926, P48a/360.
77. P48a/360.
78. P48a/57(17).
79. P48a/251(15).
80. *Irish World*, 24 April 1926.
81. P48a/42(52).
82. Mary's notes about Ard-Fheis – P48a/42(16).
83. P48a/297(3).
84. *Irish Times*, 18 Dec. 1926.
85. Countess Markievicz, *Prison Letters of Countess Markievicz*, New York, Longmans, 1934, p. 307.
86. P48a/37s(3).
87. Letter from New York, P48a/361.
88. *Ibid.*, 27 Oct. 1926.
89. *Irish World*, 9 Oct. 1926.
90. *Irish Statesman*, 13 Nov. 1926.
91. From IRA in New York – P48aa/124(24).
92. P48a/124.
93. Letter from Illinois AARIR, P48a/124(29).
94. Interview with Mrs Brugha.
95. P48a/361.
96. *Irish Freedom*, April 1927.
97. Count Plunkett to Mary, 10 Sept. 1926, P48a/42(44).
98. *Irish Freedom*, April 1927.
99. P48a/43(34) – Letter from Peadar O'Donnell to the Secretary, Sinn Féin. 27 April 1927, P48a/43(34).
100. P48a/43(32).
101. *Ibid.*.
102. P48a/43(30).
103. *Irish Freedom*, May 1927.
104. See Tom Garvin, *The Evolution of Nationalist Politics*, Gill and Macmillan, Dublin, 1981.
105. Letter to Michael Ua Domhnaill, 25 April 1927.
106. P48a/43(37).
107. P48a/43(50), 14 May 1927.
108. *Irish Statesman*, 14 May 1927.

109. Draft letter to the editor, *Irish Independent*, 25 April 1927.
110. *An Phoblact*, 8 Oct. 1927.
111. P48a/62(50), 16 June 1927.
112. *Irish Freedom*, July 1927.
113. 14 June 1927, P48a/62(6).
114. Draft of a letter, P48a/398(28).
115. P48a/62(18).
116. P48a/62, letter to Sinn Féin workers.

6. The Battle for Republicanism

1. P48a/125(16) – letter dated 29 Dec. 1927, recipient not indicated.
2. *An Phoblacht*, 3 Sept. 1927.
3. *An Phoblacht*, 29 Oct. 1927.
4. *An Phoblacht*, 22 Oct. 1927.
5. *An Phoblacht*, 12 Nov. 1927.
6. *An Phoblacht*, 9 Nov. 1927.
7. *An Phoblacht*, 29 Oct. 1927.
8. *An Phoblacht*, 26 May 1928.
9. *An Phoblacht*, 27 Oct. 1928.
10. *An Phoblacht*, 21 Jan. 1928.
11. P48a/57(17a).
12. *An Phoblacht*, 8 Sept. 1928.
13. P48a/363, recollections, 1928.
14. *An Phoblacht*, 16 June 1928 and P48a/44(3).
15. *An Phoblacht*, Dec. 1928.
16. P48a/44(2).
17. P48a/363(22).
18. P48a/44(5), letter of 8 Sept. 1928.
19. *An Phoblacht*, 22 Dec. 1928.
20. J. Bowyer Bell, *The IRA*, Academy Press, Dublin, revised edition 1979, p. 78.
21. Copy of the Constitution in MacSwiney Papers. P48a/268.
22. *Irish Times*, 22 Jan. 1929.
23. *Irish Times*, 25 Jan. 1929.
24. Bell, p. 78.
25. *An Phoblacht*, 22 Dec. 1928.
26. *An Phoblacht*, 12 May 1928.
27. P48a/364, p. 64.
28. *Irish Freedom*, August 1928.
29. P7/B224 – unidentified clip, 10 June 1928.
30. P48a/356, to USA, 10 Oct. 1939.
31. P48a/365, p. 76.
32. P48a/241(3).
33. P48a/252(1), dated 27 Oct. 1929.
34. P48a/362.
35. P48a/25(23), report on school.

36. P48a/366, 7-30 Oct.
37. *An Phoblacht*, 13, 6 July 1929.
38. *An Phoblacht*, 1 Feb. 1930.
39. P48a/362.
40. Interview with Mrs Brugha and P48aa/362.
41. P48a/58(10), copy of letter to Sceilig, 1 Jan. 1929.
42. *An Phoblacht*, 5 May 1928.
43. *Irish Freedom*, June 1928.
44. *Ibid.*
45. *Southern Star*, 28 July 1928.
46. P48a/126(2)/1, to Daithí Ceannt, 4 Feabhra 1928.
47. *An Phoblacht*, 12 May 1928.
48. P48a/45, letter to Prof. Stockley, 16 May 1929.
49. P48a/201(22), draft letter, 16 Dec. 1926.
50. *Irish World*, 14 June 1830.
51. P48a/242(i).
52. *An Phoblacht*, 6 Dec. 1930.
53. P48a/242(i).
54. See unpublished M.A. thesis, University College Dublin, 1982, Mary Banta, *The Red Scare in the Irish Free State, 1929-37.*
55. P48a/404(17), draft response to Joint Pastoral; P48a/47(1), Sinn Féin statement, 27 Oct. 1931.
56. S.P.O. S6005/17, copy of letter dated 8 May 1930.
57. P48a/386(4), 24 Aug. 1931.
58. *Cork Examiner*, 4 Jan 1933.
59. *The Catholic Mind*, Feb. 1933.
60. S.P.O., G2/8, 1 Dec. 1931.
61. *An Phoblacht*, 8 March 1930.
62. S.P.O., S5864, 1 Sept. 1931.
63. *Republican File*, Nov. 1930.
64. *Republican File*, Jan. 1931.
65. Murphy, p. 66.
66. P48a/386(5), draft letter, 31 Dec. 1931.
67. *Cork Examiner*, 28 Nov. 1931.
68. Letter to Professor Stockley, 16 May 1929, P48a/45.
69. *Ibid*
70. See Ronan Fanning, *Independent Ireland*, Helecon Ltd, Dublin, 1983, for a concise description of this period.
71. *Irish Press*, 14 Jan. 1932.
72. *An Phoblacht*, 12 March 1932.
73. *An Phoblacht*, 12 March 1932.
74. Fanning, *op. cit.*

7. *Solitude in Intransigence, 1932-1942*

  1. P48a/48(9).

2. P48a/48(10), 4 March 1932.
3. P48a/48(11).
4. P48a/48(14).
5. P48a/48(18;, circular from Sinn Féin Headquarters.
6. P48a/48(40).
7. P48a/201(19).
8. P48a/59, 2 Feb. 1932.
9. P48a/387(7).
10. P48a/252(4), to Dev, 6 June 1932.
11. Interview with Máire Óg, Mrs Brugha.
12. P48a/59(20), letter to J. J. O'Kelly, 8 June 1932.
13. *Ibid.*
14. *Irish Freedom*, Feb. 1933.
15. P48a/49(3), letter 12 April 1933.
16. *Irish World*, 17 June 1933.
17. *Irish Independent*, 24 July 1933.
18. P48a/404(49), draft letter to editor.
19. P48a/59(30), letter dated 8 June 1933.
20. P48a/59(29), letter dated only 1933.
21. *An Phoblacht*, 12 May 1923.
22. *An Phoblacht*, 24 June 1933.
23. P48a/17.
24. *Ibid.*
25. *Ibid.*
26. P48a/20(49).
27. P48a/17.
28. P48a/20(23), letter to Síghle[?], 6 June 1933.
29. P48a/10(20).
30. P48a/10(20).
31. *An Phoblacht*, 25 June 1933.
32. P48a/59(32), letter Sceilig, 20 Nov. 1933.
33. *Ibid.*
34. P48a/59(29), J. J. to Mary, 15 Oct. 1933.
35. P48a/53(39), to Sinn Féin, 3 Dec. 1933.
36. P48a/11(3)/5, Constitution of Mná na Poblachata.
37. P48a/11(3)/3, letter of 1 Nov. 1933.
38. *Ibid.*
39. P48a/11(3)/11, Mary to Eibhlín, 6 Dec. 1933.
40. *Ibid.*
41. *Ibid.*
42. P48a/389(1), letter to *Cork Examiner*, 24 Sep. 1934.
43. *An Phoblacht*, 24 Feb. 1934.
44. *An Phoblacht*, 25 Aug. 1934.
45. *An Phoblacht*, 25 Aug. 1934.
46. P48a/389(5), draft letter to *Cork Examiner*, 23 March 1934.

47. *An Phoblacht*, 13 Jan. 1934.
48. P48a/60(2), to Sceilig, 2 Feb. 1934.
49. P48a/246(4), letter from Seán Ó Diorcun, to Joint Conference, 18 May 1934.
50. P48a/62(44).
51. P48a/50(9), draft letter 23 Oct. 1934.
52. P48a/50(8), 18 Oct. 1934.
53. P15/7, Mary to Caitlín Brugha, 17 Oct. 1934 – Caitlín Brugha Papers, University College, Dublin.
54. *An Phoblacht*, 25 April 1936.
55. *An Phoblacht*, 29 April 1934.
56. *An Phoblacht*, 6 Jan. 1934.
57. P48a/252(17)
58. P48a/51(2), 18 Oct. 1935, note from Sinn Féin to Óglaigh na h-Éireann.
59. P48a/252(17), Brian O'Higgins to Mary, 13 June 1935.
60. P48a/252(16), to O'Higgins, 9 June 1935.
61. P48a/199(5), 24 Jan. 1935.
62. P48a/300(2).
63. *An Phoblacht*, 26 Jan. and 4 May 1935, 24 Nov. 1934.
64. P48a/390(5), draft of a letter to the editor, 24 May 1935.
65. *An Phoblacht*, 14 March 1936.
66. State Paper Office, S8987, official statement.
67. *An Phoblacht*, 23 May 1936.
68. P48a/257(1), 2 May 1936.
69. P48a/139(1), to Seán T., 22 May 1936.
70. P48a/257(4), 22 June 1936.
71. P48a/257(4), 30 June 1936.
72. *Irish Independent*, 6 Aug. 1936.
73. *Irish Press*, 12 Aug. 1936.
74. *Irish Independent*, 15 Aug. 1936.
75. 48. P48a/248(6), to Sceilig, 30 Sep. 1936.
76. *Irish Press*, 27 Oct. 1936.
77. P48a/248(6), to Sceilig, 30 Sep. 1936.
78. *Irish Press*, 22 Aug. 1936.
79. *An Phoblacht*, 13 June 1936.
80. P48a/392(17), Second Dáil Statement, 9 Oct. 1936.
81. P48a/403(17).
82. P48a/354(2).
83. *The Commonweal*, 16 July 1937.
84. Quoted in Ward, p. 239. For a further discussion of the reaction of women's organisations see Ward, pp. 237-245.
85. P48a/393(1), letter to Dorothy Macardle, 5 May 1937.
86. P48a/393(8), to Peadar O'Donnell, 10 Feb. 1937.
87. P48a/53(2), letter from Secretary, 11 Nov. 1937.
88. P48a/394(9), Mary to Executive Committee of Cumann na mBan, 28 March 1938.

89. Mary to Sceilig, 2 Feb. 1938, P48a/60(37).
90. P48a/57(1), draft letter, Jan. 1938.
91. P48a/250(2), to Sceilig, 3 March 1938.
92. P48a/302(56), statement of 5 May 1938.
93. P48a/202(32).
94. P48a/403(9), draft article.
95. P48a/403(26).
96. *Irish Independent*, 17 Nov. 1938.
97. P48a/394(15), draft to editor, 21 Oct. 1938.
98. *Irish Independent*, 26 Oct. 1938.
99. *Cork Evening Echo*, 14 Oct. 1938.
100. *Cork Evening Echo*, 3 Aug. 1938.
101. Interview with Mrs Brugha.
102. P48a/404(39), unidentified sheet of paper.
103. P48a/60(51), 17 Feb. 1940.
104. P48a/396.
105. P48a/60(49).
106. Interview with Mrs Brugha.

Conclusion

1. *Cork Examiner*, 9, 10, 11 March 1942, and interview with Mrs Burgha.
2. P48a/60(58), letter to Annie, 1 Jan 1943.
3. P48a/56(2), letter to Annie, 1943.
4. *Cork Examiner*, 9 March 1942.
5. *Irish World*, 4 April 1942.
6. P48a/60(54), Sceilig to Mary, June 1941.
7. P48a/333, Annie's reminiscences.
8. P48a/200(12) to Cardinal MacRory, 27 June 1940.
9. P48a/402(10), undated memo.
10. P48a/197(83), Mary's correspondence with the Holy See in Rome, her attorney and Paschal Robinson, Papal Nuncio in Dublin.
11. Interview with Mrs Brugha.
12. Terence MacSwiney, p. 121.

Bibliography

Primary Sources

Manuscripts

University College Dublin, Archives:
    Caitlín Brugha Papers.
    Máire Comerford Papers.
    Mary MacSwiney Papers.
    Richard Mulcahy Papers.
    Lily O'Brennan Papers.
National Library of Ireland, Dublin:
    Austin Stack Papers.
Holy Cross College, Dublin:
    Archbishop Byrne Papers.
State Paper Office, Dublin:
    Provisional Government Minutes.
    Executive Council Minutes.
        Both with accompanying S. Files.

Official Publications

Debate on the Treaty Between Great Britain and Ireland – 1922. Official Record.
Hansard's Parliamentary Debates. London, 1920.
Irish Catholic Directory, Dublin, 1922-1935.
Official Census of the Irish Free State, Dublin, 1926.

Interviews – all with author

Cathal Brugha, November, 1983.
Máire Brugha, October, November, 1983.
Rúarí Brugha, October, November, 1983.
Maura Tyrrell, November, 1983.

Pamphlets
Constitution of the Republic of Ireland (1929).
Ghosts of Kilmainham (1963).
Hannah Sheehy-Skeffington, *Impressions of Sinn Féin in America* (1919).
Interim Report of the Committee on Conditions in Ireland, 1921.
The Society of Friends, *Ireland Today* (1920)

Newspapers
An Phoblacht, 1923-1936.
An t-Ólgach, 1931.
Beacon Journal (Akron), 1921, 1925
Boston Globe, 1920, 1921, 1925.
Catholic Herald, 1922, 1923, 1924.
Catholic Mind, 1933.
Commonweal, 1937.
Cork Evening Echo, 1938.
Cork Examiner, 1912-1942.
Cork Free Press, 1923.
Daily Sheet, 1923.
Freeman's Journal, 1922-1932.
Irish Citizen, 1914, 1915.
Irish Freedom, 1927, 1928.
Irish Independent, 1921-1942.
Irish Press, 1936.
Irish Statesman, 1926.
Irish Times, 1914-1942.
Irish World, 1930, 1933, 1942.
The Leader, 1924.
New York American, 1921.
New York Call, 1921, 1925.
New York Evening Post, 1921, 1925.
New York Evening World, 1925.
New York Times, 1920, 1921, 1922, 1925, 1942.
New York Tribune, 1921, 1925.
New York World 1926.
Poblacht na h-Éireann, 1922.

Published sources
Books
Bell, J. Bowyer, *The IRA*, Dublin, Academy Press, 1979.

Butler, C., *Benedictine Manachism*, London, Longmans Greene, 1924.

Chavasse, Moirin, *Terence MacSwiney*, Dublin, Clanmore and Reynolds, 1961.

Conlin, Lil, *Cumann na mBan*, Kilkenny, Kilkenny People, 1969.

Coogan, Tim Pat, *Ireland Since the Rising*, London, Pall Mall Press. 1966.

Cronin, Seán, *The MacGarrity Papers*, Tralee, Anvil, 1972.

Daly, Mary, *Social and Economic History of Ireland Since 1800*, Dublin, The Education Co., 1981.

Dangerfield, George, *The Damnable Question*, London, Constable, 1976. *The Strange Death of Liberal England*, London, Granada, 1983.

Dwyer, T. Ryle, *De Valera's Darkest Hour*, Dublin, Mercier Press, 1977.

Fanning, Ronan, *Independent Ireland*, Dublin, Helicon, 1983.

Fitzgerald, William (ed.). *Voices of Ireland*, Dublin, J. Heywood, 1924.

Fitzpatrick, David, *Politics and Irish Life*, Dublin, Gill and Macmillan, 1977.

Fox, R. M., *Rebel Irishwomen*, Dublin, Talbot Press, 1935.

Garvin, Tom, *The Evolution of Irish Nationalist Politics* Dublin, Gill and Macmillan, 1981.

Gellner, Ernest, *Nations and Nationalism*, New York, Cornell University Press, 1982.

Longford, The Earl of and T. O'Neill, *Eamon de Valera*, London, Hutchinson, 1970.

Macardle, Dorothy, *The Irish Republic*, London, Corgi, 1968.

MacCartan, Patrick, *With de Valera in America*, Dublin, Fitzpatrick Ltd., 1932.

MacSwiney, Terence, *Principles of Freedom*, New York, Kennekat Press, 1970.

Markievicz, Constance, *The Prison Letters of Countess Markievicz*, New York, Kraus, 1970.

Martin, F. N., *The Irish Volunteers, 1913-1915*, Dublin, Duffy, 1963.

McCaffrey, Laurence, *The Irish Question, 1800-1922*, Lexington, University of Kentucky Press, 1968.

McNeill, Ronald, *Ulster's Stand for Union*, London, Murray, 1922.

Murphy, John, *Ireland in the Twentieth Century*, Dublin, Gill and Macmillan, 1975.

Nowlan, K. (ed.), *The Making of 1916*, Dublin, Stationery Office, 1969.

O'Connor, Frank, *An Only Child*, Dublin, Gill and MacMillan, 1961.

Phillips, W. Allison, *The Revolution in Ireland*, London, Longmans Green, 1923.

Articles

Pyne, Peter, 'The Politics of Parliamentary Abstentionism: Ireland's Four Sinn Féin Parties, 1905-1926', in *Journal of Commonwealth Comparative Politics*, Vol. 12, no. 2 (1974).

O'Neill, T., 'Irish Republicanism, 1922-1927', in *Historical Studies X*, London.

Unpublished Sources

Banta, Mary, *The Red Scare in the Irish Free State*. Unpublished MA thesis, University College, Dublin, 1982.

One Day in My Life

Bobby Sands

One Day in My Life is a human document of suffering, determination, anguish, courage and faith. It also portrays frightening examples of man's inhumanity to man.

Written with economy and a dry humour it charts, almost minute by minute, a brave man's struggle to preserve his identity against cold, dirt and boredom. It is the record of a single day and conjures up vividly the enclosed hell of Long Kesh; the poor food, the harassment and the humiliating mirror searches. Bobby Sands and his comrades were often gripped by terror at the iron system that held them and yet their courage never faltered.

Written on toilet paper with a biro refill and hidden inside Bobby Sands' own body, this is a book about human bravery and endurance and will take its place beside the great European classics on imprisonment like *One Day in the Life of Ivan Denisovich* and our own John Mitchel's *Jail Journal*.

'I wish it were possible to ensure that those in charge of formulating British policy in Ireland would read these pages. They might begin to understand the deep injuries which British policy has inflicted upon this nation, and now seek to heal these wounds.' *From the Introduction by Seán Mac Bride.*

Bobby Sands was twenty-seven years old when he died, on the sixty-sixth day of his hunger strike, on 5 May 1981. He had spent almost the last nine years of his short life in prison because of his Irish Republican activities. By the time of his death he was world-famous for having embarrassed the British establishment by being elected as M.P. to the British Parliament for Fermanagh/South Tyrone and having defiantly withstood political and moral pressure to abandon his hunger-strike.